TREFIGNATH
and
DIN DRYFOL
The Excavation of Two
Megalithic Tombs in Anglesey

by C. A. SMITH, B.A., Ph.D. and F. M. LYNCH, M.A., F.S.A.

The Cambrian Archaeological Association 1987

ISBN 0 947846 01 8
ISSN 0266-593X

Series Editor: Robin G. Livens, F.S.A.

Published by the Cambrian Archaeological Association
with the aid of a grant from the Welsh Office

Cambrian Archaeological Monographs may be obtained from:
Robin G. Livens,
Department of History,
University College of North Wales,
Bangor,
Gwynedd LL57 2DG

Printed by Qualitex Printing Limited, Tudor Street, Cardiff

Editor's Preface

This volume marks a new departure for the Series, in that it records the excavation of two monuments which are in the care of the Welsh Office and which were excavated as part of a programme of research and conservation. Neither monument was threatened by any form of development and both still survive. Trefignath, in its newly restored form, is one of the more impressive and informative monuments of Anglesey, whose history and explanation have been much amplified by the work published here and it is to be hoped that the monument will attract the increasing public attention which it deserves.

The observant reader will note that the text was substantially completed in 1982 and that the study of the monuments takes no account of developments since that date. The delay in publication is regretted and was entirely due to financial constraints. I must record my personal indebtedness to the number of people who have helped in the production of this study: first of all, to the two authors, for producing a concise and acceptable typescript with commendable speed; Dr H. N. Savory read the typescript in draft and gave much guidance about it and Miss B. L. R. Jones undertook a vast amount of routine work in preparing the text for publication. Mr Richard Avent, Principal Inspector of Ancient Monuments of the Welsh Historic Monuments Service ('Cadw') smoothed the administrative part of the exercise. I must also pay a personal tribute to the Cambrian Archaeological Association's Management Committee, under the chairmanship of Mr H. N. Jerman for their support, advice and assistance.

ROBIN G. LIVENS

Joint Preface

Few areas in Britain have a greater density of megalithic tombs than Anglesey and Figure 1 records the position of all sites at present known to the authors. It is based mainly on lists published by one of us in 1969 (Lynch in Powell *et al* 1969, 296-308). These lists include surviving sites, well authenticated but destroyed sites, and sites of natural origin previously wrongly classified as megalithic tombs. It is the first two categories that are illustrated in Figure 1. Each site shown is annotated with the number allocated to it in the 1969 list.

In addition, the Ordnance Survey record cards for Anglesey provide details of a further nineteen sites where no remains survive and where records are insufficient to establish the authenticity of the site. Often the available information amounts to no more than a single, early reference, a field name, or an inclusion on an early map. It is unlikely that the authenticity of these sites will now be established and it is improbable that all were genuine tombs. But some almost certainly were and in the interests of completeness all of these imponderables are shown in Figure 1, although the conventions used highlight the well authenticated sites.

The excavations at Trefignath and Din Dryfol were not carried out as part of a carefully designed programme of research into the megalithic tombs of Anglesey and the publication of their reports in a single volume owes something to historical accident, both projects having been brought to a successful conclusion at roughly the same time. The 1969-70 excavations at Din Dryfol were undertaken with a limited objective in view and the complete investigation of the site was not contemplated. The further work in 1980 was undertaken partly to resolve questions left outstanding in 1970 and partly in the light of the experience gained by one of us at Trefignath between 1977 and 1979. At that site work was first prompted by concern over the stability of the surviving burial chamber. However, it was decided from the outset that if any work was to be undertaken it would have to be preceded by the complete excavation of the site and followed by its partial restoration so that the main outline of its history could be made intelligible to interested visitors.

The two projects reported in this volume had different objectives, employed different approaches, and had different results—both in archaeological terms as evidenced by the reports and in the field as will be clear to anyone who pays them a visit. Their common ground lies in the fact that for a long time certain superficial similarities led to their classification as similar types of tomb. Both were regarded as segmented gallery graves and with the site at Hen Drefor (ANG 11) constituted the distinct group known as the Anglesey Long Graves. Our excavations show that this classification is no longer tenable within the terms in which it was originally employed. The history of both sites is far more complicated than previously supposed. However, similarities remain—both tombs underwent several periods of development and both ended up as rather 'long graves'—and their reports are presented here as a further contribution to the continuing megalithic enquiries in the west of Britain.

Christopher Smith
Frances Lynch
Autumn 1982

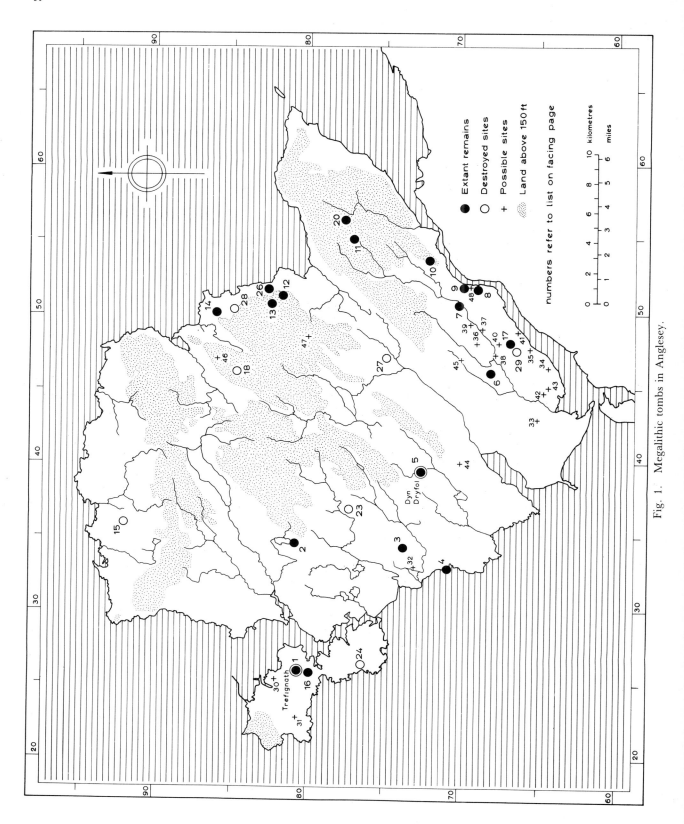

Fig. 1. Megalithic tombs in Anglesey.

Megalithic Tombs in Anglesey

The following list is divided into three parts, the first two of which are a simple repetition of the lists published by Lynch in 1969 (in Powell *et al* 1969, 296-308). Further details and references to these sites will be found there. The third part has not been published before and is presented here as a supplement to the earlier lists. The county numbering system has been extended to include these additions and the entry for each site includes details of its parish and the principal published reference.

Part 1—Surviving remains

ANG 1	Trefignath	SH259805
ANG 2	Presaddfed	SH348809
ANG 3	Ty Newydd	SH344738
ANG 4	Barclodiad y Gawres	SH329707
ANG 5	Din Dryfol	SH396725
ANG 6	Bodowyr	SH463682
ANG 7	Bryn Celli Ddu	SH508702
ANG 8	Bryn yr Hen Bobl	SH519690
ANG 9	Plas Newydd	SH520697
ANG 10	Ty Mawr	SH539722
ANG 11	Hen Drefor	SH551773
ANG 12	Glyn	SH514817
ANG 13	Pant y Saer	SH509824
ANG 14	Lligwy	SH501860
ANG 16	Trearddur	SH259800
ANG 17	Perthiduon	SH480668
ANG 20	Cremlyn	SH567776
ANG 26	Benllech	SH518825

Part 2—Destroyed but well authenticated sites

ANG 15	Llanfechell	SH361920
ANG 18	Bodafon Mountain	SH462846
ANG 23	Treban	SH370773
ANG 24	Rhoscolyn	SH263766
ANG 27	Tregarnedd	SH472748
ANG 28	Llanallgo	SH503849
ANG 29	Carreg y fran	SH479667

(The following have been discounted as natural features: ANG 19, ANG 21, ANG 22, and ANG 25.)

Part 3—Possible sites

ANG 30	Holyhead, Holyhead Urban W. O. Stanley, 1868 map opposite page 385	SH253821
ANG 31	Plas Feilw, Holyhead Rural E. N. Baynes, 1911, 11	SH22?80?
ANG 32	Llanfaelog, Llanfaelog E. N. Baynes, 1911, 12	SH33?73?
ANG 33	Rhoscolyn, Llangeinwen W. O. Stanley, 1870, 58	SH43?65?
ANG 34	Lon Caerau Mawr, Llangeinwen E. N. Baynes, 1911, 15	SH465644
ANG 35	Barras, Llanidan E. N. Baynes, 1911, 10	SH479655
ANG 36	Bodlew, Llanddaniel Fab OS Card SH46NE23	SH481690
ANG 37	Cerrig Gwydryn, Llanidan E. N. Baynes, 1911, 10	SH491677
ANG 38	Llyslew, Llanidan E. N. Baynes, 1911, 11	SH473688
ANG 39	Rhos y Cerrig, Llanddaniel Fab E. N. Baynes, 1911, 11	SH494693
ANG 40	Barclodiad y Gawres, Llanidan E. N. Baynes, 1911, 14	SH481675
ANG 41	Old Church, Llanidan H. L. Jones, 1854, 206	SH49?66?
ANG 42	Cae'r Llechau, Llangeinwen E. N. Baynes, 1911, 10	SH447647
ANG 43	Tan Twr, Llangeinwen E. N. Baynes, 1911, 15	SH451645
ANG 44	Plas Bach, Trefdraeth W. O. Stanley, 1870, 58	SH40?70?
ANG 45	Myfyrian, Llanidan E. N. Baynes, 1911, 11	SH47?70?
ANG 46	Fedw, Penrhos Lligwy E. N. Baynes, 1911	SH47?86?
ANG 47	Llech Talmon, Llanddyfnan E. N. Baynes, 1911, 15	SH486800
ANG 48	Tyddyn Caesar, Llanddaniel Fab E. N. Baynes, 1911	SH51?69?

Contents

PART 1

The Excavation of the Trefignath Burial Chambers —1977 to 1979

by Christopher Smith

WITH CONTRIBUTIONS FROM

Pauline Beswick, James Greig, Elizabeth Healey, Vernon Hughes, David Jenkins, Helen Keeley, and Tomos Roberts

List of Figures (Trefignath)

List of Plates (Trefignath)

(between pages 88 and 89)

List of Tables (Trefignath)

"On reaching Trevigneth, we examined some relics of Druidism, called cromlechs. Where did these unhewn massive stones come from? How were such giants brought to their position, all the buried centuries ago? Their solemn, silent solitude awes us. They remain as century-links, 'twixt Past and Present—'twixt superstition's night, and that new morn, when God's great light lit up an abject world, and Mind's immortal glory blessed the land, while we walked around, and gazed upon the mouldering and mysterious remains before us, the breeze seemed fraught with the mysteries of the past, and we felt that we were breathing the atmosphere of a remote age; our imaginations were led back to the period when the horrid rites of Druids, of whom at a very early period this island was a stronghold, were celebrated on this spot. Here the Druid priests once offered their dreadful sacrifices, and performed their idolatrous worship, in their long white garments, their temples enwreathed with chaplets of oak-leaves, the magic wand in their hand, and on their head a serpents egg, an ensign of their order; thus attired they went forth to sacrifice, standing round the crimson-stained altar, shrouded with superstition, mystery, and death. Here the victims, bound with cords for slaughter and sacrifice, filled the air with shrieks of agony and screams of horror. Well for us we lived not Then, but Now. Here once lived and worshipped another race of beings, who from their forest haunts came forth in mystic power to invoke their awe-throned deity with human sacrifices. Beneath the same sun which rolls over our heads, and the same moon that smiles on us, the ancient Britons, bent in humble, though blind adoration, and worshipped a mysterious Divinity." (Jackson, Thomas 1856 *Reminiscences of Five Days in the Isle of Holyhead in the month of September, 1856,* 25.)

Preface

Although the excavations at Trefignath were undertaken as part of a programme of work designed to ensure the stability of the eastern chamber they were extended far beyond the part of the monument immediately affected. In fact the opportunity was taken to investigate the whole site and lay it out in such a manner that interested visitors would be able to see and appreciate the main outlines of its history. The excavations took place over three seasons in 1977, 1978, and 1979 but the laying out of the monument was only completed in the autumn of 1982 with the replacement of orthostat XV after it had been repaired at Caernarfon.

This report is divided into three principal sections, the first of which comprises the initial two chapters. The first chapter gives a general introduction to the site and a history of archaeological interest in it. The chapter concludes with a brief account of the excavation and a summary by Vernon Hughes, Ancient Monuments Architect, of the structural problems involved in the investigation. Chapter 2 provides a detailed account of the archaeological discoveries made and discusses their implications for the history of the site. That history proved a good deal more complicated than had been anticipated, three main periods of development being identified encompassing up to ten distinct phases. For this reason I have adopted the somewhat unusual approach of treating each major stage as a distinct subject and include alongside the archaeological evidence from Trefignath a discussion of comparanda and all other matter relevant to an interpretation of that evidence. I felt this was preferable to leaving such material to a later chapter by which time the details of the Trefignath evidence could easily become lost in the overall complexity of the site. However, this approach necessarily involves some anticipation of evidence in respect of finds which is more fully presented elsewhere in the report.

The second section of the report includes two chapters dealing with the soil and palynological studies undertaken as part of the project. These chapters are contributed by Helen Keeley and James Greig respectively. They are complementary and provide an account of the environment in which the burial chambers were built.

Section three consists of four chapters in which the various finds made during the excavation are discussed. The first chapter in this section deals with the radio-carbon dates obtained from two small finds of charcoal. These, and other radio-carbon dates are frequently referred to throughout the report. In quoting such dates I have followed the convention of using bc or bp for radio-carbon years and BC or BP for calendar years. The following chapter deals with the chipped stone industry found at Trefignath. This material has been studied in detail by Elizabeth Healey and the chapter has been written jointly with her. Chapter 7 discusses the pottery and includes a detailed consideration of its petrology by David Jenkins. A final chapter in this section describes the remaining rather heterogeneous finds.

These eight chapters make extensive reference to the primary data recovered during the project. These data reside in the unpublished excavation archive but as far as has been considered feasible as much as possible has been summarised here in a series of appendices. These deal with archaeological contexts, finds, and samples. All but the most ardent specialist should find sufficient information in the report and these appendices. References are presented Harvard style and Trefignath shares a bibliography with Din Dryfol at the end of the volume.

The finds from the excavation have been deposited with the National Museum of Wales in Cardiff pending the provision of appropriate museum facilities in North Wales. At the time of writing no final decision has been taken on arrangements for the storage of excavation records in the Principality. Until such a decision is taken the records will be retained by the Conservation and Land Division of the Welsh Office.

I should like to conclude these opening remarks by expressing my sincere thanks to all those who helped with the project, both on site and in the subsequent preparation of this report.

First thanks must go to the numerous volunteers and Ancient Monuments Branch staff who carried out the work on site. There are rather too many of them to mention individually but should any read this report they will know whom I mean. My site assistants over the three years were Pat Lynch (1977), Keith Dallimore (1977 and 1978), John Samuels (1978), Rosemary Clarkson (1978), Julie Wilson (1979), Martin de Lewandowicz (1979), and Dave Fine (1979). They ensured the smooth running of the excavation and the accurate recording of our discoveries. I could not have managed without them. After the excavation help with the finds has been provided by George Boon, John Lewis, Richard Brewer, Mark Webster, Rosemary Powers, and Frances Lynch. Frances was also a great source of advice and support throughout the excavation and during the preparation of the report. It is a great pleasure to share a monograph with her. The skilful work of Jean Williamson is responsible for most of the illustrations.

Jack Scott very kindly read and commented on a draft of the entire monograph and helpful comments on the Trefignath text have also been received from William Britnell, Frances Lynch, and Siân Rees. I am most grateful to them all.

C. A. SMITH

Chapter 1—Introduction

In sharp contrast to mountainous Snowdonia the former County of Anglesey, comprising Ynys Gybi and the much larger Ynys Môn, is predominantly a low lying area of comparatively good farmland. With the exception of a few isolated uplands the topography of Anglesey is dominated by a series of parallel, gently undulating ridges crossing the area on a north-east/south-west alignment. Streams flow along the intervening depressions and further emphasise the distinct grain of the landscape (Fig. 1).

This pattern extends to small-scale features and there are few areas the potential monotony of which is not mitigated by frequent small rocky crests or damp hollows. This is especially true of Ynys Gybi which, apart from Mynydd Twr at its northern extremity, is entirely characterised by low rocky ridges and intervening damp depressions. The Trefignath Burial Chambers occupy just such a ridge about 2km south-east of Holyhead railway station and a few metres north of a minor road from Holyhead to Trearddur Bay (NGR SH259805) (Fig. 2). To the north, east, and south the ground drops to low lying, and at one time, marshy hollows. It appears local topography may be reflected in the name of the site itself and I am most grateful to Tomos Roberts of U.C.N.W. Archives Department for providing the following note on the Trefignath place name. His remarks are preceded by a list of all the known forms of the name.

1624	Trefignerth	*Bodewryd*
c. 1659	Tre-figneth	*Bodleian*
1695	Trefigneth	*Penrhos* vii.130
1715-		
1733	Trefignath	*Penrhos* vii.506
1723	Trefigneth	*Penrhos* vi.155
c. 1737	Tre Fignerth	*LWLM* 85
1741	Trefigneth	*Penrhos* i.1309
1753	Trefigneth	*GAG/M. WQT*/12/2
1769	Trefignedd	*Penrhos* ii.775.f.6
c. 1807	Trefignedd	*Penrhos* vi.157
1823	Trefigneth	*Penrhos* ii.721
1833	Trevignedd	*AL1/HIM* 208
1846	Trefignerth	*GAG/M.WQC/Œ/*11
1853	Trefignaeth	ibid.
1860	Trefignerth	ibid.
1869	Trefignerth	ibid.
1871	Trefignerth	ibid.
1908	Trefignaeth	*TM/ELIM* 181

To my knowledge no forms of this name, recorded before 1624, still exist. The forms that do exist show no logical development or consistency. The name does not refer to a medieval township or hamlet and does not appear in the 1352 extent of Anglesey (*Baron Hill* 6714). Trefigneth was a small farm, part of the Tre'r-go estate, and was also known as Pen-y-lôn (e.g. *Penrhos* ii.772). John Owen of Penrhos inherited the Tre'r-go estate on the death of Robert Wynn in the mid seventeenth century. No deeds earlier than the sixteenth century referring to the Tre'r-go are to be found among the Penrhos Papers. Although Tre'r-go estate rentals for the period 1619-1624 do exist (*Penrhos* vii.489), the name *Trefigneth* does not occur in them.

Documentation of the name is therefore incomplete, and it remains difficult to interpret. The first element *tref-* means 'farm, homestead, hamlet'. The *-r-* in the second element in the 1624 form may be intrusive, but it does occur again in the *c.* 1737 form, and several times during the nineteenth century. The *c.* 1737 form was recorded by the antiquary Lewis Morris at the time when he was a customs officer at Holyhead. However the *-r-* does not occur in any of the forms in the Penrhos rentals of the period. The 1769, *c.* 1807, and 1833 forms (Trefignedd), and the 1853 and 1908 forms (Trefignaeth) are probably late interpretations of the name.

If the original form of the name was *Trefignerth* then it is possible that the second element is an unrecorded personal name, itself containing the element *-nerth*. This element occurs as the second element of several Welsh personal names e.g. *Cyfnerth, Gwaednerth, Gwrnerth Idnerth*. It also occurs as the first element of *Nerthach* and as a simplex *Nerth* in 'Fictional names' in *WM* 231.

If, however, the *-r-* in the second element is intrusive, and the original form was *Trefigneth,* then the second element may contain *mign* 'swamp, quagmire', and an unknown suffix *-eth*. The element *mign* occurs in several Welsh place-names e.g. Talymignedd, Llanllyfni (*mignedd* is the plural form of *mign*) and Trefign, Monington, Dyfed. The modern oral form *Trefignath* would be a natural development of *Trefigneth*.

Sources
AL1/HIM   Angharad Llwyd, *A History of the Island of Mona or Anglesey*, Ruthin 1833

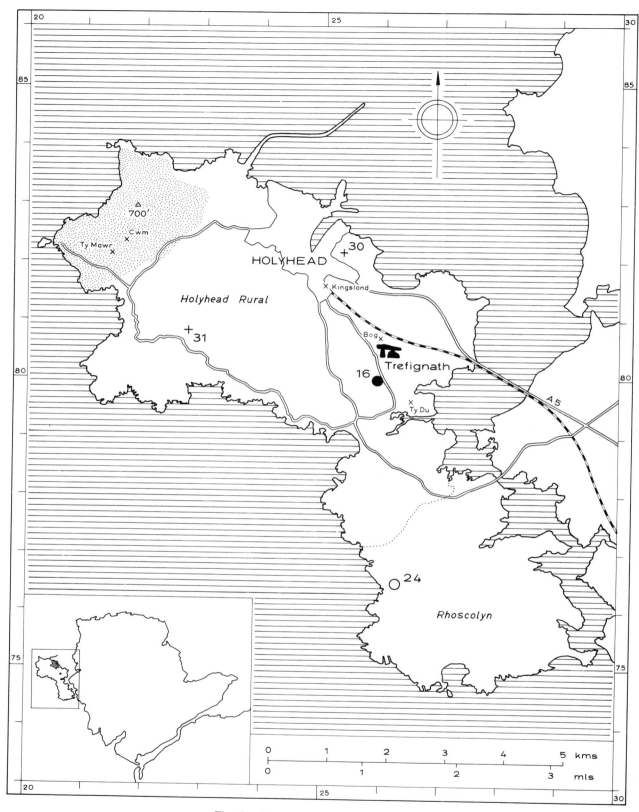

Fig. 2.   Neolithic sites on Ynys Gybi.

Baron Hill   Baron Hill Mss. at U.C.N.W.,
                  Bangor

Bodewryd   Bodewryd Mss. and Documents at
                  N.L.W., Aberystwyth

Bodleian   Bodleian M.S. Top.Gen., c25; 39
                  and 34-35

GAG/M   Papers of the Gwynedd Archives
                  Service, Area Record Office,
                  Llangefni

LWLM   *The Life and Works of Lewis Morris,* ed.
                  Hugh Owen, 1951

Penrhos   Penrhos Papers at U.C.N.W., Bangor

TM/EL1M   R. T. Williams (Trebor Môn), *Enwau Lleoedd yn Môn a'u Tarddiad*, Bala, 1908

W.M.   *The White Book Mabinogion,* ed. J. Gwenogvryn Evans, Pwllheli, 1907

Tomos Roberts

The topographical significance of the location is further discussed in Chapter 2 while full details of the local soils and geology are provided by Helen Keeley and David Jenkins in Chapters 3 and 7 (cf. Figs. 22 and 29). In the remainder of this chapter we are concerned with the history of antiquarian and archaeological interest in Trefignath.

Antiquarian Interest

The recorded history of the Trefignath Burial Chambers began in the mid Seventeenth Century when the site was visited by John Aubrey and described by him in his *Monumenta Britannica.* The recently published facsimile of part of this work does not include the section dealing with Trefignath and I am deeply indebted to Aubrey Burl who has kindly provided a full transcript of the relevant sections from his photocopy of the entire work. This transcript is of such interest that it is reproduced here in full. The original document is in the Bodleian Library.

"In *Anglesey,* about a mile from *Holyhead,* on a hill near the way that leads to Beaumaris are placed certain great rude stones much after ye fashion of this draught here:"

(in the margin Aubrey has a very simple sketch, reproduced here as Fig. 3)

"for want of an Interpreter I could not learne the name of it. the cavity is about five foot, I remember a mountain Beast (or two) were at Shade within it. (Aug.)

"Sr Timothy Littleton, Serjeant at Lawe, and one of ye Judges that went this Circuit, did me the favour to obtain this following account from M^r ... W . a Justice of ye Peace at Holyhead. sc.

"There is a mile from Holyhead, etc." as in the originall, hereto annexed."

"There is about a mile from Holy-H^d a Monum^t wch I conceive to be y^t meant in y^r paper of great rough stones about 20 in number & about 30 paces from one of ye roades leading from HolyH^d to Bewmaris between 4 & 5 foot high, at ye Northern End whereof stand two stones on End about two yards high above ground; The fashion of them can hardlie be exactlie described, by reason some are sunk deep & some fallen flat wch are almost overgrown wth earth & grasse. They are *Y-Lleche,* they stand upon a hillock in a farm called Tre-figneth in the p.ish of *Caer-Gybi* att Holy-Head. But ye p.ticul^r Inclosure wch they stand in is called (from them as I conceive) Cae-r-lleche, Cae in y^e

British "tongue Signifyinge as Inclosure; llech most comonlie in our Language (as I conceive) is rendered for a flat stone, & most of these are of y^t kinde, for I have observ'd in sevrall places where these great stones are set on end, as they be in sevrall pts of y^{is} p.ish & ye countie, If it be a stone somew^t flat or thinne it's called lleche; but if a thick bulkie or round stone it's rendred Maen or Carreg; I doe conceive *llech* signifies upon this acc^t wch Doct. Davies in his British Dictionarie (omitting Lapis, Scandula etc) renders it to be Tabula Saxea, wch epithet makes me fancie his Translacan Tabula, Kyfr-Cof, A Book of Remembrance, for all ye Acc^t y^t ever I could come by of these stonie monum^{ts} was y^t they were set up to preserve ye remembrance of some Notable Actione; His other words for Tabula being Astyllen ·Bwrdd wch is a piece of a board, and Llifwydden a slit-deal or firre etc. wch sort p.chance might be their Table-booke for things of lesse Importance; & lleche being ye plurall may Signifie Tabula Saxea, & Tabula he renders to signifie in our language Ysgrifenadau Writings, Rhwymedigaethau Obligacons, Ysgrifenadau Cyffred in Comon Writins, Hen Gogion—Ancient Remembrance & it is a comon Tradicon y^t many of these were used for evidences & conveyances. My Neighb^{rs} can give me noe Acc^t in pticul^r how these or any of y^r kinde were set up. There is a gent Mr Jo^n Gryffyth ye elder of Llan-ddyfnan in this counties who lives about 5 or 6 miles from Bewmaris who hath ye repute of an Antiquarie & may give some satisfaction in In gen^{ce} touchinge these ancient monum^{ts} (But I conceive most of ye pticul^{rs} are lost) wth whom I had not ye opportunitie to confir.

"Llech hath another Signification as Latebra, Latit.. etc. & llechu Lateo Abscondo etc. but I conceive it's not ye meaning of these Monum^{ts} unles some might be buried under them.

  fro Mr Win
  of   in
  ye pish of Holyhed
  Justice of peace"

(then, in Aubrey's own hand)

"I must not forget here to acknowledge my Obligation to S^r "Timothy Littleton who was judge in this Circuite and made diligent Enquiry after these Monuments for me. He was since made one of the Barons of ye Exchequer. This letter, and another he brought for me."

(Bodleian M.S.Top.Gen., c.25 39 and 34-35).

According to Stanley (1871, 96) Aubrey's visit to Trefignath should be dated to 1660 when he returned from Ireland via Holyhead. However, Aubrey Burl has drawn to my attention a parallel drawn by John Aubrey between Trefignath and a site near Pain's Castle which he is known to have visited in 1656 (Bodleian M.S.Top.Gen., c.25; 48). Aubrey's wording suggests a pre-existing knowledge of Trefignath and it is therefore possible that he saw it as part of a journey he made through Wales in 1655 (Hunter 1975). Whatever the precise date of his visit John Aubrey's description of Trefignath is the earliest of any megalithic tomb in Anglesey.

Aubrey's observation that "a mountain Beast (or two) were at Shade within it" indicates that at least one of the chambers was open and the accompanying sketch suggests that a structure of three compartments could be recognised. Apart from this most of the information about the condition of the site is contained in Mr Win's letter, although a large part of this is taken up by a somewhat opaque discourse on the meaning of the field name Cae'r lleche. He precedes this with a description and concludes by noting that sites of this type may have been used for burial.

Over a century passes before any further information becomes available. The entry in Gibson's edition of *Camden's Britannia* does no more than quote Aubrey (Gibson 1695, 675) and Henry Rowlands, who otherwise wrote so much about the megaliths of Anglesey, does not mention Trefignath (Rowlands 1723). In 1775 the site was visited by Nicholas Owen who records that there "are some rude stone monuments supposed to have been three cromlechs; they join each other, though the upper stones are now fallen off their supporters" (Owen 1775, 33-36). This brief reference encompasses all the themes dealt with by later writers on Trefignath; firstly, how many chambers were there?, secondly,

were they joined or separate? Thirdly, what happened to the monument until the time it was placed in State care in 1911? It will be convenient to deal with each of these themes individually.

Apart, perhaps, from John Aubrey's sketch (Fig. 3) Nicholas Owen was the first to suggest that burial chambers had been built at Trefignath, although it was not until the excavations in 1979 that this was finally established to be the case. Gough's edition of Camden's *Britannia* records the site as a 'double cromlech' (Gough 1789, 571) and in 1816 Pugh provided a confused description of a double cromlech at 'Tre Iarddur' (*sic*) (probably Trearddur) which is almost certainly meant to be Trefignath (Pugh 1816, 64). Longueville Jones' list of 1855 notes two cromlechs at Trefignath (Jones 1855, 25) and at the time of the Cambrian Archaeological Association's visit in 1870 doubts were expressed as to whether the remains comprised two or three chambers (C.A.A. 1870, 362). Meanwhile, in 1818 Lewis Morris was of the view that the site comprised three monuments "... erected over the graves of some great men" (Morris 1818, 217), and in 1870 Stanley noted three chambers at Trefignath (Stanley 1870, 58). It appears that Stanley may have changed his mind on this point for his 1867 account, although not enumerating the chambers, is accompanied by an engraving (Plate I) which shows only the eastern and central chambers (Stanley 1867, 234) whereas a later engraving, published by Stanley in 1874 (Plate II) shows all three, and his accompanying account describes the site in those terms (Stanley 1874, 1).

John Aubrey's Sketch of Trefignath c.1656

Fig. 3. John Aubrey's sketch of Trefignath from *Monumenta Britannica*
(after Bodleian M.S.Top.Gen., c.25; 39)

Arguments about the contiguity of the chambers at Trefignath may also be taken back to John Aubrey's sketch (Fig. 3) which, although diagrammatic, does depict three, contiguous structures. Owen (1775, 36) specifically states that the three cromlechs 'join each other' and Longueville Jones believed the two he listed to be connected by a stone passage (Jones 1855, 25). According to Stanley, while Trefignath appeared to be three distinct cromlechs, "... on closer examination it is evident that it consisted of one continuous covered way" (Stanley 1874, 1). It is presumably statements such as this that led to the inclusion of Trefignath in some *Ward Lock Guides* as a Bronze Age souterrain! In 1910 Baynes described the site as a 'gallery grave' and it is as such that it has since appeared in archaeological literature (Baynes 1910, 42; RCAHM 1937, 22-23; Grimes 1936, 119-20; Daniel 1950, 86; Piggott 1970, 179; Powell *et al* 1969, 113-14; Lynch 1970, 30-32). Dissenting voices were few and far between (Morris 1818, 217; C.A.A. 1870, 362; Baynes 1914, 55), and Frances Lynch has been the only writer in recent years to acknowledge the difficulties of this interpretation and suggest a possible alternative (in Powell *et al* 1969, 113-14; Lynch 1970, 30-32).

It is evident from the entry in *Monumenta Britannica* that the site had been considerably disturbed by the middle of the Seventeenth Century. Part of the cairn had been removed exposing the chambers, some of the orthostats had fallen, but the twenty stones noted were three more than the number remaining on site at the time of the excavation and at least one chamber survived to provide shelter for 'mountain Beasts'. Aubrey's sketch (Fig. 3) is almost certainly a conjectural reconstruction and has little to tell us about the condition of the monument. The most detailed account of the partial destruction of Trefignath is provided by Stanley in two notes in *Archaeologia Cambrensis* (1867, 234; 1874, 1). According to Stanley most of the cairn and many orthostats were removed in about 1790. Total destruction was averted only by the intervention of Lady Stanley, his grandmother. This was probably the occasion on which the 'urns and bones' mentioned by Longueville Jones were recovered (Jones 1855, 25), and Stanley refers to a sketch in his possession that shows the central chamber as complete until then. Sadly, neither 'urns and bones' nor sketch can now be located. This account cannot be entirely reconciled with Owen's statement that at the time of his visit in 1775 the upper stones had fallen off their supporters (Owen 1775, 36). Either Stanley's dating is incorrect or Owen misunderstood what he saw, which is, perhaps, more likely. At all events Owen's statement is repeated without acknowledgement by Llwyd (1833, 208) and may have given rise to Baynes' view that some of the stones had 'evidently' been replaced (Baynes 1910, 43). There is no record of any work being carried out at Trefignath before it was placed in State care in 1911.

Stanley's 1874 illustration (Plate II) shows the site in much the same condition in which it remained until 1971, the only changes being the breaking of the central capstone and the partial collapse of the northern portal to the eastern chamber. Both these events had occurred by 1900, according to a photograph published by Griffith (1900, Plate I).

Maintenance and Care

On 16 August 1911 Trefignath, along with five other Anglesey monuments including Din Dryfol, was placed in the care of the Commissioners of Works by the owner, Edward Lyulph Stanley of Penrhos, Lord Sheffield. Since then the site has been looked after by the various government departments with responsibility for the preservation of ancient monuments in Wales, currently the Conservation and Land Division of the Welsh Office. Departmental records suggest that a timber prop supporting the capstone of the eastern chamber was either already present in 1911 or was introduced soon after. No developments occurred at the site for nearly sixty years.

At the beginning of 1971 it was noticed that the capstone of the central chamber had finally collapsed completely, breaking one of the supporting stones in the process. This capstone had been precariously balanced for over a century (Plate IV) and its ultimate collapse was inevitable. The precise date of the collapse is not known but it must have occurred in the spring or summer of 1971. It was decided that while the restoration of the central chamber was not feasible attention should be paid to ensuring the stability of the surviving eastern chamber. It was planned that the capstones of the eastern chamber should be lifted and the side stones re-set in a vertical position. As a temporary measure an internal masonry support was provided for the capstones and a buttress built against the leaning northern side slab. This work was completed by December 1971 but in the event nothing further was done and the temporary arrangements became more or less permanent.

In May 1976 the condition of the timber prop, which had rotted at ground level, began to give cause for concern (Plate V). In August it was decided that the programme of work begun in 1971 should be resumed as soon as possible. However, it was felt that any further work on site should be preceded by a thorough archaeological investigation and the potentially complex nature of the site argued against such an investigation being limited to a small portion only. Accordingly, in October 1976 plans were put in hand for the total excavation of the Trefignath Burial Chambers, with work to commence the following spring.

The Progress of the Excavation

The total excavation of the site was accomplished in three seasons of work carried out each spring between

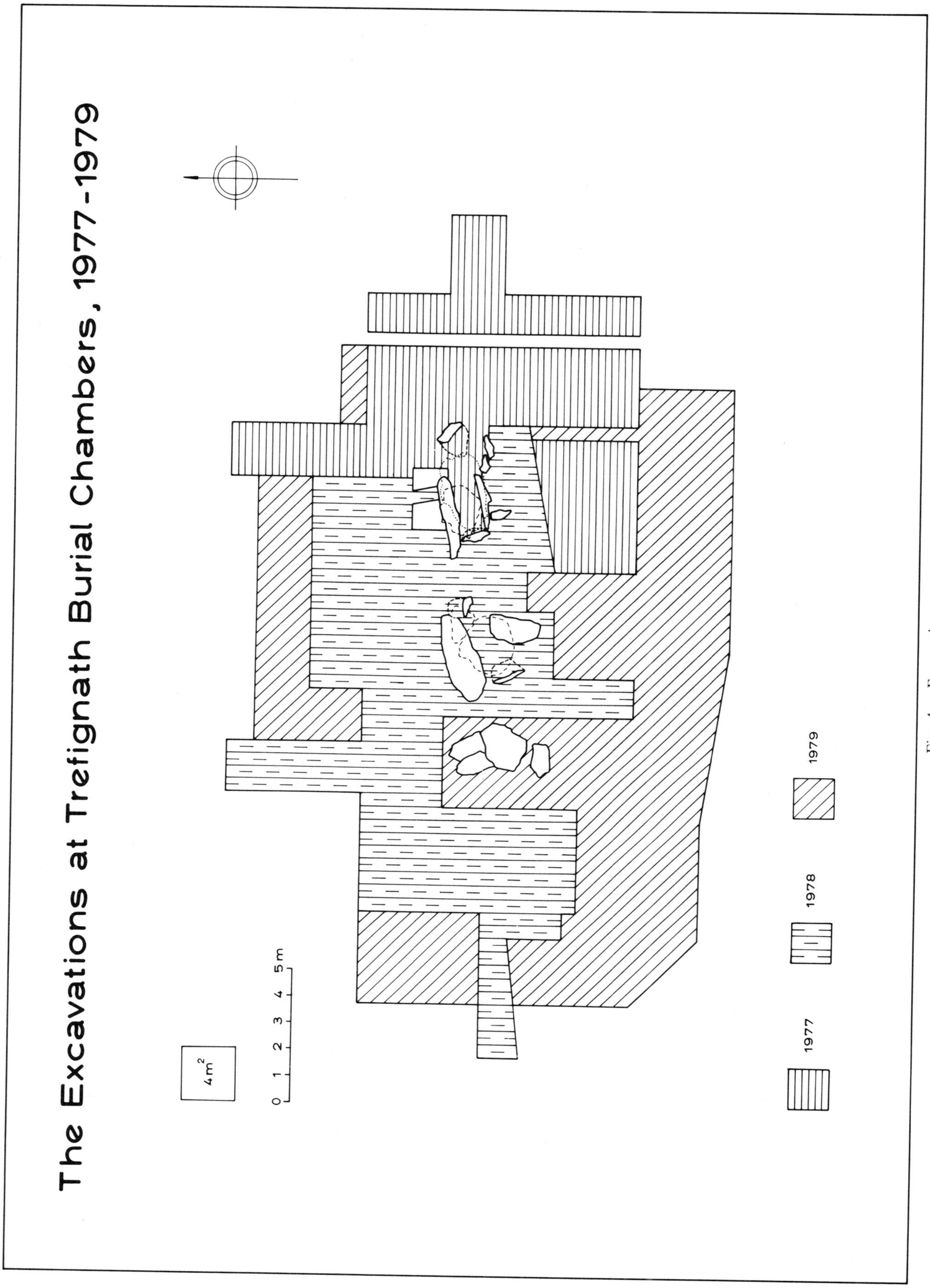

The Excavations at Trefignath Burial Chambers, 1977-1979

4 m²

0 1 2 3 4 5 m

1977

1978

1979

Fig. 4. Excavation sequence.

TREFIG

Contour

4 m²

TREFIGNATH

Excavations 77-79

4 m²

0   1   2   3   4   5 m

Fig. 6.   General excavation plan.

1977 and 1979. Post-excavation consolidation and reconstruction continued into 1982. The progress of the excavation is illustrated in Figure 4 and briefly outlined below. Work was organised and recorded on the basis of a 5 x 5 metre grid provided by staff of the Ancient Monuments Drawing Office, and details will be found in the archive. The drawing office staff also produced a contour plan of the site before any excavation began, provided a temporary bench mark, and drew the elevations of the eastern chamber before any of its stones were moved. The presence of the surviving chamber and the collapsed orthostats of the two others did present special problems and the solutions devised to deal with them are described by Vernon Hughes in the final section of this chapter. Mr Hughes also deals with the consolidation and reconstruction of the site.

An indication of the appearance of the site before the excavation is provided by the contour plan (Fig. 5). This also shows the positions of the orthostats surviving on site at that time. Each has been given a Roman numeral and they are identified by this numbering throughout the report.

The first season, in 1977, saw the excavation of the eastern chamber and its forecourt. Cuttings to the north and south enabled the extent of the surrounding cairn to be established, although its examination immediately around the chamber was prevented by the scaffolding supports employed that year (Plate VI). A 'T'-shaped cutting was also excavated east of the main area but as it revealed no ancient remains was promptly refilled. It is not referred to again in the report and does not appear in any other illustrations.

By the spring of 1978 the scaffolding around the eastern chamber had been removed and it was possible to examine the cairn on either side. The removal of all but Stone X of the central chamber, as described below, enabled the whole of the central area to be excavated along with virtually the full extent of the northern side of the cairn. Cuttings were also opened across the western end, down the outcrop to the west and to the south of the central chamber in order to establish the position of the cairn perimeter in this direction.

The final season in 1979 concentrated on the excavation of the western chamber, the stones of which had been removed, and the south side of the cairn. The excavation was extended well beyond the known limits of the cairn and further small cuttings to the NW, N, and NE completed the investigation of the site.

The cairn, which had at one time surrounded and covered the chambers was found to have been extensively robbed. Throughout most of its extent hardly more than a single layer of stone survived. In some areas not even this marked the former position of the once substantial pile of stones and all that remained was a distinctive mauve-brown soil horizon. This is described fully by Dr Keeley in Chapter 3. It appears to be the remnants of the old ground surface on which the monument was built, but somewhat altered by its long burial under the stones of the cairn. The extent of this deposit is indicated in Figure 6 by the denser grade of stipple. This old ground surface and the three successive phases in the construction of the cairn provide the main stratigraphical units into which the history of the site can be divided. They are described in full in Chapter 2 and summarised in Table 1.

Planning on site was undertaken at a scale of 1:20 and sections drawn at 1:10. A selection of these records is reproduced here at scales of 1:40, 1:80, and 1:160, as appropriate. Figure 6 is a general excavation plan while Figures 9, 13, and 17 provide more detailed illustrations of the main structural periods identified, and Figure 7 is a conjectural reconstruction of the topography of the site before construction of the burial chambers began. The principal sections are illustrated in Figures 10, 14, and 18, and details of the chambers are given in Figures 15 and 19.

All features and other contexts are identified by Arabic numerals in a simple running sequence. However, many features initially allocated individual numbers were subsequently found to be part of features already identified. In this report only the earliest numbers allocated in such cases are used. A full index of contexts is provided in Appendix 1.

Finds, other than obviously recent material from the topsoil, were also recorded in a simple numerical sequence. A total of 666 numbers were allocated on site but substantial numbers of these were subsequently deleted for various reasons and the total finds from Trefignath now number 514. These finds are discussed in full in Chapters 6, 7, and 8 while further details will be found in Appendix 2.

Archaeologically significant finds of pottery and stone tools occurred in three kinds of context. Firstly, a large amount of material was found on or close to the old ground surface below the cairn. Because of the sequential nature of the tomb's development it is impossible to be sure that all of this ante-dates the construction of the earliest chamber and cairn. Some could belong to later stages in the construction of the monument. However, for the sake of simplicity all the material found associated with the old ground surface is treated together. Its distribution is illustrated in Figure 8. Secondly, a few finds were recovered from contexts which enable them to be specifically associated with one or other of the phases in the development of the tomb. Their positions are shown on the appropriate phase plans (Figs. 9, 13, and 17). Thirdly, over half the recorded finds came from within the surviving remnants of the cairn itself, or from beyond its known limits. Strictly speaking this material is unstratified and there is no way of telling to which phase in the development of the site it belongs. The distribution of these finds is shown in Figure 26.

A number of samples were collected during the course of the excavation for soil pollen analysis and radio-carbon dating. These too were simply numbered in sequence. In the event only a few proved suitable for analysis and details of these are given in Appendix 3. Their distribution has been plotted in Figure 8. The results of the analyses are described in Chapters 4 and 5.

In addition to work on site the opportunity was taken of sampling the surviving portion of the Trefignath bog (Fig. 2), most of which had been filled in during the construction of the railway in the Nineteenth Century and the aluminium works in the 1970s. James Greig and the author took a monolith sample on 21 April 1978 and the pollen sequence from this is discussed with the other palynological work in Chapter 4.

WORKS AT TREFIGNATH, 1977 TO 1982
by Vernon Hughes

When Lord Sheffield placed the Trefignath Burial Chambers in the care of the Commissioners for Works in 1911 no specific arrangements were made about the land around. The monument is on a flat rocky outcrop which forms a large portion of a small field. In 1977 this field was no longer used for farming but served merely as an access to a larger field beyond. All this land belongs to the Anglesey Aluminium Co. Ltd., which is part of the Rio Tinto Organisation, and the firm farms the land itself. In order to present the monument to its best advantage it was felt that the part of the field in which it stood should be fenced off leaving the remainder as an access strip to the larger field. Thanks to the public-spiritedness of the Company and the good offices of Mr Morris, the farm manager, this was agreed to.

This fencing was carried out and a gate provided for works traffic. The stile entrance to the site from the lane was retained and a length of wall removed to provide an adequate turn-off into the new access area. The Post Office also collaborated by moving a telegraph pole to one side of the new turn-in. There were several large stones lying near the original entrance and being of similar material and proportions to the orthostats of the monument they were moved onto the site and placed in a pile just to the right of the stile.

By 1977 the oak post in the centre of the eastern chamber was in a rotten state and there was increasing danger of the whole monument collapsing. Rather than renew the post it was decided to replace both it and the temporary supports erected in 1971 with a permanent stone column built to replace a missing orthostat. The carrying out of this permanent work necessitated an investigation of the site for the new support. As it would involve the

adjustment of some of the other orthostats, with a consequent disturbance of archaeological deposits, it was decided to carry out a complete investigation of the whole monument in parallel with the remedial structural work. It was planned that the work should be divided into three phases. The first phase was to concentrate on the eastern chamber with its immediate and urgent problems, and the second phase to deal with the central chamber and any outstanding work from the first. The western chamber would be treated in the third phase which would include much of the preservation work for the whole monument.

The first year's (1977) work was dominated by the problem of lifting the two capstones of the eastern chamber so that the supporting orthostats could be returned to the vertical position, the new support built, and the old temporary supports removed. It was also necessary to ensure that the archaeological excavation of the chamber could proceed in safety. It is not known how long the capstones had been in position. The probability is that they had been there since first erected so it was decided that they should not be moved away from the chamber but merely raised into the air. To do this the Ancient Monuments Branch, using its own workforce, erected a scaffolding gantry with metal beams above and across the monument from which, with the aid of chain slings and pulley blocks, both stones were hoisted about 0.6 m above their initial positions (Plate VI). The stones were protected from damage by the chains with timber wedges. It is estimated that the weights of the two stones are 1.5 tonnes (IV) and 1.25 tonnes (VII) respectively. The northern outer portal stone (I) was supported while its stone hole was excavated. It was then fixed in a vertical position by the hole being filled with weak concrete. The recumbent orthostat on the north side (VI) was returned to a vertical position as was the end stone (VIII). The other stones were not moved. The internal stone pier and timber prop (Plate V) were removed and the chamber excavated. It was hoped that the buttress to the north of the chamber could be removed also, but as the stability of Stone VI was rather suspect it was retained bearing in mind that it could be concealed during the proposed partial reconstruction of the site. The new support was built in the space between orthostats I and VI. There had almost certainly originally been an orthostat here but all trace of it had been removed during an earlier disturbance of the site. The two capstones were then gently lowered into position and required very little adjustment for them to site firmly (Plate VII). The scaffold was removed but the excavation of the two areas where it had stood was left until the following season.

The excavation revealed a low dry-stone retaining wall along the southern limits of the cairn. This wall turned in a sweep towards the portal area. At this stage it was agreed that the final presentation of the monument should seek to show its original extent by surrounding the chambers with a pile of loose stones formed so as to partially simulate the original appearance of the cairn. The dry-stone walling was very fragile and its top course was therefore mortared to retain it in position. Larger stones were carefully laid along the top of this wall so as to prevent any damage to it and to act as a limit to the stones to be piled behind. On the north side, where little trace of dry-stone walling survived, the limit of the cairn was left deliberately broken and indistinct, though roughly corresponding to the plan on the south. This was a policy generally adopted throughout the site.

Before work began in 1978 it was agreed that because the central chamber was collapsed it would be easier if the capstone, which had broken into two pieces (XI and XII), and the other orthostats not in position (XIII, XIV, and XV) could be moved away from the monument to allow an uninterrupted area for excavation. It was decided that it would be quicker and cheaper if these stones could be lifted by crane. In the event the machine hired for the job could not gain access to the site because of the soft ground and a large crawler excavator was used instead. The jib of this machine, working without its bucket, was used to lift the stones which were then carried and placed on the north side of the monument. The machine was working to its limit when lifting the larger portion of the broken capstone (XII), an estimated weight of 3 tonnes. The large orthostat (XIV) was lying on its side and a small piece had broken off. Both parts were removed and orthostat XV, which was also broken, was taken to Caernarfon for repair. Orthostat X was propped up and then wedged in its original vertical, position, while XIII was removed by hand, and replaced after the excavations. The positions of these stones before removal can be seen in Plate IV. With the completion of the 1978 season of excavation these stones, except XV, were returned to approximately their fallen positions. Orthostat XV, after being repaired, was finally re-erected on site in November 1982.

The western chamber was the scene of activity during the third season of work. Stone XVII was lying on its side, while XVIII was leaning over and XVI resting on both (Plate III). The bases of all three were found to be partly in their original stone holes. Orthostat XIX was away from the others lying on its side to the south. All these stones were moved away from their fallen positions using a Land Rover with tackle and rollers. On completion of the excavation orthostats XVI, XVII, and XVIII were replaced erect in their original stone holes and XIX was erected in a stone hole discovered between orthostats XVI and XVIII. This was very likely its original hole.

During the excavation the waste material dug out had been placed in a neat pile near the NE corner of the Guardianship area. With the completion of the excavation the stones from this pile were used in the partial reconstruction of the cairn and the soil was levelled, spread over the grass area, and re-seeded. Other stones were brought from the boundary wall to the east of the monument and used to further build up the cairn around the chambers. The cairn was carefully formed so as to mask the northern buttress and show the original sequence of building. The western chamber and the central forecourt were roughly paved with layers of very small stones to ensure that they may be easily distinguished from the surrounding cairn.

It is the intention that the orthostats which form the chambers will be maintained in good structural order and the surface of the cairn kept free of large weeds, although small rock plants and lichen will be allowed to grow. The remainder of the site will be kept as mown grass so that visitors can see and appreciate the monument to its best advantage.

Chapter 2—The Structural Sequence

The excavations at Trefignath established that there had been three main periods of activity at the site, the principal one of which was the construction and use of the burial chambers. This activity was preceded by a brief period of occupation and followed by a prolonged period of denudation and destruction. In this chapter the history of the site is described within the framework of these three periods of activity and their subdivisions as set out in the following table.

Table 1 — Structural Periods

Period	Events at Trefignath
III	Denudation
II$_{3c}$	Closure of the eastern chamber
II$_{3b}$	Use of the eastern chamber
II$_{3a}$	Construction of the eastern chamber and closure of the central and western chambers
II$_{2b}$	Contemporary use of the central and western chambers
II$_{2a}$	Construction of the central chamber
II$_{1b}$	Use of the western chamber
II$_{1a}$	Construction of the western chamber
I	Pre-tomb activity

However, we must first give some consideration to the conditions existing at the site at the time the burial chambers were built for this also provided the setting for the pre-tomb settlement.

The main feature of the site, a smooth ridge of rock running from ENE to WSW, can still be readily appreciated today and we may be sure that this appreciation was shared by the builders of the burial chambers for the site greatly enhances the appearance of the monument. The highest point of the ridge, at 19.6m OD, lies slightly to the west of the centre of the site (Fig. 5) and it was here that the earliest of the burial chambers was erected. To the east a cleft divides the ridge in two and it was along the resulting hollow that the monument developed. About four metres to the west of the highest point the ridge terminates in a near vertical rock face dropping about 1.5m to the present ground surface. The configuration of the ridge, smoothed and gently rising to the west but stopping abruptly, suggests the characteristics of a *roche moutonnée*, a boss of rock shaped by the smoothing and plucking action of an ice sheet moving, in this case, from NE to SW during the Pleistocene Period. The plucking action will have

taken place at the down flow end and probably produced a talus of large rock slabs which were later used to build the burial chambers. The sections, profiles and elevations recorded during the excavation have made possible a conjectural reconstruction of the topography of the site before construction of the burial chambers began. This is illustrated here as Figure 7 which includes a small group of features also thought to ante-date the tomb. The extent to which the site was covered with soil at this time is difficult to judge owing to the incomplete survival of the old ground surface under the more heavily robbed portions of the cairn. But it may reasonably be assumed that virtually the whole site was covered with at least a thin layer of soil, although bare rock may have protruded in a few places. The soil and palynological studies described in Chapters 3 and 4 indicate that while some fairly open woodland could be found in the vicinity the site itself was free from tree cover and occupied mostly by grassland. It was to this rocky and grassy knoll that one or more groups of the local Neolithic population came first to camp and then to bury their dead.

Period I — Pre-tomb activity (Figs. 7 and 8)
The first period of activity at Trefignath was represented by a small group of features and a large assemblage of finds found within the buried soil preserved beneath the cairn. The incomplete survival of the cairn meant that the old ground surface was a truly sealed context in a few places only. However, its millennia-long burial by the cairn had insufficiently altered the soil profile for it to be easily recognised even on those parts of the site from which the cairn had more recently been removed. Its extent is indicated by the denser grade of stipple in Figure 6. But in places the destruction of the monument had been so thorough that not even this vestigial buried soil survived and the distribution of both features (Fig. 7) and finds (Fig. 8) is partly a reflection of this accident of survival as it is also a reflection of the original situation.

The pre-tomb activity at Trefignath may be tentatively dated to the earlier part of the fourth millennium BC by a radio-carbon date of 5050 ± 70 bp (HAR 3932) obtained from wood charcoal found beneath the first phase of the cairn (sample 8, Fig. 8). This date is more fully discussed in Chapter 5.

TREFIG
Pre-Tomb

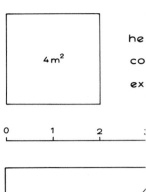

4 m²

he
co
ex

0   1   2   :

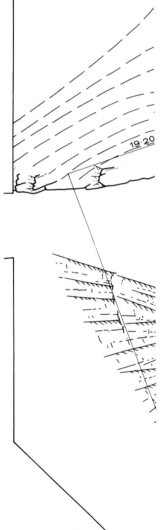

19·20

TREFIGNATH
Pre-Tomb finds

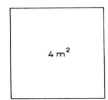

4 m²

0   1   2   3   4   5 m

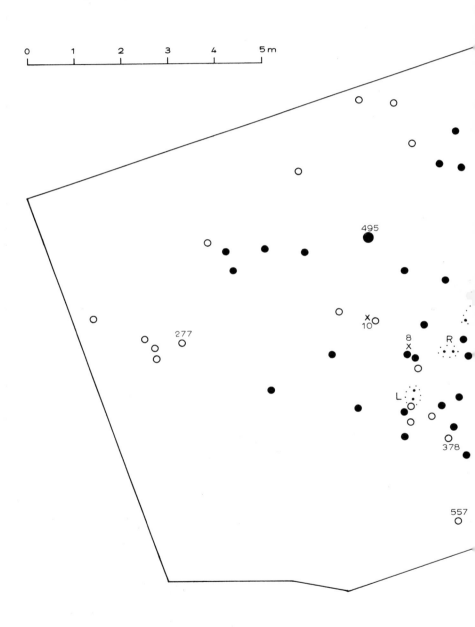

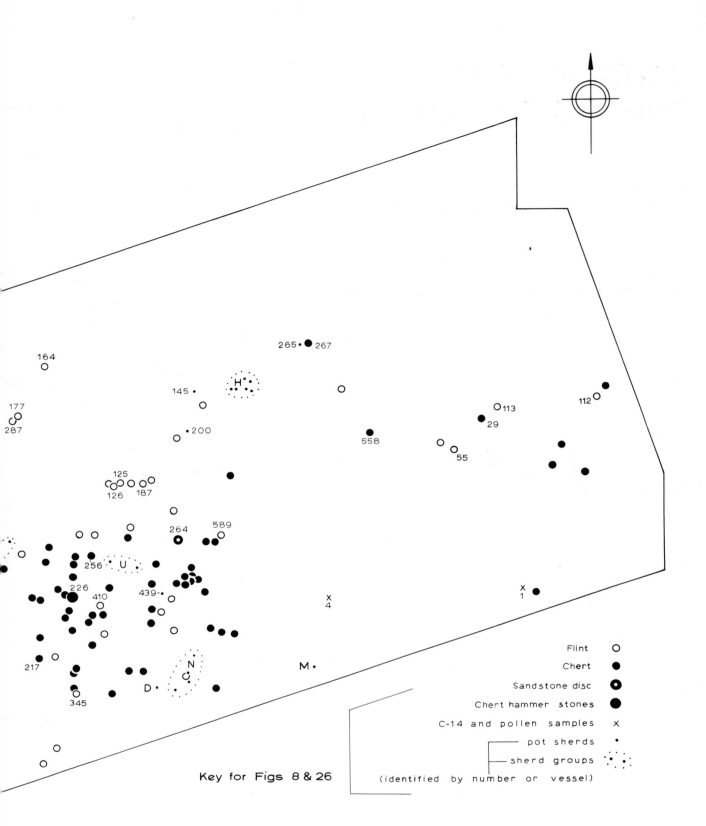

Fig. 8 — Pre-tomb finds

Of several features recorded as having penetrated the old ground surface (12) one group only (31, 32, 33, and 55) may be associated with pre-tomb activity. These features were found below cairn material associated with the central chamber and, accordingly, must ante-date its construction. On stratigraphical grounds these features could be contemporary with the earlier western chamber but this is thought unlikely as they would have stood very close to the perimeter of its cairn. There is also a hint in the finds distribution (see below and Fig. 8) that the features in question were part of a larger structure most of which would have lain under that primary phase of the cairn.

The excavation and recording of these pre-tomb features were not entirely satisfactory. This is partly due to the fact that they lay at the junction between two seasons' work, and partly because, being unexpected and in places cut away by later features, they were not at first recognised for what they were. All were at least recorded in plan and their lower levels profiled. The inset to Figure 7 shows their plan in detail with the accompanying profiles, which have been reconstructed in diagrammatic form.

Although regarded as broadly contemporary these features do not all appear to have been cut at the same time, 31 being partly cut by 55 which is itself cut by 32. Only the bottom of 31 survived, the upper portion having been removed by 30, a later stone hole. Like the other features considered here it appears to have been the socket for a timber upright about 0.2m in diameter, the initial rather irregular and large size of the pit being due to an outcrop of rock which had to be dug around in order to provide a firm footing for the post. The reconstructed profile suggests that although 55 must have been cut after 31 had been partly refilled the two posts could have been *in situ* contemporaneously. This was also the case with 55 and 32 and all four features were probably part of a single structure. The full plan of this structure cannot now be established for it must have included other features which did not survive or were not noticed during the excavation.

These remains are too fragmentary to merit detailed comparison with the few other sites where Neolithic timber structures have been identified, but some general remarks will help to place them in context. Most such structures are rectangular and employ a variety of construction techniques, including posts set individually in the ground, wall trenches, and stone footings. Occasionally more than one technique has been recognised in a single structure. Size varies considerably. At Ballyglass, County Mayo, a building 13m by 6m included both wall trench and post construction (Ó'Nulláin 1972), while at Gwernvale, Powys, two buildings, one of wall trench type and one employing post holes, measured 3.8m by 2.4m and 3.5m by 2.3m respectively (Britnell 1979). At both these sites the Neolithic buildings were found stratified beneath chambered cairns and in this respect can be said to have something in common with the fragmentary structure discovered at Trefignath. A similar structure, of post hole type measuring 14m by 8m, was found during the excavation of a complex of crop-marks at Llandegai, Gwynedd (Houlder 1968), about 40 km east of Trefignath. This building has a radio-carbon date of 5240 ± 150 bp (NPL 223). This, and a similar date of 5050 ± 75 bp (CAR 113) for the pre-tomb activity at Gwernvale (Britnell 1980), are both very similar to the date obtained at Trefignath and quoted above.

One of the features that distinguished Trefignath from the other excavated tombs in North Wales, with the exception of Bryn yr Hen Bobl (ANG 8), is the number of finds made. This is as much a reflection of the extent of the excavation as it is of the richness of the site, for Trefignath is the first to be completely excavated. These finds are described in detail in Chapters 6, 7 and 8. In this chapter we are concerned with the contribution they can make to our understanding of the nature and date of the prehistoric activity at Trefignath.

The finds of pottery, chipped flint and chert and other items that can be associated with the first period of activity at Trefignath are plotted in Figure 8. The basis for this association is that they were found on, or within 0.1m of, the old ground surface identified below the cairn. Because of the sequential nature of the cairn's development we cannot be sure that all this material ante-dates its first phase, and a similar problem has already been raised in the consideration of the pre-tomb features. Nevertheless these finds do constitute the principal assemblage of stratified material from the excavation and for this reason it has been considered best to treat them together at this stage. The point is that Period I may be more a stage in the history of the site than a distinct chronological period, but I shall return to this problem below.

The finds that may be attributed to Period I consist of twenty-four groups of pottery sherds, including remains of eight vessels (D, H, L, M, N, R, S, and U), 131 chipped flint and chert artifacts and three other items.

Although the pottery of Period I includes the remains of eight vessels all are very fragmentary and no complete profiles can be reconstructed. What diagnostic fragments there are (Fig. 35) show that the assemblage includes both globular and carinated bowls. Tentatively this assemblage may be ascribed to the group known as Irish Sea Wares and the Trefignath radio-carbon date of 5050 ± 70 bp (HAR 3932) is consistent with dates obtained for this type of pottery elsewhere (Lynch 1976, 65). The petrographic and heavy mineral analyses of the Trefignath pottery described in Chapter 7 have established that all the Period I vessels were probably made in the immediate locality. The fragmentary nature of the assemblage is what would be expected in the case of pottery in domestic use as opposed to vessels deliberately buried as part of a funerary ritual.

The chipped stone artifacts were not distributed evenly throughout the area covered by the cairn (Fig. 8). A Chi^2 Test of the kind described more fully in the introduction to Chapter 6 establishes that the probability of this distribution occurring by chance was about 1 in 1,000. It is therefore significantly non-random in the statistical sense. Although this may be partly due to the differential survival of the old ground surface comparison of Figure 8 with Figure 7 does suggest some concentration of stone artifacts immediately to the SW of the small group of features identified as belonging to this period. It is tempting to see this association of features and finds as defining the main area of activity in Period I and, perhaps, even the extent of the structure of which features 31, 32, 33 and 55 were the only tangible remains. The area in question was approximately 6m by 3m and was overlain by both the first and second phases of the cairn. However, before any further inferences are wrung from this meagre evidence it is as well to remember that the number of stone artifacts involved need constitute the remains from the reduction of no more than a few nodules. We do not appear to be dealing with activity of long duration and a very substantial structure is perhaps unlikely.

In her analysis of the flint and chert assemblage from Trefignath, including the material distinguished here as belonging to Period I (Chapter 6), Elizabeth Healey has come to the conclusion that it is relatively homogeneous and probably dates from the later, rather than the earlier, part of the Neolithic period. At first sight this may seem a little difficult to reconcile with the radio-carbon date for the Period I activity and the stratigraphical position of part of the assemblage below the primary cairn. This problem is partly bound up with that of the rather ambivalent status of the Period I material at Trefignath, and we shall consider this further shortly. However, none of the diagnostically later Neolithic pieces came from precisely the same context as the charcoal used to obtain the radio-carbon date and they can probably be associated with one or the other of the later stages in the development of the cairn. The part of the assemblage from under the primary cairn was comprised of rather more indeterminate pieces. Nevertheless I feel we should be prepared to accept the possibility that technological features usually regarded as typically later Neolithic, such as *écaille* knapping, may already be discernible in assemblages dating from the mid-fourth millennium.

The other Period I finds consist of a chert hammerstone (495; Fig. 38), a fragment of another (226) — both of which can be associated with knapping activity — and a small sandstone disc with central perforation (264; Fig. 37). This is too small to have served as a spindle whorl and may have been a bead or button.

It is now necessary to return to the twice deferred question of the status of the Period I finds at Trefignath. In the foregoing account they have been treated as a single assemblage reflecting activity on site before the construction of the burial chambers. However, the sequential nature of the tomb's development means finds which stratigraphically ante-date the second phase could be contemporary with the first, while finds ante-dating the third phase could be contemporary with both the first and second. The only absolute date is that from charcoal sample 8. Strictly speaking this can only be applied to finds from below the primary cairn, and not those below its later extensions, although there are some grounds for tentatively extending it to the structure represented by features 31, 32, 33, and 55. Other finds, still stratigraphically of Period I, could be considerably later, as may be the case with some of the stone artifacts.

The Period I finds at Trefignath probably arise from either one of two kinds of activity, or perhaps both. Firstly, they could reflect occupation of the knoll of an entirely domestic kind having nothing to do with funerary activity. Secondly, they could reflect the activities of the tomb builders. In the former case I would expect all such activity to antedate the use of any part of the site for burial, though this is an admittedly Twentieth Century AD view of the impropriety of squatting in a cemetery. In the second case the activity would have been repeated every time work was required on the monument.

In my view the Period I assemblage at Trefignath derives material from both kinds of activity. In the first place the rocky knoll seems to have been selected for some kind of temporary settlement. Whether the group responsible had a permanent home elsewhere or had not yet adopted a sedentary way of life can only be conjectured. The raw materials used in the manufacture of their pottery suggest their activities may have been confined to Ynys Gybi and palynological evidence suggests some forest clearance and cereal cultivation, but we cannot be sure that the Trefignath people were responsible for this. For whatever reason, about the middle of the fourth millennium the site became the focus of funerary activity with the construction of the first of the series of burial chambers. Domestic activity ceased, but each time there was further work on the monument more artifacts were added to the assemblage. This accumulation of material remains could have continued for over a millennium.

Other finds from Ynys Gybi dating from before the second millennium BC, while not providing a complete picture of the early settlement of the island, do enable the Trefignath finds to be seen within some kind of context. Although cut off from the mainland of Anglesey by the beginning of the fifth millennium the initial post-glacial settlement of the island may have taken place while it was still possible to cross dry shod. However, apart from two doubtful, but possibly earlier, sites at Penrhos and Trearddur Bay

TREFIGNATH
West Chamber and
Putative Cairn

V
'P' ⎤ Sherds

1m²

0   1   2   3m

Fig. 9. Plan of the western chamber and cairn (Period II₁)

(Williams 1950, 51; Burton 1914) evidence for fourth and third millennium activity on Ynys Gybi consists in the remains of two megalithic tombs and references to three others, unassociated finds of four polished stone axes and two settlements on the SW slopes of Mynydd Twr (Holyhead Mountain).

A little over 500m to the south of Trefignath lie the remains of the Trearddur Burial Chamber (ANG 16). This is the only other site on Ynys Gybi where such remains survive and it will be referred to again later in this chapter. Of the three tombs which are known only from early records, that at Plas Feilw (ANG 31) is very doubtful. If we discount this one the remainder give a density of one tomb per 9.5 km². It would be rash to take this figure as indicating the size of territorial units in the fourth or third millennia and in spite of many attempts, such as those of Renfrew (1976, 146-52), no convincing evidence has emerged for any precise correlation between tomb and territory. Nevertheless, it is interesting to note that the southern portion of Ynys Gybi—virtually a separate island—has an extent of 11 km² and the site of a single tomb (ANG 24) (Fig. 2).

Three of the four unassociated polished stone axes were found at Kingsland and the fourth about 500m SE of the Treaddur tomb (ANG 16) (Fig. 2) find spots derived from Holgate 1980, 33)). Two of the Kingsland specimens are of Group VII rock but the others are unidentified. Presumably these axes may be associated with the forest clearance indicated in the pollen record.

Stone axes of flint, chert, and unidentified material have also been found in the settlements on Mynydd Twr. One of these, at Cwm (Fig. 2), has been known for over a century (Stanley 1847b, 296-97). A group of four flint axes, a flint rough-out and a group of flakes were reported to have been found in a hut circle, a type of site normally thought to belong to a somewhat later period in prehistory. Radio-carbon dates for the nearby Ty Mawr Hut Circles indicate that they may have been occupied during the third millennium BC and a similar dating for the site at Cwm need not be regarded as exceptional. The Ty Mawr site has also produced stone axe finds, a fragment of a chert axe and an unidentified polished specimen.

Period II—The Burial Chambers

The second, and main, period of activity at Trefignath saw the erection and use of the burial chambers and their surrounding cairn. The most important discovery of the excavation was that the burial chambers were not part of a single, contemporaneous structure but had been built as three distinct phases of activity. These phases are summarised in Table 1 above. The study of the development of megalithic tombs is hampered by the paucity of extensively excavated sites providing comparative data and by speculation over un-excavated or partly excavated sites (Corcoran, 1972, 31-63). However, the composite tomb has now been recognised as so widespread a class of monument that there must be some doubt about the contemporaneous development of all but the most unitary structures.

The first chamber to be built at Trefignath was erected at the western end of the site on the highest point of the rocky knoll. This chamber was surrounded by a cairn, probably round, although very little of this survived. This cairn partly overlay the site of the settlement activity described earlier in this chapter. After an unknown interval a second chamber, the central one on the site, was erected immediately to the east. The cairn was now considerably enlarged to incorporate this new chamber and at the same time replanned so as to form a wedge-shaped long cairn defined by dry-stone walls, and with a deeply recessed forecourt at the east end onto which the chamber opened. After a further interval the third, surviving chamber was erected partly within this forecourt and the cairn was further extended so as to incorporate this third chamber. These three phases are illustrated in Figure 21 along with details of two other composite sites by way of comparison. Each of the three phases at Trefignath is now described in detail.

Period II phase 1a and b: The Western Chamber (Figs. 9 and 10; Plates III, VII, IX, X).

Until its excavation in 1979 there was some doubt about the existence of this chamber which survived only as a jumbled pile of orthostats (Fig. 5; Plate III, (Smith 1979, 340; 1978, 445)). This doubt disappeared immediately it became clear that orthostats XVI, XVII, and XVIII had occupied well-defined stone holes (contexts 42, 43, and 36 respectively)—in fact XVIII was still partly erect—and had collapsed virtually *in situ*. A fourth stone hole (49) appeared, from its shape, to have been occupied by orthostat XIX which was displaced about two metres to the south. Perhaps this was one of the stones being removed when Lady Stanley intervened in *c.* 1790 (pp. 000).

Given the collapsed state of this chamber (20) the precise details of its plan cannot now be established with complete certainty, but it evidently consisted of two distinct units; a short passage about 1.25m by 1.0m defined by orthostats XVII and XVIII, and a small polygonal chamber about 1.75m by 1.0m. The long axes of these two units were at right-angles giving the structure an 'L'-shaped plan. The gap between orthostats XVIII and XIX was probably filled with dry-stonework and the bedrock here had been deliberately levelled to provide an even footing (54). The distinct chamber and passage ground plan suggest that this chamber may be regarded as an example of a Passage Grave, albeit of a very simple form. This interpretation seems all the more likely

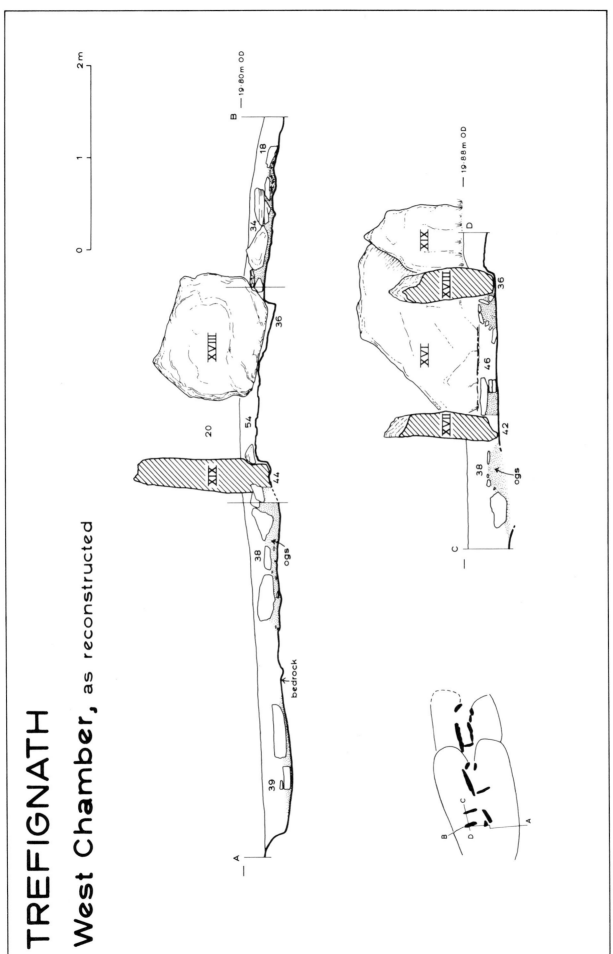

Fig. 10.   Sections through the western chamber and cairn (Period II₁).

when the elevation of the chamber is considered in addition to its plan (Fig. 10), the passage evidently being rather lower than the chamber proper. This feature is very characteristic of Passage Graves and has been achieved in this case by varying the axes on which the orthostats have been erected, those of the passage having their long axes approximately horizontal whereas at least one of the chamber orthostats (XIX) has its long axis vertical. Orthostat XVI is more irregular in shape but was nevertheless erected so as to obtain maximum height. The height difference between the chamber and passage would have presented considerable difficulties if the entire structure was to be roofed with a single capstone and in the conjectural reconstruction two are proposed (Fig. 11). There is no evidence on this point either way but the use of separate capstones for the passage and chamber would be consistent with the interpretation of this chamber as a Passage Grave. In Figure 11 the western chamber at Trefignath is compared with an Iberian tomb, the Anta 2 da Caeira, Alentejo, which exemplifies the chamber and passage arrangements particularly well.

Although the cairn around the western chamber (38) had been severely robbed sufficient survived to show that it had been built of naturally weathered boulders of about the maximum size that can be manoeuvred by a single individual without too much difficulty. Such material was probably to be found on the site, a relic from Ice Age times and contrasted in terms of colour and surface texture with the stone used in subsequent phases in the development of the cairn, some of which appears to have been specifically quarried for the purpose. This is particularly true in the case of the material used for the retaining walls and Plates IX and X illustrate the contrast between the light coloured, tabular, quarried blocks of the Period II_2 retaining walls and the darker, rounded boulders of the period II_1 cairn.

Little survived of the arrangements immediately outside the entrance to the western chamber, although the weathered boulders remaining on the western side (Plates IX and X) suggest that it may have had a small, shallow, outward curving forecourt which was later squared-off with dry-stonework in Period II_2. Apart from this little can be said about the shape of the primary cairn, though in common with most other Passage Graves it was probably round.

No ancient deposits survived within the chamber or passage, both of which had previously been cleared to bedrock, and the blocking material in front of the entrance (35) belonged to a later phase in the tomb's development. A number of finds of Neolithic pottery and stone artifacts were made within the area of the western chamber and its cairn, but apart from the few fragments of Vessels P and V none can be specifically associated with either the construction or use of this chamber.

The remains of Vessels P and V are indeed very fragmentary amounting to no more than 20 grammes in all, and the tiny pieces of P were found on analysis to be so heterogeneous that more than a single pot may be represented. Notwithstanding these limitations it is noted in Chapter 7 that neither P nor V is at all similar to the Irish Sea Ware vessels of Period I and they have more in common with the later Neolithic vessels (A, C, and G) found in the eastern chamber. The presence of such vessels in the western chamber need imply no more than it remained accessible for a long time. They certainly do not date its construction.

However, the radio-carbon date of 5050 ± 70 bp (HAR 3932) was obtained from charcoal (sample 8) found immediately below the primary cairn and provides a *terminus post quem* for its construction. I do not think the deposition of the charcoal and the beginning of building operations on site can have been separated by much of an interval, and suggest that the western chamber at Trefignath was built around the second quarter of the fourth millennium (i.e. 3750-3500 BC).

Passage Graves are one of the best known and most widely distributed categories of megalithic tomb in Western Europe. Major concentrations occur in Iberia, Brittany, Ireland, and the Northern Isles while individual tombs or small groups are found in most of the areas in between. Anglesey is one such area with the famous Passage Graves of Bryn Celli Ddu and Barclodiad y Gawres the best-known of the island's prehistoric monuments. These two sites are both classic Passage Graves with long, clearly defined passages and imposing chambers. They differ considerably from the tiny western chamber at Trefignath. But the classic sites are not necessarily typical of the full range of Passage Grave architecture and many simple, small tombs have been identified which nevertheless comprise distinct chamber and passage elements (Fig. 12). Daniel (1950, 8) was the first to draw attention to this category of tomb and proposed the name 'B-Passage-Dolmen' as a variant of his 'B-Dolmen' type. More recently Lynch (1976, 75) has used the term 'small chamber and passage' tomb to describe sites of this type. With specific reference to the western chamber at Trefignath I have preferred the phrase 'Simple Passage Grave' (Smith 1981, 134-36).

Simple Passage Graves occur throughout the area of Passage Grave distribution and are essentially so simple as to make any attempt to draw specific parallels unrewarding. Figure 12 illustrates a selection of ground plans but it should be remembered that it may only be in elevation that the distinction between chamber and passage becomes really evident. Unfortunately elevations are not as common as ground plans in publications dealing with megalithic tombs in spite of the very obvious three-dimensional quality of such sites.

In areas where they occur in their greatest density Passage Graves are commonly found in groups, the great cemeteries of Lough Crew, Carrowkeel, and Carrowmore in Ireland being well-known examples.

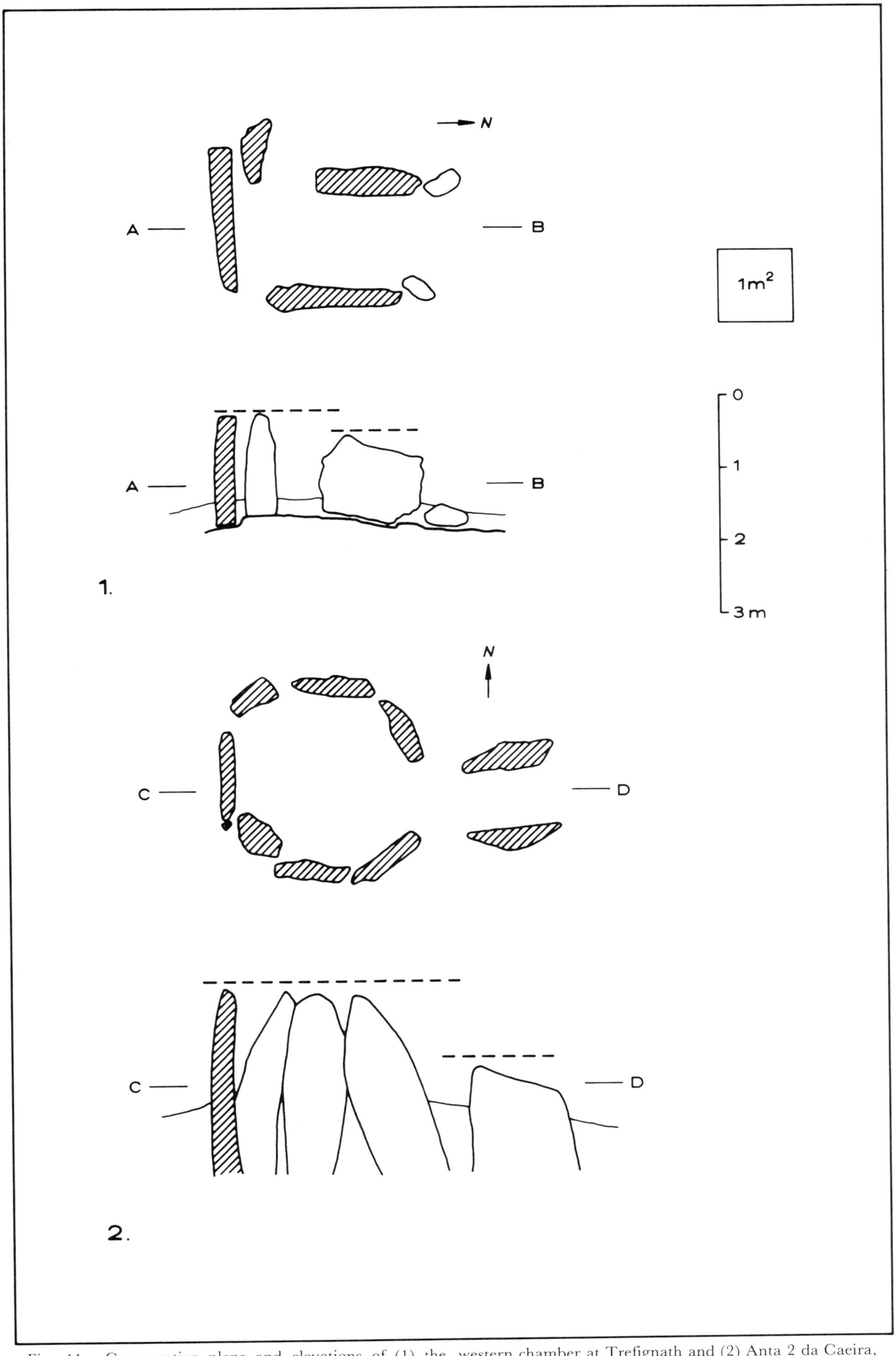

Fig. 11. Comparative plans and elevations of (1) the western chamber at Trefignath and (2) Anta 2 da Caeira, Alentejo (after Leisner, G and V 1965, I Lieferung, Tafel 9 no. 4).

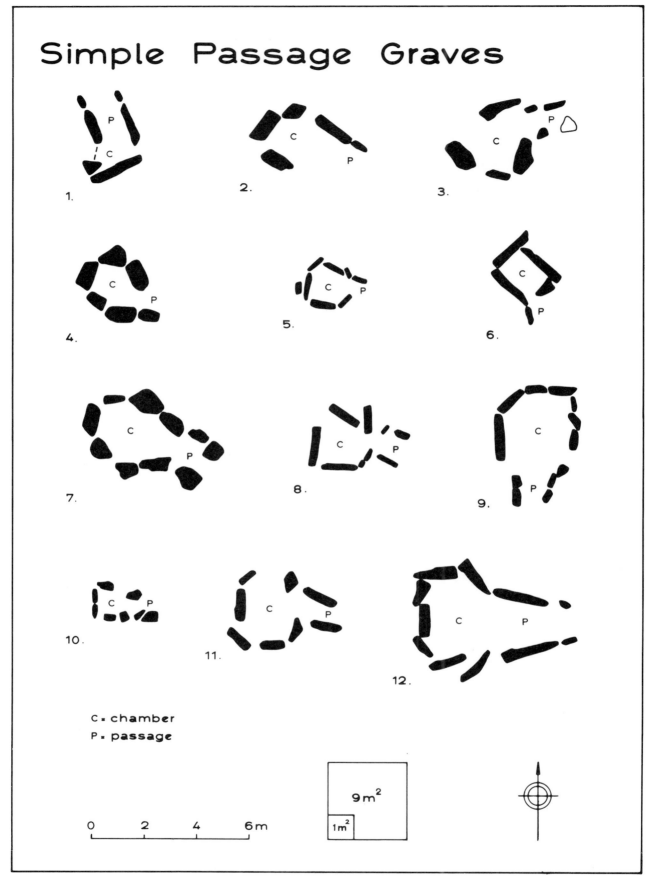

Simple Passage Graves

C = chamber
P = passage

9m²

1m²

0   2   4   6m

Fig. 12.   Comparative plans of Simple Passage Graves in Britain and Europe: (1) Trefignath, Anglesey; (2) Ty Newydd, Anglesey; (3) Hanging Stone, Pembs.; (4) Carrowmore 7, Co. Sligo; (5) Fenagh Beg 3, Co. Leitrim; (6) Scregg, Co. Roscommon; (7) Achnacreebeag, Argyll; (8) Balvraid, Inverness; (9) Quelvezin, Carnac, Brittany; (10) San Martinho 2, Alentejo, Portugal; (11) Nogueira, Alentejo, Portugal; (12) Chã das Arcas 4, Traz os Montes, Portugal (sources: 2, 3 (Lynch 1976), 74, Fig. 8); 4 (Burenhult 1980, 24); 5, 6 (Herity 1974, 84); 7 (Ritchie 1970, 32); 8 (Corcoran 1972, 33); 9 (L'Helgouach 1965, 57, Fig. 24.1); 10, 11, 12 (Leisner, G and V 1965, 2 Lieferung Tafel 13 no 16 and Tafel 5 no 11; 1 Lieferung Tafel 29 no 6)).

In peripheral areas such as Wales and Scotland the cemetery tradition does not appear to have been present and Passage Graves are usually found singly or as components in composite monuments.

About 500m to the south of Trefignath lie the remains of the Trearddur Burial Chamber (ANG 16, Fig. 2), the only other surviving tomb on Ynys Gybi. Even here only two orthostats survive, one of which has fallen. The situation of this tomb is very similar to that occupied by the western chamber at Trefignath and the surviving orthostats at Trearddur resemble more those employed in that structure than in either of the later chambers. I therefore tentatively suggest that Trearddur was also a Simple Passage Grave. Trefignath and Trearddur are clearly intervisible and are close enough to have been part of a cemetery on the Irish model. However, two tombs hardly constitute a cemetery and better parallels for Trefignath are provided by Scottish sites such as Balvraid, Mid Gleniron II, and Achnacreebeag (Corcoran 1972, 33 and 37) where Simple Passage Graves occur as parts of composite monuments.

Whilst views on the absolute, and even relative, dating of the various types of megalithic tomb are constantly changing (*Antiquity*, 1981, 82-85) there is widespread agreement that Simple Passage Graves stand early in the sequence and may be ancestral to the Passage Grave type as a whole (Giot 1960, 42, 87; Herity 1974, 75; Lynch 1976, 77; Burenhult 1980, 111-15). This relatively early chronological position is well demonstrated at Trefignath where the Simple Passage Grave occupies the primary position in what was to become a complex sequence of tomb development.

Period II phases 2a and b; The Central Chamber (Figs. 13, 14 and 15; Plates IV, XII, XIII, XIV and XV)

The next stage in the development of the monument was the erection of a second burial chamber immediately to the east of the Simple Passage Grave and the enlargement of the primary cairn so as to encompass both chambers. The interval of time involved is not apparent but soil pollen samples from below both the primary cairn (samples 10.1 and 10.2) and its enlargement (sample 4b) show that it was of sufficient duration for some change in the environment to be registered. Both samples have similar amounts of tree pollen but the sample from below the enlarged cairn records an increase in the pollen from both grasses and arable plants. This suggests that there had been some progress in the conversion of the landscape to farmland between the construction of the western chamber and the addition of that in the centre.

The newly erected chamber was of a completely different type. With the exception of orthostat X this chamber had completely collapsed before the excavation began (Fig. 5 and Plate IV), although orthostat XV had continued to support one end of the capstone (XII) until 1971, as described in Chapter 1. Given that the positions of orthostats X and XV are known and that that of XIV can be inferred from the way in which it had collapsed, the original plan of the chamber may be established with reasonable certainty. It was basically rectangular, about 2.8m long and with an entrance at the eastern end. On the north side this entrance was flanked by a low portal stone (X) and the excavation revealed a stone hole (25) for a similar portal stone on the southern side. The entrance thus created was narrow, being only about 0.5m wide, and had a slightly different axis to the chamber itself, a feature repeated in the later eastern chamber. Like the southern portal stone the southern side slab of the chamber was represented by a stone hole (30) only. From this it appears that the chamber was about 1.25m wide. Orthostat XIII, found broken and lying on cairn debris immediately to the south of the chamber, was probably originally the southern portal stone and like orthostat XIX of the western chamber may have been saved from removal altogether by the timely intervention of Lady Stanley in *c.* 1790 (p. 5). The capstone is now broken in two (XI and XII) and has been in this state at least since the preparation of the engraving published by Stanley in 1867 (Plate I). It appears that even when complete it could not have rested on both the end stone (XV) and the portals (X and XIII). In the conjectural elevation illustrated in Figure 15 it has been assumed that the capstone rested in a level position on two side slabs and the end stone while the portal stones rose in front of its leading edge.

With the exception of the southern side slab and portal stone, which were erected in stone holes (30 and 25), the other upright elements in this chamber stood directly on bedrock gaining stability by being wedged against natural fissures and ledges. Two natural rock benches occur within the area of the chamber and it is likely that these formed a feature at the time of its use, one a platform within the chamber proper, the other a kind of threshold between the portal stones.

The erection of the central chamber (14) entailed some disturbance of the primary cairn (38) but the main development in this respect was its enlargement and total replanning; the primary, small, and putatively round cairn being replaced by a much larger wedge-shaped long cairn (10). This enlarged cairn possessed a number of distinct features which allow comparison with other long cairns elsewhere in western Britain. The first of these is the wedge-shaped ground plan. From a maximum of 8.4m near the eastern end the width diminishes westwards to about 5.0m at the top of the outcrop where the cairn terminated. The structure was approximately symmetrical along its central axis and this appears to have been an important consideration for had the southern margin been displaced even 0.5m farther south the edge of the cairn would have been brought up against a substantial rock ridge which would have provided greater lateral stability than the dry-stone

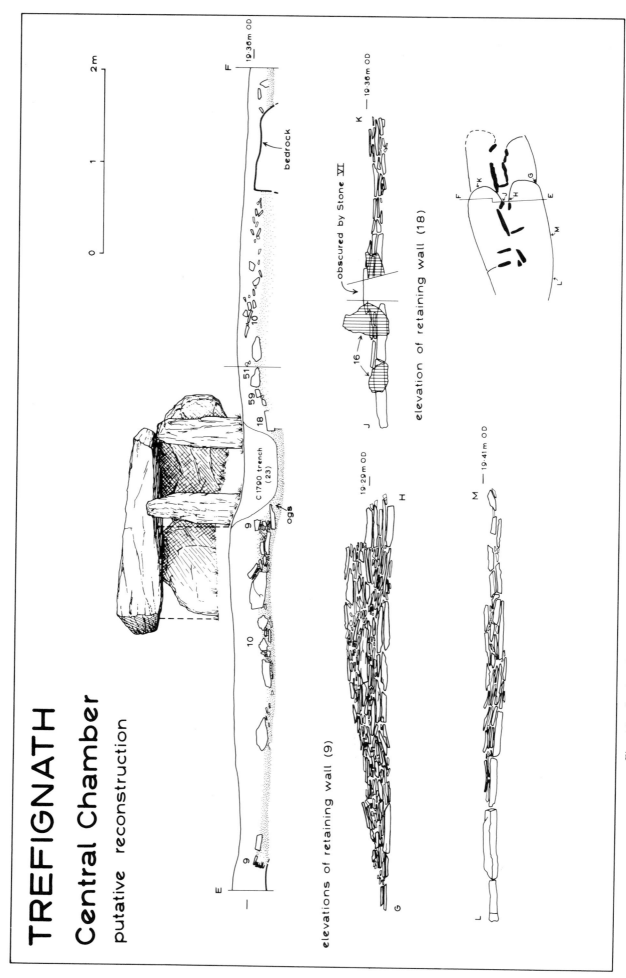

Fig. 14.   Section through the wedge-shaped cairn and, elevations of the retaining walls (Period II₂).

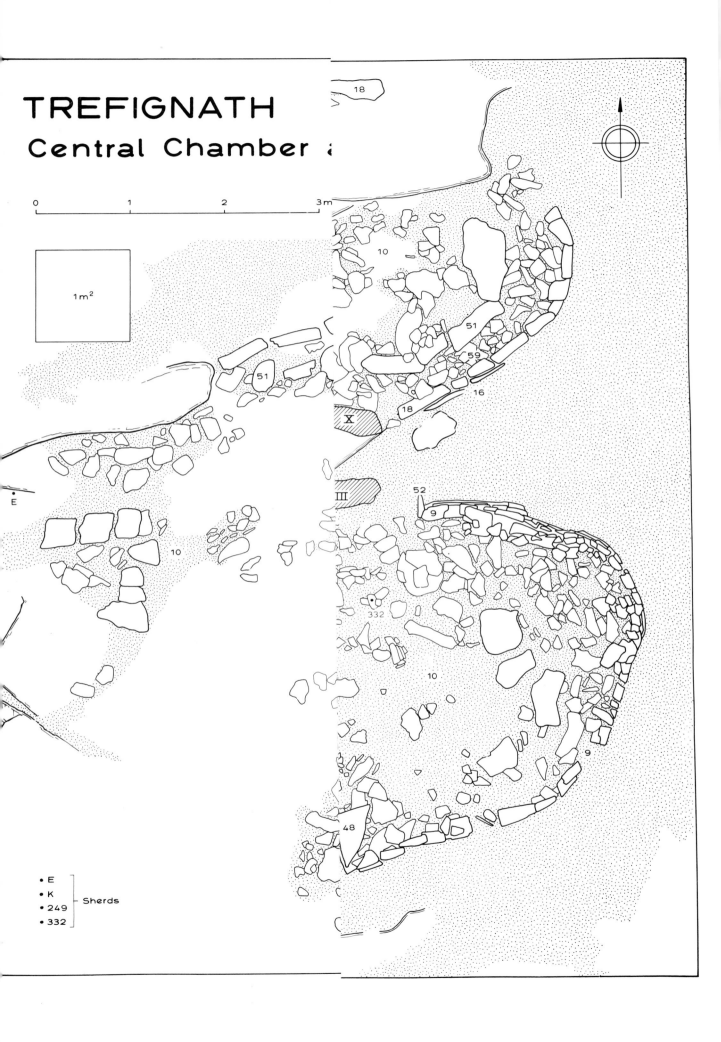

TREFIGNATH
Central Chamber

retaining wall actually used. Secondly, at the eastern end of the cairn lay a deeply recessed forecourt onto which the central chamber opened through its portals. Thirdly, the long cairn was delimited to the north and south by dry-stone retaining walls (9) which were continued around the eastern end and into the forecourt. No corresponding feature was traced at the western end and the natural rock outcrop probably provided sufficient demarcation in this direction. The retaining walls were poorly preserved, little more than one or two courses surviving throughout most of their length, with wide gaps on the north side. Preservation was better in the forecourt and on its southern side up to nine courses remained, rising to nearly 1.0m in height (Plate XII). Where the retaining wall survived to its highest it exhibited a marked tendency to lean inwards, towards the body of the cairn. This was at first surprising as it might have been expected that the weight of the cairn material would have pushed the retaining wall outwards. The answer was provided by the excavation of the portion of the cairn lying to the north of the forecourt. Here clear traces survived of an inner retaining wall of substantial blocks (51), the space between it and the outer wall being filled with small rubble (59) (Plate XII; Fig. 13). This implies that, at least in the vicinity of the forecourt, the outer retaining walls were little more than a facing and served no structural function. Destruction of the long cairn had been too extensive for the full extent of the inner retaining wall to be established, but traces along the northern side indicate that it was not confined to the forecourt alone. The last of the generally distinctive features is the presence within the long cairn of one, or perhaps two, lateral walls. On the south side of the cairn, about 3.5m from its eastern end, a spur of dry-stone walling (48) projected at right-angles from the retaining wall towards the body of the cairn. It could be traced for a little over a metre but had no obvious structural function. A similar feature was found on the north side of the cairn but its status is somewhat equivocal owing to its proximity to the entrance to the western chamber. This short length of dry-stonework (34) ran inwards from the edge of the cairn and abutted the remnants of the primary cairn on the west side of the entrance to the western chamber (Plate IX). On excavation this feature was regarded as an extension to the entrance passage and was taken to imply that the western chamber remained accessible during the use of the central chamber. Proof of this interpretation was not forthcoming for no trace could be found of the opposite side of this putative extended passage and the possibility remains that 34 need have been no more than a lateral wall similar to 48 but fortuitously placed in relation to the entrance to the western chamber. However, I still prefer the former view, and the material immediately to the east of 34 is regarded as entrance blocking (35) rather than cairn material.

The outer retaining walls were built of neat dry-stonework, the blocks having been carefully selected and laid. The bedrock at Trefignath does split into convenient tabular blocks and sufficient material could have been provided by a limited amount of quarrying. Traces of this were identified on the outcrop at the west end of the site where a series of ledges had been produced by the removal of substantial tabular blocks (53) (Plate XI). The quarrying method employed is not known but natural fissures in the rock would have facilitated the use of wedges and levers. The broken remains of Vessel E, a carinated bowl of Irish Sea Ware (Fig. 35; Plate XX), lay on one of the quarried ledges.

Like the western chamber, that in the centre contained no ancient deposits owing to disturbance in earlier times. Archaeologically, this disturbance was represented by a substantial robbers' pit (23) which had removed most of the deposits in the forecourt (Fig. 15) and by the discovery of a sherd of post-Medieval pottery (243) at the bottom of stone hole 25. Many finds of Neolithic pottery and stone artifacts were made within the vicinity of the central chamber but most of this material is thought to belong to Period I. The three sherds (186) which comprise the remains of Vessel K provide an exception (Fig. 36; Plate 00). These were found within the area of the central chamber and differ sufficiently from the Period I material to be regarded, tentatively, as part of the contents of the tomb. Vessel K, which is distinct in both appearance and petrology is described in Chapter 7. Here it is enough to note that it appears to belong to the widespread class of later Neolithic pottery known as Grooved Ware. Hitherto finds of Grooved Ware have been a rarity in Wales, the Lligwy Burial Chamber (ANG 14; Fig. 1) being one of the few places where material of this kind has been recognised. Recently, excavations at Gaerwen, also in Anglesey, have produced some finds of Grooved Ware associated with domestic occupation (White 1981, 17-20) and a considerable assemblage of Grooved Ware has been recovered from a settlement at Trelystan, Montgomery (Britnell 1981, 201). Radio-carbon dates from these sites indicate that Grooved Ware was in use in North Wales by the middle of the third millennium BC. Two other anomalous sherds (332 and 249) were close to the central chamber. In fabric they are similar to Vessel V and the later Neolithic vessels found in the eastern chamber (A, C, and G). From this limited evidence we may tentatively infer that the central chamber at Trefignath was in use (i.e. Period II$_{2b}$) during the middle of the third millennium BC.

Although no trace of burials survived within the central chamber a Nineteenth Century reference seems to imply that one or more inhumations were found there in *c.* 1790 (Chapter 1). The reference in question (Jones 1855) states simply that urns and bones were found at Trefignath but does not say in which chamber. However, as the western chamber,

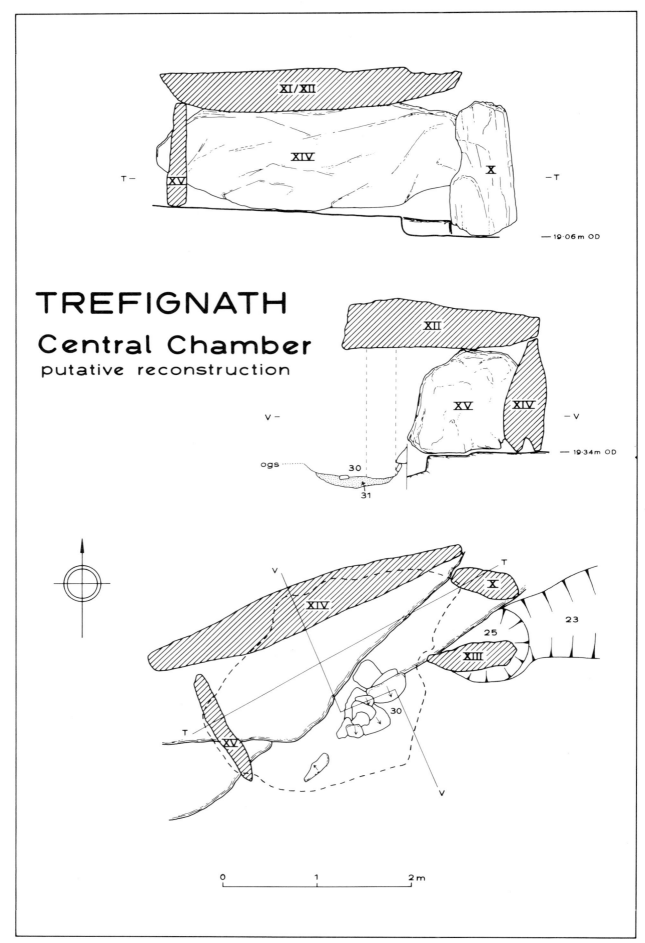

Fig. 15. Plan and sections through the conjectured central chamber (Period II₂).

being a Passage Grave, is more likely to have contained cremations, and the eastern chamber, according to Aubrey (Chapter 2), had been disturbed long before the Eighteenth Century, these discoveries may be attributed to the central chamber.

The construction of the central chamber (Period II_{2a}) is dated by the Irish Sea Ware carinated bowl, Vessel E, which was found on one of the ledges from which blocks had been quarried for the retaining walls. Vessels of this type have hitherto been dated to the fourth millennium and the Trefignath example can be taken to suggest that the central chamber may have been under construction as early as the beginning of the third millennium, if not even earlier.

The central chamber at Trefignath is architecturally undistinguished and can be paralleled in many areas where megalithic tombs are found. Masters' (1981, 171-72) recent attempt to ascribe it to the Portal Dolmen class is not accepted here. Similarly the wedge-shaped long cairn may be widely paralleled, but it is sufficiently distinctive for it to be assigned to a class of monument with which it has a lot in common. Long cairns enclosing megalithic chambers are found in several parts of the British Isles, notably in Ireland, SW Scotland, Wessex, and the Cotswold-Severn area. The detailed features of the long cairn at Trefignath, enumerated above, find their best parallels among the long cairns of the Cotswold-Severn group. Corcoran (1969, 41-68) divided the sites in this group into three classes according to the type of megalithic chamber the long cairn encloses. His classes are 'Cairns with simple terminal chambers', 'Cairns with terminal transepted chambers' and 'Cairns with lateral chambers'. The simple terminal chamber at Trefignath invites comparison with the first of these classes (Fig. 16, numbers 1 and 2). All the principal features—the wedge-shaped long cairn with dry-stone retaining walls, the deeply recessed forecourt, and the simple terminal chamber—can be paralleled among sites in the Cotswold-Severn group and it is only the relatively small size of Trefignath (Fig. 16, number 3) and its considerable distance from the main Cotswold-Severn area that lead to any reticence in formally assigning it to that group. However, the size of the Trefignath cairn is more likely to be a reflection of the availability of resources—both of materials, for some quarrying was necessary, and labour—than a specifically architectural feature of tomb design. The problem of distance is also reduced when it is recalled that several sites with Cotswold-Severn affinities have been identified in North Wales. The best known of these is the Capel Garmon long cairn (Fig. 16, number 4). Others in the group are Carnedd Hengwm North and South (Lynch 1976, 68-71) and Tyddyn Bleiddyn (Lynch 1969, 144-45). There seems to me little reason why the Period II_2 tomb at Trefignath should not be included in this North Wales group of Cotswold-Severn tombs. The spread of Cotswold-Severn architectural forms to this area may be seen as part of a much wider dissemination, the repercussions of which have been detected in SW Scotland and the north of Ireland (Daniel 1963, 19-20; Scott 1969, 206-12; Corcoran 1969, 103; 1972, 49-53).

Some slight evidence survived of the arrangements for blocking the entrance to the central chamber. Most of the material in the forecourt had been removed by later disturbances (23), and it is not clear whether what remained was part of a formal blocking or simply cairn material added when the eastern chamber was built. The evidence consisted of a few flat slabs (16) which had been carefully laid against the face of the retaining walls (Plate XIII), presumably to protect them when the forecourt area itself was filled with stone and soil. However, at the inner end of the forecourt a single stone (52) was found to project at right-angles from the southern retaining wall into the chamber entrance. This stone was quite firmly in place and did not appear to have slipped out of position (Fig. 13 and Plate XII). It has been assumed that it was an intentional feature and formed part of the arrangements for blocking the entrance. With only a single stone for evidence it is difficult to be more specific, but if originally there were others at higher levels and on both sides of the entrance they may have provided keying by which a blocking wall across the entrance was tied to the retaining walls. Such features can be paralleled at other long cairns where dry-stone walling has been extensively used such as Gwernvale (Britnell, 1984), and would have facilitated repeated access to the chamber.

It has already been suggested that the western chamber at Trefignath remained in use during the construction and use of the central chamber. The evidence for this is that when the cairn was enlarged and replanned to accommodate the central chamber (Period II_{2a}) instead of simply blocking the entrance to the western chamber provision was made for continuing access by the construction of a short dry-stone passage, one side of which survived (34). This passage was built in what had been the shallow forecourt of the western chamber and its effect was to extend the entrance passage of that chamber to the edge of the enlarged cairn (Plates IX and X). Slight but further confirmation for the continuing use of the western chamber is provided by the remains of Vessels P and V. These were found in the chamber and its entrance passage and are best paralleled by the coarse, heavily gritted wares represented in the central chamber by sherds 232 and 249 (Period II_{2b}) and later still by Vessels A and C in the eastern chamber (Period II_3). This may be taken to imply that the western chamber remained accessible as long as the central chamber, that is down to Period II_{3a} when the eastern chamber was built.

The arrangements for closing the western chamber seem to have been similar to those suggested in the case of the central chamber. The surviving, western side of the extended entrance passage was of the same

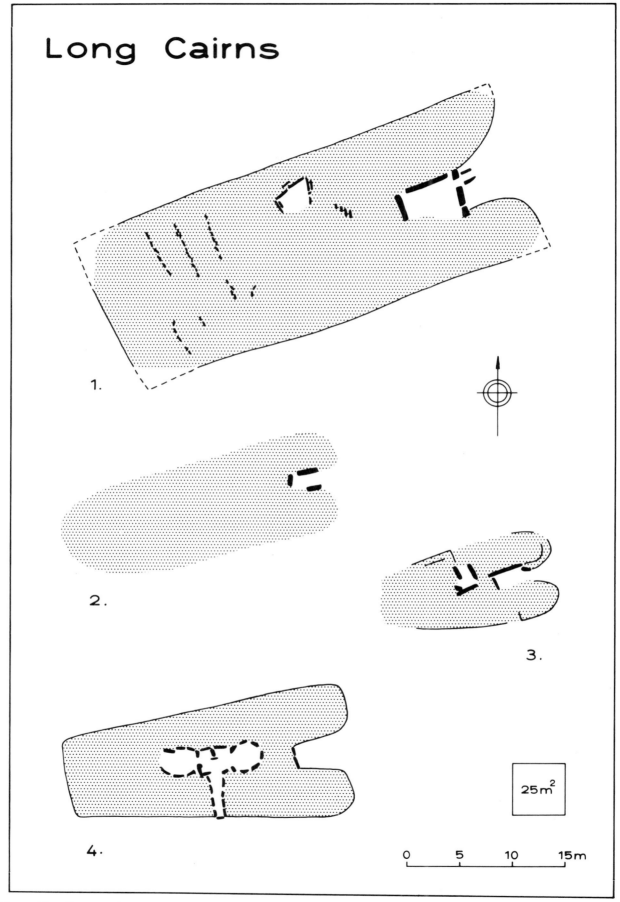

Long Cairns

Fig. 16. Comparative plans of long cairns; (1) Tinkinswood, Glamorgan (GLA 9); (2) Maes y Felin, Glamorgan (GLA 10); (3) Trefignath Period II₂, Anglesey (ANG 1); Capel Garmon, Denbighshire (DEN 3) (sources: 1, 2 (Corcoran 1969, 42 Fig. 9, 15 Fig. 1); 4 (Lynch 1969, 144 Fig. 51)).

character and material as the retaining wall of the long cairn and of one build with it. In spite of this no attempt was made to create a neat jamb (Plate X), the slabs of the retaining wall giving the impression that they had continued without a break across the entrance. This suggests that like the central chamber, provision was made for the entrance to be walled-up. Arrangements such as these have been noted at other Cotswold-Severn Long Cairns (Britnell, 1984; Corcoran 1969, 91). Such a blocking wall could easily be removed and replaced as occasion demanded but the passage itself contained remains of what is taken to be the final blocking of this chamber. This consisted of a compact mass of soil and stones (35), confined on the west by the passage wall (34) but petering out to the east. This material must have been put in place when the western chamber was closed for the last time. This event cannot be dated, but as indicated above it could be at least as late as Period II_{3a}.

It finally remains to consider the status of the extensive spreads of stone found beyond the retaining walls of the long cairn, to both the north and south. Such spreads of stone are a common feature at excavated sites of the Cotswold-Severn group and have attracted much comment, the main consideration being whether such material represented a fortuitous collapse of the cairn or a deliberately placed structural element. Daniel (1950, 41-42) was one of the first to suggest that such material, called by him and others 'extra-revetment', was part of the design of the cairn and not later collapse. From this it followed that both outer and inner retaining walls were no more than structural devices within the body of the cairn and that the neat trapezoidal ground plan recorded at many sites was something of an illusion; the actual, original, plan being more simply ovate or oblong, although the absence of a clearly defined outer limit made this difficult to appreciate today. Grimes (1960) has given this problem the most exhaustive treatment to date in the course of the Burn Ground long cairn report. In a very careful consideration of the evidence Grimes makes out a strong case for regarding the extra-revetment at Burn Ground as part of the original structure of the long cairn and from this basis argues for a similar interpretation of the evidence from a number of other, less thoroughly investigated, sites. Since the publication of Grimes' work the view that extra-revetment was structural rather than simply collapse has been widely accepted (Corcoran 1969, 93; Saville 1979, 89), but some problems remain.

It is still difficult to accept that the great skill displayed in the laying out of most of the long cairns that have been thoroughly investigated arose from structural considerations alone and that the main architectural elements of the cairn, which have such a widespread occurrence, were never intended to be manifest. Similarly it is hard to appreciate why such care was lavished on the construction of neat dry-stone retaining walls if they were to be immediately obscured by extra-revetment. In fact greater structural stability would have been provided if the retaining walls had been keyed into the material on both sides.

The answer to these problems may lie, in part at least, in the interval of time that elapsed between the construction of the outer retaining walls and the placing of the extra-revetment. This question has hitherto received little attention, although Corcoran (1969, 92) expressed the view that these two events were 'separated by no great interval of time'. In the recent excavation of the Gwernvale long cairn the excavator paid particular attention to the status of the material found lying beyond the line of the outer retaining wall. Whilst concluding that this material was indeed part of a deliberately placed extra-revetment, probably intended to mask the outlines of the trepezoidal long cairn, this actual masking may not have occurred until several hundred years after the original construction of the cairn (Britnell, 1984).

Although fragmentary and disturbed, the remains of the long cairn at Trefignath can contribute some information on this point. The stratigraphical relationship between the original long cairn built around the central chamber and its extension eastwards when the eastern chamber was erected was very clear (Plate XV), the retaining wall of the extension abutting at right-angles the retaining wall of the original cairn. Had that original retaining wall been obscured by extra-revetment some traces of it might have been expected to survive below the later extension. No such trace survived and it seems likely that no extra-revetment was in place at the time the cairn was extended eastwards. Furthermore, it has already been pointed out that the retaining walls on either side of the forecourt in front of the central chamber fulfilled no structural function, the mass of the cairn being retained by an inner, more substantial, structure. It may be concluded from this that the outer retaining wall, at least in the vicinity of the forecourt and perhaps elsewhere, was entirely cosmetic and therefore intended to be seen, not masked by extra-revetment. I have also drawn attention to the symmetry of the long cairn at Trefignath. Greater stability could have been achieved by a small displacement to the south which would have enabled the cairn material to be retained by a ridge of bedrock. But in the interests of the overall layout this option was not adopted, and I believe that this is a further indication that the details of the layout were important and intended to be seen. Finally, although considerable quantities of stone did lie beyond the retaining walls none of this material appeared to have been deliberately placed nor did it exhibit any of the characteristics of extra-revetment as identified at other sites, and specially by Grimes at Burn Ground (Grimes 1960, 47-59). Instead, this material had every appearance of being debris which had slumped from the cairn on the partial collapse of the retaining walls the basal courses of which could be seen to be displaced in several places. In summary, there is no evidence that the original wedge-shaped long cairn at Trefignath was masked by deliberately placed extra-revetment. On the contrary it seems that the layout of the cairn and its carefully built retaining walls were intended to be seen and represented the finished appearance of the monument, at least until the construction of the eastern chamber and the extension of the cairn.

Period II phases 3a, b and c; The Eastern Chamber (Figs. 17, 18, and 19; Plates V, VI, VII, VIII, XIV, XVI, XVII, and XVIII).

The third stage in the development of the monument was the erection of a further chamber (5) to the east. Because it was built partly within the forecourt of the central chamber and blocking access to it we may assume that this chamber was not in contemporaneous use. Soil pollen samples from under the extension of the cairn built around the eastern chamber (4) (samples 1a and d) indicate, by a marked decline in tree pollen, that the landscape had been further opened up during the period the central chamber was in use.

The eastern chamber survives virtually intact (Fig. 19; Plate V) and consists of two elements; the chamber itself (5) and a complex portal (8). The chamber proper is rectangular and measures 2.5m by 1.0m, the long axis being approximately the same as that of the central chamber. Single, recumbent orthostats (V and VI) provide the south and north sides while a polygonal slab (VIII) closes the west end. In plan and size this chamber is very similar to the central chamber but the design is so simple that this may not be significant. The portal, which has an axis slightly different to that of the chamber—again repeating a feature of the central chamber—is defined by what were originally two pairs of upright orthostats (II and III, I and ?), although the innermost one on the northern side is missing and has now been replaced by a masonry pillar. The stones on the south imbricate with each other and with the side slab of the chamber. The surviving inner portal stone stands to a height of 1.2m and supports the eastern end of the more easterly of the two capstones (IV). The outer pair of portal stones rise to a height of 2m and are of such monumental proportions that there must be some doubt that they were ever covered by cairn material. The chamber was divided from the portal by a low wall of deeply set overlapping slabs (13; Fig. 19) the southern end of which had been displaced when the chamber was disturbed, probably towards the end of the Eighteenth Century. The chamber and portal had been so thoroughly disturbed that no ancient deposits survived *in situ*.

During this third phase of development the long cairn was extended eastwards (4) so as to surround the new chamber, this extension being delimited to the north, south and east by a further series of drystone retaining walls (6). On the south side the new

retaining wall abutted that of the earlier cairn and provided a clear stratigraphical relationship. The same thing undoubtedly also happened on the north side but the relationship here had been destroyed. These retaining walls were more substantial than the outer walls of the original long cairn, being built of large blocks, and appeared from overlapping joints to have been laid from west to east. They were also keyed directly into the main body of the cairn and in the absence of any inner retaining walls must have taken its full thrust. The body of the cairn was very disturbed to the north of the chamber but to its south preservation was somewhat better, several layers of large stones surviving in places. At the eastern end the extended long cairn had a recessed forecourt onto which the chamber opened through its monumental portal. This forecourt was similar to that provided in front of the central chamber but was flatter and had sharper angles with the sides of the cairn.

During the second phase of the tomb's development (Period II$_2$) it was the wedge-shaped long cairn that had the most distinctive features and enabled the architectural affinities of the site at this stage to be established. In the third phase it is the chamber that is most distinctive and allows comparisons with other sites in Britain.

The principal features of the eastern chamber are the simple rectangular chamber itself and the portal with its outer pair of monumental stones erected on roughly the same axis as the chamber. These features can all be found in a number of sites in SW Scotland, thought by Scott (1969, 181) to lie early in the sequence he has proposed for the development of tombs in the Clyde area. Once again I do not accept Masters' (1981, 172) description of this chamber at Trefignath as a Portal Dolmen. Several Clyde chambers are illustrated in Figure 20 where they may be compared with Trefignath, The similarity is striking and may imply a fairly close connexion. Just as the affinities of the central chamber and wedge-shaped long cairn document the arrival in North Wales of architectural influences from the south and east, those of the eastern chamber appear to document a similar process, but one emanating from the north.

Although all ancient deposits in both the portal and chamber had been disturbed, considerable amounts of ancient pottery and a fine flint sickle (48) were recovered during the excavation. These finds can probably be attributed to the use and final closure of the eastern chamber. Remains of three vessels (A, C, and G) were found within the portal, although a further sherd of Vessel G came from within the chamber while sherds of A were also found in the forecourt. All three are heavily decorated and although fragmentary can be identified as belonging to the Peterborough Ware class of late Neolithic pottery, Vessels A and C being apparently of its Fengate subdivision. Such vessels are rare as grave goods in megalithic tombs except in secondary contexts, and even this is not common (Megaw and

TREFIGNATH
East Chamber and

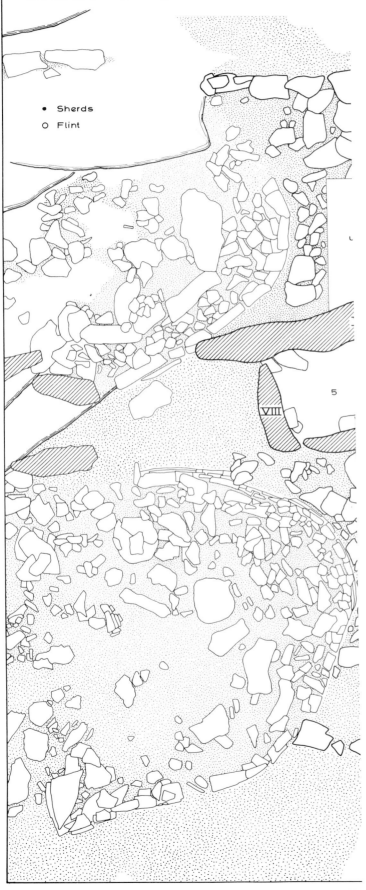

● Sherds
○ Flint

VIII

5

Fig. 17.   Pla

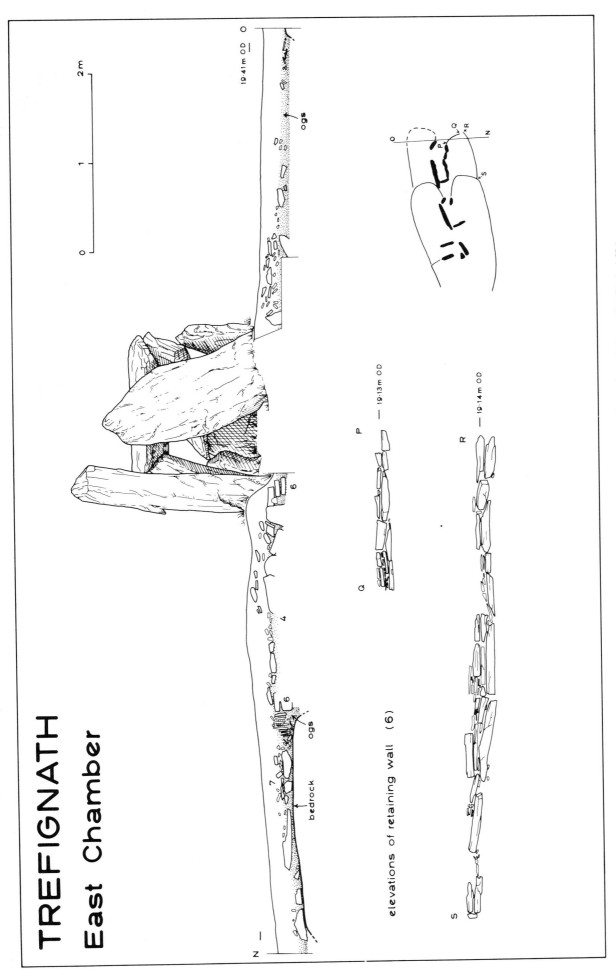

TREFIGNATH
East Chamber

elevations of retaining wall (6)

Fig. 18.   Section through the extended cairn with elevations of retaining walls (Period II₃).

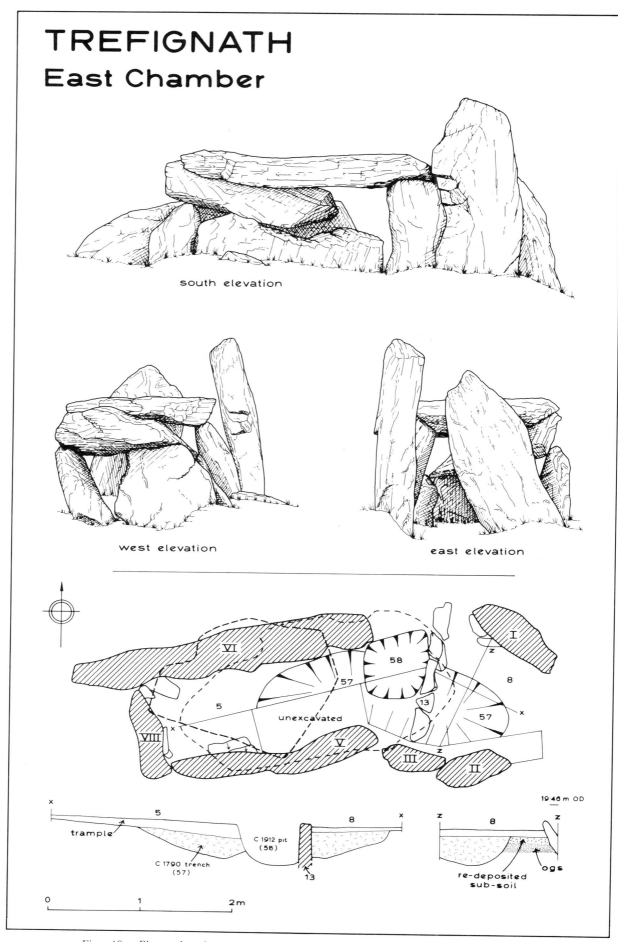

Fig. 19. Plan, elevations, and sections through the eastern chamber (Period II$_3$).

Simpson, 1979, 166-68). They are more usually found on settlement sites and the best parallels for the Trefignath vessels are among the many sherds from the settlement at Bryn yr Hen Bobl (Lynch 1970, 69) and the few from the putative henge at Castell Bryn Gwyn (Wainwright 1962, 49). Smith (1974, 112) dates the development of the Peterborough Ware series from the first quarter of the third millennium to the first quarter of the second and places the Fengate variant at the end of this sequence. The implication of this for Trefignath is that the Fengate vessels were part of a secondary deposit and nothing, except perhaps the two sherds of Vessel G, remains of the primary deposit. Petrographic analysis of sherds from Vessels A, C and G indicates that they were probably manufactured locally, implying that the eastern chamber was used as a burial vault by a group living on Ynys Gybi.

It has been proposed above that the central chamber was in use by the middle of the third millennium and the sequence established on site requires that the construction of the eastern chamber occurred after this. A date for this during the third quarter of the third millennium would seem reasonable from the evidence on site but it is difficult to reconcile this with the considerably earlier date suggested by Trefignath's Clyde analogies. The tomb at Glenvoidhean (Fig. 20, 2) has a radio-carbon date of 2910 ± 115 bc (I 5794) (*Antiquity*, 1981, 83) implying a date in calendar years a millenium earlier than that suggested for Trefignath. However, it would be rash to infer too much from a single date and judgment on this issue should be suspended until more dates are available from both Scotland and Wales.

Several features were noted within the forecourt area below a layer of stone that probably constituted the disturbed remnants of the blocking. These features consisted of an arc of stake holes (26, 27, 28, and 29), of uncertain function, and a pit (11). This pit may have played some part in the rituals that we can assume took place within the forecourt, or it could have contained a secondary burial. The remains of Vessel B, amounting to little more than a few rim and body sherds, were found close by. If vessel B had originally held a cremation within pit 11 it could easily have been smashed and its sherds scattered when the chamber was broken into and disturbed, but there was no trace of any cremated bone to support this interpretation. The disturbance was so thorough that it was not possible to establish whether pit 11 had been sealed by forecourt blocking or cut through it.

In the outer part of the forecourt and along the southern side of the enlarged long cairn considerable quantities of stone were found beyond the retaining walls (Fig. 6) and it is necessary to turn again to the question of extra-revetment material. Had this material been deliberately placed as an extra-revetment or had it simply collapsed from the cairn with the displacement of its retaining walls? The

evidence at this eastern end of the site does seem to suggest, in contrast to that associated with the original wedge-shaped long cairn of Period II$_2$, that much of this material was deliberately placed *in situ*, perhaps fairly soon after the completion of the retaining walls. It could be seen to be regularly disposed in the vicinity of the retaining walls, small slabs having been laid vertically against the wall face and other slabs and blocks firmly wedged against them at an angle (Fig. 18; Plates XVI and XVIII). This closely resembles the situation described by Grimes (1960, 58-59) and accepted by him as evidence for a deliberately placed extra-revetment at the Burn Ground Long Cairn.

The final phase in the development of the Trefignath Burial Chambers (Period II$_{3c}$) appears to have been the deliberate placement of extra-revetment around the eastern end of the enlarged long cairn and into the forecourt to serve as blocking. The absence of such a feature around the entire monument probably means that the original wedge-shaped long cairn had already suffered some collapse by the time it was decided to add an extra-revetment around the eastern chamber. If the purpose of such a decision was to disguise the outline of the tomb it might only have been necessary to build an extra-revetment at the eastern end in order to give the whole monument a homogeneous appearance.

Summary of developments in Period II and the status of Trefignath as a composite monument.

This chapter began with a brief statement of the main stages in the development of the Trefignath Burial Chambers and readers may find it convenient to have the broad outline reiterated here before proceeding to an account of the denudation of the site and its partial destruction.

The first phase (Period II$_1$) saw the erection of a Simple Passage Grave within a putatively round cairn of weathered boulders. This was on the highest part of the site and over the remains of some earlier activity. By this time the landscape was already fairly open, the tomb being built in an area of grassland. Some woodland did survive not far away but the soil pollen samples also include evidence for arable land in the vicinity. The entrance to the Simple Passage Grave faced north onto a shallow forecourt but this, and the chamber itself, had been thoroughly disturbed. The few remaining finds—sherds of Vessels P and V—suggest that the chamber continued in use until a fairly late stage in the history of the monument. There was no trace of any burials but analogies with other Passage Graves suggest these would have been cremations.

After an unknown interval the monument was enlarged by the addition of a second chamber to the east and the extension and replanning of the cairn (Period II$_2$). Although the soil pollen samples record little change in the extent of woodland cover, arable land appears to have increased, though the site itself

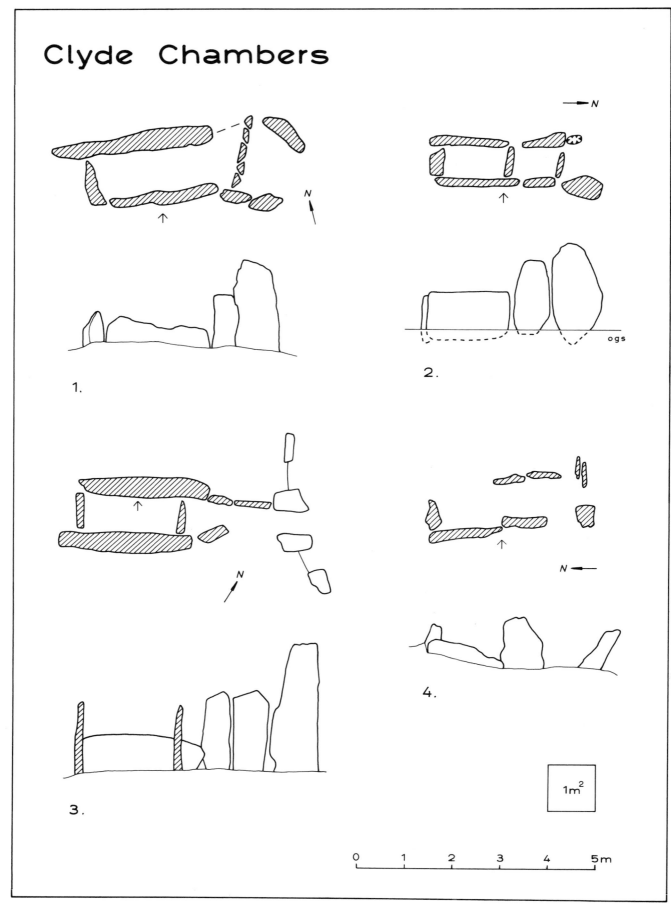

Clyde Chambers

Fig. 20. Comparative plans and elevation of Clyde Chambers (1) Trefignath East; (2) Glenvoidean Axial; (3) Cairnholy I; (4) Gort na h'Ulaidhe south central (sources: (2) (Marshall 1977, Fig. 3 and 4); (3) and (4) (Scott 1969, 192, Fig. 66 and 231, Fig. 81 A).

remained surrounded by grassland. Several features
of the enlarged cairn, especially its wedge shape,
deeply recessed forecourt, and dry-stone retaining
walls of quarried blocks betray the arrival in the area
of architectural ideas from the south and east and
enable Trefignath, during this phase, to be regarded
as an outlier of the Cotswold-Severn group of long
cairns. It appears that during this phase both the
western chamber—the Simple Passage Grave—and
the central chamber were in contemporaneous use.
The central chamber had also been extensively
disturbed and few finds and no burials survived.
However, an earlier account of the site implies that
this chamber contained one or more inhumations
accompanied by 'urns'. There is no evidence that the
original wedge-shaped long cairn was provided with
a deliberately constructed extra-revetment but rather
the cairn was left to collapse naturally.

After a further interval a third chamber was
constructed to the east, partly within the forecourt of
the central chamber and blocking access to it. At the
same time the cairn was extended eastwards so as to
incorporate the new chamber (Period II₃). By now
tree pollen had declined markedly and the landscape
appears to have been completely open. The eastern
chamber possesses a number of distinctive features
which suggest that its design was influenced by
developments in tomb architecture taking place in
south west Scotland. Finds of Peterborough Ware in
the portal area indicate that this chamber may have
remained in use until the end of the third
millennium.

Finally, some attempt appears to have been made
to disguise the main elements of the monument by
the construction of an extra-revetment around the
eastern end of the enlarged long cairn, natural
collapse having already made the outlines of the rest
of the tomb sufficiently obscure. Although known
mainly as a feature of Cotswold-Severn long cairns
the presence of extra-revetment has been noted
elsewhere as for example at Beacharra in south west
Scotland (Scott 1964, 139-50). These developments
appear to have spanned the period from the middle
of the fourth millennium to the end of the third. On
the whole the finds associated with the chambers date
from the latter part of this period and imply that each
of the chambers remained in use for a long time after
their initial construction.

Until the recent excavations the Trefignath burial
chambers had been regarded by most writers as a
Segmented Gallery Grave, a simple unitary structure
reflecting a single period of construction (Grimes
1936, 119-20; Daniel 1950, 86; Piggott 1954, 179;
Lynch 1970, 30-32). As such it was compared with
two superficially similar Anglesey tombs, Din Dryfol
and Hen Drefor, and the three grouped together to
form a class of monument known as Long Graves
(Lynch 1969, 113-16). These sites were thought to be
characterised by their length—Trefignath was
believed to be about 15m long—and by the presence
of tall portal stones, both features thought to indicate

some connexion with other long graves in the north
of Ireland, south-west Scotland, and the Isle of Man.
Sufficient differences could be discerned to make a
very direct connexion unlikely. In particular
attention was drawn to the closed nature of the
chambers on the Anglesey sites and the absence of
any trace of the monumental facade which forms a
usual feature of Long Graves in the other areas
mentioned. Lynch (1970, 32) pointed out that while
the absence of a monumental facade could be
paralleled among the earlier tombs in south-west
Scotland these were usually considerably smaller
than the Anglesey sites.

Lynch (1969, 114) was also the first to suggest that
Trefignath might be a composite monument, the
chambers having been added over a considerable
period. The excavations have demonstrated this to be
the case. Lynch's own excavations at Din Dryfol
(reported in this volume) have shown that that site
also developed over a series of phases, and the same
may well be the case at Hen Drefor. From this it
follows that the original view of these sites as Long
Graves, i.e. Segmented Gallery Graves reflecting a
single period of construction, is no longer valid.
Trefignath and Din Dryfol may now be classified as
composite tombs.

Composite, or multi-period, tombs are now
established as a widespread class of monument and
examples are known throughout the British Isles. All
three sites excavated in North Wales during the past
two decades—Din Dryfol, Dyffryn Ardudwy, and
Trefignath—have proved to be of this type (Figs. 21
(1) and (3); Din Dryfol Fig. 14) and there is doubt
about the contemporaneous development of all but
the most unitary or simple structures. Corcoran
(1972) gave very full consideration to the
phenomenon of multi-period development in
megalithic tombs throughout Britain and Ireland and
most of the points made remain valid after a decade
of further research (Masters 1981, 17-73). However,
Corcoran did not consider the validity of the
composite tomb as a class in itself, reflecting the
conscious choice of its builders as opposed to the
fortuitous coming together on a single site of a
succession of architectural styles.

Multi-period developments of two kinds can be
distinguished, sometimes at a single monument. The
first may be termed architectural embellishments
such as the addition of trapezoidal long cairns and
monumental facades to existing monuments. The
provision of an extra-revetment, perhaps after
several centuries, could also be considered as such an
embellishment. The second development is of a more
strictly practical nature and consists in the provision
of additional space for burial. This might involve the
inclusion of additional chambers within the cairn, as
at Dyffryn Ardudwy and Trefignath, or the
elaboration of an existing structure, as at Din Dryfol.
At all three sites trapezoidal long cairns were added
and Trefignath received the further addition of an
extra-revetment at the eastern end.

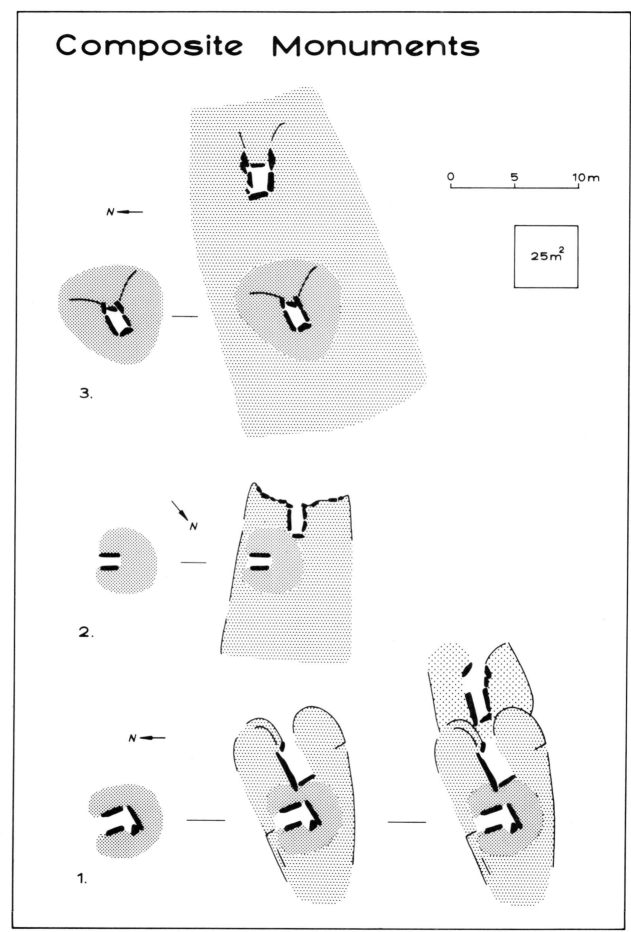

Composite Monuments

Fig. 21. Comparative plans of composite cairns; (1) Trefignath; (2) Mid Gleniron II, Wigtown; (3) Dyffryn Ardudwy, Merioneth. (sources: (2) Scott 1969, 213 Fig. 73; (3) Lynch 1969, 134 Fig. 45).

As the evidence from large-scale excavations accumulates it becomes apparent that architectural embellishment may have occurred at many, if not most, sites and appears in itself to be too general a phenomenon to provide the basis for a distinct class. No single type—Passage Grave, Portal Dolmen or Protomegalith, Clyde, Carlingford or Cotswold-Severn tomb—is without examples of such developments and they may be seen as analogous to the kind of architectural developments that embellished the cathedrals and churches of the Middle Ages. However, the provision of additional burial spaces within a single cairn is a different matter and should be considered more closely.

It is understood that most megalithic tombs functioned as collective burial vaults and it is not entirely an accident that sites recognised as early are usually small. This may be attributed to the size of the population as a whole and in particular of the individual groups responsible for building the tombs. As the population, both generally and within the group, increased so did the funerary population and more space was required. The response to this was either the building of more tombs or the elaboration of existing ones. The choice was a clear one and had a cultural basis. There is no obvious reason why further Passage Graves should not have been built at Trefignath thus leading to the development of a cemetery which was usual in areas where this type of tomb predominates. But instead an existing monument was elaborated, implying both the absence of the cemetery tradition and the importance of the original Trefignath site. It is the decision to maintain funerary activity at a single monument rather than within a generalised area that is the significant aspect of sites such as Dyffryn Ardudwy, Din Dryfol, and Trefignath and identifies them as a distinct class. The linking element is the site itself, the recurrent use of which implies an importance transcending architectural styles and different cultural backgrounds.

Period III—Denudation and partial Destruction.

Following their final closure and partial concealment the Trefignath Burial Chambers have remained a prominent feature in the landscape of Ynys Gybi to the present day. During this period the superincumbent cairn has been almost entirely removed and the western and central chambers demolished. Records, discussed in Chapter 1, suggest that most of this destruction has taken place during the past three hundred years. However, there is some evidence of disturbance at a much earlier date.

The second of the two radio-carbon dates (sample 15, HAR 3933) obtained for the site appertains to charcoal found in association with late Neolithic pottery in the portal of the eastern chamber. It was hoped that this would provide a date for the pottery and the final phase of use of burial chambers. In the event the date obtained was 2210 ± 70 bp (260 bc) and clearly many centuries later than anticipated. The charcoal and pottery were recovered from the northern half of the portal area (Fig. 17) and had not been disturbed by the intrusions affecting the area to the south and the chamber (Fig. 19). Accordingly, it appears that the eastern chamber had been entered towards the end of the first millennium BC and the burial deposits therein disturbed. The late Neolithic pottery was therefore in a derived context, which probably accounts for its fragmentary nature. The intruders appear to have lit a fire, and a number of animal bones (54 Appendix 2) recovered from one of the later intrusions may be the remains of a meal. Several finds made during the excavation—three spindle whorls (116, 119, 518; Figs. 26 and 37), and two perforated stones (30, 189; Figs. 26 and 37)—may belong to this squatter occupation while two sherds of Romano-British pottery and a much abraded coin (102, 559, and 4; Fig. 26) indicate that such visits may have continued over a long period. Such visits to megalithic tombs by later peoples are widely recorded and need cause no surprise. Their occurrence at Trefignath is interesting because they imply that the eastern chamber was open, and probably empty, long before the recorded disturbance of the site in the late Eighteenth Century, and the finds reported at that time can be assumed to have come from one of the other chambers.

The earliest description of the site is that provided by John Aubrey, and this has been quoted in full in Chapter 1. At the time of his visit Aubrey noticed several animals 'at shade' within one of the chambers and from the evidence discussed above we may assume that this was the eastern one. Aubrey's correspondent Mr. Win recorded that at that time the monument comprised about twenty 'great rough stones', three more than the number remaining on site in 1977. Each chamber seems to be missing at least one large stone; the inner northern portal of the eastern chamber, the southern side slab of the central chamber, and the capstone (or -stones) of the western chamber. If the three additional stones noted by Mr. Win could be restored we might find that the site was virtually intact at the time of his visit, although the very fact that so many orthostats were visible suggests that the cairn was already considerably denuded.

The documentary sources discussed in Chapter 1 suggest that the condition of the monument in the mid Nineteenth Century should be mainly attributed to its systematic demolition about seventy years earlier. The removal of several orthostats probably occurred at this time and as we have seen the site was only saved from further destruction by the intervention of Lady Stanley (Stanley 1867, 234; 1974, 1). This was probably the occasion when the 'urns and bones' mentioned by Longueville Jones were found (Jones 1855, 25), probably in either the central or western chambers. The disturbances noted in the central and eastern chambers should also be attributed to this late Eighteenth Century activity. Both were irregular trenches dug, presumably, in search of finds. One (23) had almost entirely cleared the forecourt of the central chamber, while the stone hole for its southern portal (25) appears also to have been emptied and refilled at this time. The other main disturbance had removed most of the ancient deposits from the eastern chamber and its portal (57), and had displaced the southern end of the low septal wall (13) separating the two. Doubtless it was also at this time that most of the blocking in the forecourt of the eastern chamber was removed but this disturbance could not be traced as a clearly defined feature.

Finally, the eastern chamber was disturbed yet again when a pit (58) was excavated and refilled with concrete in order to provide a firm footing for the timber prop placed under one of the capstones (IV) earlier in the present century. The precise date of this is not known but departmental records suggest that it occurred shortly before or soon after the site was placed in State care in 1911.

The surviving remains of the cairn were covered with a layer of soil and small stones (1) which included many fragments of recent pottery and a small number of metal objects and coins. Details of these are given in Chapter 8 and Appendix 2. None is of particular interest and all may be attributed to the use of the site as a refuse dump by the occupants of Trefignath Farm. The farm was demolished in the early 1970s and soon after the fourth period of acitivity at the site began. This has consisted of the excavation and restoration of the burial chambers and forms the subject of this report.

Chapter 3, The Soils

by Helen C. M. Keeley

The soils of Anglesey have been mapped by the Soil Survey of England and Wales (Roberts 1958; Ball 1963) at a scale of 1:63360. Physical features and soil distribution are shown in Figs. 1 and 22.

Anglesey is relatively flat but the sharp escarpment of the Carboniferous limestones, the rugged outcrops of the Mona Complex area, the igneous rocks of the Ceodana granite, the wind-blown sands of Newborough, Aberffraw, and Trewan, and the glacial features around the districts of Beaumaris-Llangoed, Pentraeth and Cemaes Bay to Cemlyn, give considerable variations to the land surface. The several cycles of erosion, and especially those earlier ones which are supposed to have caused the pene-planation of the island, are responsible for the present land surface and for the general system of drainage (Roberts 1958).

Dominating the solid geology is the Mona Complex which occupies approximately two-thirds of the island's surface. It is divided into three major groups: (1) The Gneisses, (2) The Bedded Series, and (3) The Plutonic Intrusions. The Bedded Series are the most extensive, but many have been so metamorphosed that they now behave as hard igneous rocks. The dominant rock types of this series appear as pale green holocrystalline chlorite schists and these are the parent materials found in the Trefignath area.

There is abundant evidence that North Wales was subjected to an intense glaciation during the Quaternary Ice Age. This ice is thought to have advanced and retreated twice, giving rise to two distinct deposits—the 'upper' and 'lower' boulder clays—separated by beds of sand and gravel. The lower boulder clay is grey or bluish-grey in colour and contains much Carboniferous and shelly material, which accounts for its highly calcareous nature. The upper deposit is reddish-brown in colour and with a calcareous matrix, overlying interglacial sands and gravels (Roberts 1958), but this occurs only in a narrow strip along the eastern margin of Anglesey. It gives way fairly abruptly towards the south west to locally derived drifts. Extensive areas of post-glacial deposits occur, mainly marine alluvium, fluviatile and lacustrine deposits and windblown sands, but not at Trefignath.

The soils are mapped in the area of Trefignath as belonging to the Rocky Gaerwen Series and are developed on the Pre-Cambrian schists of the Mona Complex. The soils were originally classified as low base status brown earths (Roberts 1958; Ball 1963) and represent the rocky, shallow phase of the Gaerwen Series, developed on glacial drift derived from rocks of the Mona Complex. The surface soil is stony, reddish-brown sandy loam overlying a yellowish-brown stony or pebbly material with a high proportion of rock fragments. Surface pH is usually about five and the soils are low in phosphorus and potassium. They are well-drained.

The normal phase represents useful general purpose soils which can carry arable crops or excellent pasture (Roberts 1958) and are agriculturally the most important on Anglesey. Grimes (1945, 169-74) noted that the most densely populated areas of Anglesey in prehistoric times were those of the light to medium textured soils developed on rocks of the Mona Complex, which would include the Gaerwen Series. These soils, therefore, have obviously been of prime importance to agriculture throughout man's occupation of the Island.

The Rocky Gaerwen soils are generally shallow and rock outcrops occur frequently. Consequently farms and fields are smaller than on the deep Gaerwen soils (Ball, 1963).

Soil Studies at the Trefignath Burial Chambers

Examination of soils was carried out at Trefignath during excavations in 1977 and 1978, and this work formed the basis of two interim reports (Keeley 1977 and 1979). Soil profiles adjacent to the site and buried soils were investigated and representative profile descriptions are given below:

(a) *Modern soils*

A pit was dug on top of the outcrop south south west of the eastern chamber, about five metres from the retaining wall of the cairn (6). The site was level, moderately drained and with a vegetation cover of grasses. An apparently worked piece of chert was found at a depth of 30cm, indicating that the soil may have been disturbed.

0 to 2cm	Root mat.
2 to 30cm Ahg	Very dark greyish-brown (10YR3/2) friable silty clay loam with moderate medium angular blocky structure. Roots abundant, medium to fine fibrous and stones rare, gravel to medium. Common medium distinct strong brown mottles.

SKETCH MAP OF THE SOILS OF YNYS GYBI (after Roberts, 1958)

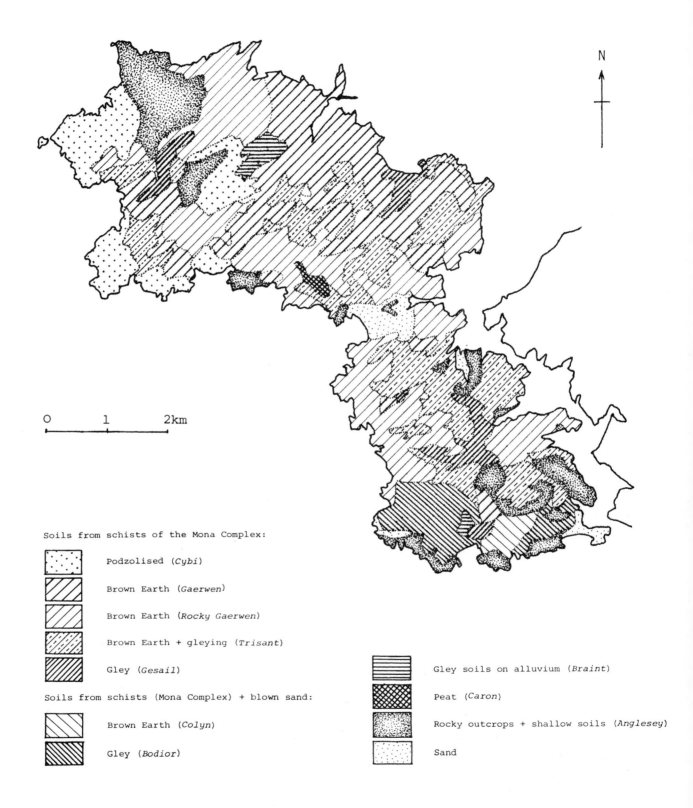

N

O   1   2km

Soils from schists of the Mona Complex:

Podzolised (*Cybi*)

Brown Earth (*Gaerwen*)

Brown Earth (*Rocky Gaerwen*)

Brown Earth + gleying (*Trisant*)

Gley (*Gesail*)

Soils from schists (Mona Complex) + blown sand:

Brown Earth (*Colyn*)

Gley (*Bodior*)

Gley soils on alluvium (*Braint*)

Peat (*Caron*)

Rocky outcrops + shallow soils (*Anglesey*)

Sand

Fig. 22.   The soils of Ynys Gybi.

30 to 40cm Brown/dark brown (10YR4/3) friable
Eb   silty loam with weak medium
           subangular blocky structure. Roots
           abundant, fine fibrous and stones
           common, gravel to large. Occasional
           distinct medium strong brown mottles
           associated with stones and root
           channels.

40 to 42cm Yellowish-brown (10YR5/4) friable
Btg   silty clay loam with weak medium
           subangular blocky structure. Roots
           common, fine fibrous and stones
           abundant, gravel to large (mainly
           weathering schist fragments, with
           some quartz and flint and chert
           pebbles). Occasional distinct medium
           strong brown mottles were noted,
           associated with weathering rock
           fragments.

Below 42cm Soil matrix similar to above but
BCg   dominated by large schist boulders.

A shallower soil was found to the south south east of
the eastern chamber, on a 5° slope under grasses and
herbaceous plants, and the site was freely drained.

0 to 3cm   Root mat (roots coarse to fine fibrous).

3 to 10cm Very dark brown (10YR2/2) humose
Ah   silt containing abundant medium to
           fine fibrous roots. Fine weak granular
           structure, friable, mottles absent and
           stones few (gravel to medium). pH (in
           distilled water) 5.1.

10 to 18cm Dark brown (7.5YR3/4) silt loam,
AB   friable, with weak medium subangular
           blocky structure; mottles absent. Roots
           common, fine to medium fibrous and
           stones common (gravel to medium).
           pH 5.0.

18 to 24cm Mixed horizon of dark brown
B/Cgf   (10YR3/3) silt loam and dark reddish-
           brown (5YR3/4) slightly concreted
           coarse gravelly silt loam, with about
           40% yellowish-red (5YR4/6) mottles.
           Weak medium granular structure,
           moderately friable, stones abundant
           (gravel to large fragments of weather-
           ing schist). Roots common, fine
           fibrous. pH 4.7.

Below 24cm Large schist boulders.

There appeared to be some variations in the soils
around the monument related to drainage and parent
material.

(b) Buried soils

Two buried soil profiles were examined from
contexts sealed by the long cairn. In area A the
profile lay to the north of the eastern chamber and
was sealed by cairn material belonging to Period II_3,
the extension of the long cairn.

0 to 10cm Dark brown (10YR3/3) friable humose
BAh   sandy silt loam with weak to moderate
           subangular blocky structure, contain-
           ing many gravel to small stones,
           including occasional quartz fragments
           (up to 5 mm diameter) and very small
           iron/manganese oxide concretions.
           Occasional charcoal fragments were
           present.

10 to 13cm Dark yellowish-brown (10YR4/4)
bAB   moderately friable sandy silt loam with
           weak to moderate fine subangular
           blocky structure, containing a few
           yellowish-brown (10YR5/6) fine
           distinct mottles. Stones many, gravel
           to medium, including occasional
           quartz fragments (5mm diameter).
           Roots common, fine fibrous.

13 to 23cm Dark yellowish-brown (10YR4/4)
bBg   moderately friable sandy silt loam
           containing abundant fine, distinct
           strong brown (7.5YR5/6) mottles.
           Patches of very dark greyish-brown
           (10YR3/2) organic material also
           present, associated with root channels.
           Weak medium granular structure.
           Stones common, gravel to small, and
           roots common, fine fibrous.

23 to 30cm Dark yellowish-brown (10YR4/4)
bBC   moderately friable sandy silt loam with
           common distinct fine strong brown
           (7.5YR4/6) mottles. Also a few
           coatings of light brownish-grey
           (2.5Y6/2) material. Structure was
           moderate medium subangular blocky,
           stones common, gravel to small, and
           roots few, fine fibrous.

Below 30cm Light brownish-grey (2.5Y6/2) friable
bCg   sandy loam with moderate medium
           subangular blocky structure contain-
           ing common dark yellowish-brown
           (10YR4/6) prominent medium
           mottles. Stones abundant, gravel to
           small, consisting of weathering schist
           fragments. Roots few, very fine
           fibrous. Small iron/manganese con-
           cretions, up to 5mm diameter, were
           noted.

In area B the profile lay to the south of the forecourt
in front of the central chamber and was sealed by
cairn material belonging to Period II_2, the original
wedge-shaped long cairn. The profile was examined
below the baulk of section EF (Fig. 14). The top of
the buried topsoil was indistinct but could be
distinguished at about 39cm depth.

39 to 42cm Very dark brown (10YR2/2) friable
bAh   humose sandy silt loam with moderate
           fine subangular blocky structure con-
           taining common gravel to small stones,
           including occasional small quartz
           fragments, and abundant fibrous
           roots. A few small organic pellets were
           noted.

42 to 47cm bAB	Dark brown (10YR3/3) moderately friable sandy silt loam with moderate medium subangular blocky structure. Patches of very dark brown (10YR2/2) material similar to the layer above, were noted. Stones common, gravel to small, including occasional quartz fragments, and roots common, fine fibrous. Few iron/manganese oxides/organic matter concretions, 1 to 2cm diameter, occurred.
47 to 62cm b Bgf	Dark yellowish-brown (10YR4/4) moderately friable sandy loam with moderate medium subangular blocky structure. Common fine, distinct strong brown (7.5YR4/6) mottles occurred. Stones common, gravel to small, and roots few, fine fibrous. Concretions of iron/manganese oxides/organic matter, up to 1cm diameter, were fairly common.
62 to 70cm bCgf	Dark greyish-brown (2.5Y4/2) moderately friable sandy loam with weak medium subangular blocky structure containing common, prominent, medium strong brown (7.5YR4/6) mottles. Stones many, gravel to small, including occasional small quartz fragments, and roots very few, very fine fibrous. Many Fe/Mn/organic matter concretions up to 2cm diameter.
Below 70cm bCg	Dark greyish-brown (2.5Y4/20) moderately friable sandy loam with strong medium subangular/angular blocky structure, containing common medium/fine prominent dark reddish-brown (5YR3/4) mottles. Stones many, gravel to medium, consisting of weathering schist fragments, and roots few, fine fibrous. A few Fe/Mn concretions (up to 1cm diameter) were noted.

Table 2 shows values for loss on ignition (%) for the two buried soil profiles.

Table 000

cm	Area A	cm	Area B
0-10	13.76	39-42	22.18
10-13	9.79	42-47	7.99
13-23	12.86	47-62	7.82
23-30	9.20	62-70	5.93
Below 30	3.45	Below 70	3.06

Discussion

The modern soil profiles did not conform exactly to the expected Rocky Gaerwen type, but such soil variation over a small area is not unusual and soil mapping is not carried out in sufficient detail to detect these differences. The first profile described had impeded drainage and the shallower soil appeared to have been subjected to differential water movement in the subsoil, probably due to textural variation.

Several episodes of activity have been delineated: Period I preceding the construction of the earliest burial chamber and cairn (charcoal found lying on the old ground below this cairn has been dated to 5050 ± bp)(HAR3932); Period II representing the construction and use of the burial chambers (the buried soils from Areas B and A being sealed by cairn material of the second and third phases of this period respectively); and Period III representing the history of the site following the final closure of the burial chambers.

The buried soils, particularly in Area B, showed considerable post-depositional iron and manganese movement, as evidenced by the presence of concretions. The presence of charcoal fragments, and the lower organic matter content, in the buried soil in Area A suggested that the soil had been disturbed prior to the construction of the overlying part of the cairn, but in Area B the buried soil had a high loss on ignition value, consistent with the Ah horizon of an undisturbed soil, perhaps under grassland. Results of pollen analysis by James Greig of samples from the nearby bog (Chapter 4) have indicated the presence of trees in the early Neolithic although the environment was essentially open and very grassy.

Soil pollen from Period I showed that more trees were present than in later periods but substantial clearance had occurred by this time. By the second phase of Period II (Area B) there had been little change in the soil pollen record although more cereal pollen occurred. However, by the third phase (Area A) there was much less tree pollen. Soil pollen results for Area B fit in well with the soil evidence. Disturbance of the soil in Area A no doubt resulted from human activity in the locality during cairn construction, possibly including burning off the vegetation, and indirectly relates to the soil pollen evidence for this period, which indicates the increasing impact of man on the environment in this area.

Chapter 4, Pollen and Plant Macrofossils

by J. R. A. Greig

This work was undertaken to find out about the landscape in which the megalithic monument was constructed and altered. To date, pollen analysis has apparently not been done on material from Anglesey (J. A. Taylor, *pers. comm.*) although there are many pollen diagrams from neighbouring parts of Wales, mainly the uplands at altitudes greater than 300m. Anglesey is a very promising place for such investigations into prehistoric landscapes because there are many peat deposits, acid soils and a great range of signs of past occupation.

Field work

A peat bog lying a few hundred metres north west of the megalith (Fig. 2) was sampled. A hole was dug so that monolith boxes could be hammered into the upper part of the profile (0-75cm), and a Russian type peat borer was used to collect samples from deeper down, to just below two metres. The stratigraphy of the bog here is as follows:

0-25cm	Peaty alluvium with some stones
25-30cm	Peat with some traces of silt
30-130cm	Well-humified monocotyledonous (probably *Phragmites*) peat with very little mineral matter
130-145cm	Woody peat
145-153cm	Peat as above, without wood
153-175cm	Peat with marl
175-195cm	Reddish fibrous peat
195-210cm	Darker fibrous peat
Below 210cm	Minerals, borer failed to penetrate

Soils buried underneath parts of the cairn were sampled by H. C. M. Keeley and C. Smith and some of these have been analysed to provide a complementary set of pollen records to those from the peat bog (Appendix 3).

Results

The pollen results are presented in the form of a pollen diagram from the peat bog samples (Fig. 23). There are also some plant macrofossil and charcoal results from the bog. The soil pollen spectra are presented in pollen diagram form, although they must be regarded as distinct from one another rather than being a sample series as in the case of the peat samples. The amount of time available for this work has been strictly limited. The intervals between the peat samples are wider than desirable, and there are

only a few macrofossil and soil pollen results. Even so, a substantial body of data is presented.

A number of pollen assemblage zones (parts of the pollen diagram with broadly similar pollen values) can be seen in the pollen diagram. These are discussed in terms of the well-known Godwin pollen zones for the sake of clarity.

Lower peat (pre-Neolithic development of soils and vegetation)

The lowermost sample analysed, 175cm (not drawn on the diagram), has a late-glacial type pollen assemblage (Zone III). The presence of *Betula* (birch), *Salix* (willow), and *Juniperus* (juniper) suggests that there was a shrubby sub-arctic vegetation with a range of grasses and other herbs characteristic of this period in Britain such as *Helianthemum* (rock rose), *Koenigia* (Iceland purslane), and *Thalictrum* (rue). Cyperaceae (sedges), *Sparganium* (bur-reed), and *Potamogeton* (pond-weed) are the most abundant members of a fairly rich wetland community growing on the sedge peat as it formed. The mineral bottom of the bog probably consists of glacial debris, and after the end of glacial action restricted drainage appears to have led to peat formation. There does not seem to have been deep water here, as in a kettle-hole, because the lower deposits are not mineral in origin like the late-glacial clay deposits found at other sites. The bog probably covered a fairly extensive area, but it has been cut by the main Holyhead to Chester railway line, and more recently by the grounds of the aluminium works, so it is hard to map.

The sample at 125cm (not drawn on the diagram) is dominated by *Betula* (birch) and Gramineae (grass) pollen, without the arctic flora of the previous sample, and probably represents Zone IV, when woodland development was at a comparatively early stage. The samples from 75 to 47.5cm (on the pollen diagram) show the final stages of pre-Neolithic forest development (Zones VI and VIIa). The very large amount of *Salix* (willow) pollen in the 75cm sample seems peculiar, for it is not usually a very abundant producer of pollen. The large amount of *Quercus* (oak) pollen shows that oak forest had developed by this stage. The samples at 50 and 47.5cm show the development of "climax forest" containing *Quercus* (oak), *Ulmus* (elm), and *Hedera* (ivy), with *Corylus* (hazel) perhaps growing as a forest understory and

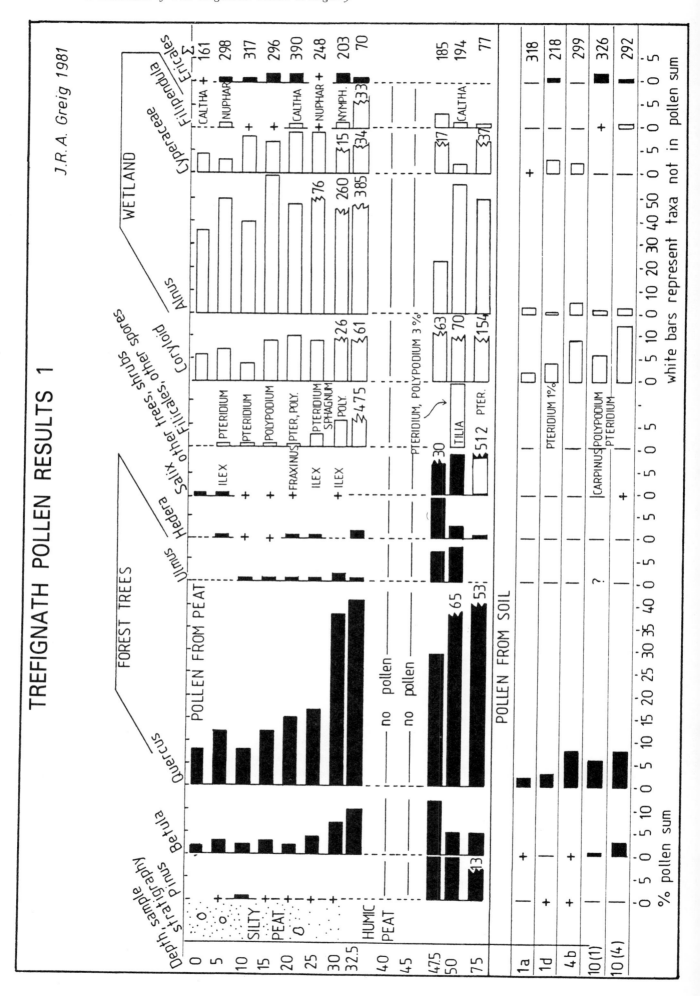

TREFIGNATH POLLEN RESULTS 1

J.R.A. Greig 1981

white bars represent taxa not in pollen sum

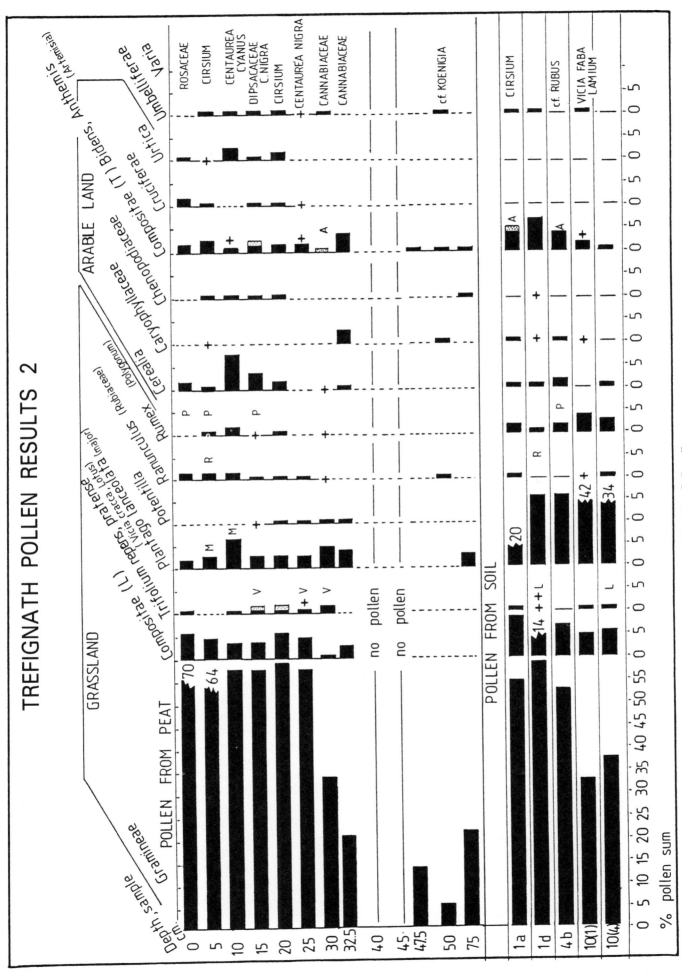

Fig. 23. Pollen diagrams.

round forest edges. This seems to be typical of maximum forest development in Wales, and *Tilia* (lime), which was a very important forest tree at this time in eastern England, is only represented by one grain here. The small number of pollen records from herbaceous plants shows that the forest covered most of the land. Tidal coast edges and steeper parts of Holyhead Mountain would have probably been the only unwooded parts of the landscape. The peat bog itself seems to have had a wetland vegetation with Cyperaceae (sedges) growing on the peat, and a carr of *Alnus* (alder) and *Quercus* (oak) on wet land generally. The soil that developed under this kind of natural vegetation cover would have been deep and well drained with a good supply of the kinds of leaves which promote the formation of rich humus (as opposed to modern soil degradation under conifer plantation) and very little erosion, for the peat has practically no inorganic matter.

Middle peat; initial forest clearance

At this stage there is a band of peat, not distinguishable by eye from above and below it, in which no pollen was preserved. The samples prepared from 30, 35, and 40cm did not contain significant amounts of pollen, and in the case of further samples prepared at 32.5 and 47.5cm the pollen was not as abundant as usual, so the counts are low. It would appear that the bog dried out enough for the pollen to become oxidised, either from local factors such as drainage changes, or more widespread ones.

In order to obtain some information, in the absence of pollen, small samples of about 100cc of peat were collected from the sample boxes at 30-35cm and 40-45cm, washed, sieved on a 0.3mm mesh, and sorted under a microscope for macrofossils. The 40-45cm sample was very poor in remains, but seeds of *Carex* cf. *disticha* (brown sedge) were present, a plant which prefers areas with a fluctuating water table (Jermy and Tutin 1968). A few small charcoal fragments, pieces of stone and carbon spheroids were also found. The 30-35cm sample was much richer, with a range of plants (Table 3), remains of Coleoptera (beetles) and Trichoptera (caddis flies), carbon fragments and spheroids in great numbers. These last are a somewhat mysterious but not uncommon find, and could possibly be the result of tarry matter having been spattered out of burning fuel, such as wood. The increasing amount of carbon and mineral fragments seems to be a sign that there were fires, and that erosion was taking place in a small way (although on the basis of only two small samples), so the Elm Decline horizon (of initial forest clearance at around 3,000 bc) seems to be at around 40cm depth, and therefore disappointingly poorly represented.

Upper peat; later landscape clearance

Where pollen is present, once again, at 32.5cm the pollen assemblage is one of the Zone VIIb type with

Table 3—Macroscopic remains from peat

	30-35	40-45cm
Ranunculus flammula L. (lesser spearwort) seeds	1	—
R. subgenus *Batrachium* (water crowfoot) seeds	1	—
Nuphar lutea (L.) Sm. (yellow water lily) seeds	2	—
Viola cf. *palustris* L. (? marsh violet) seeds	2	—
Rubus fruticosus agg (bramble) seeds	2	—
Umbelliferae	2	—
Lysimachia ? *nemorum* L. (creeping jenny) seeds	1	—
Alismataceae (water plantains) seeds	1	—
Juncus spp. (rush) seeds	4	—
Carex cf. *panicea* L. (carnation grass) seeds	1	—
Carex cf. *disticha* Huds. (brown sedge) seeds	—	4
Carex sp. (sedge) seeds	3	—
Monocotyledons stem nodes	.	.
Charcoal fragments	.	.
Carbon spheroids (0.5—2.0mm)	13	2
Coleoptera (beetle fragments)	14	—
Trichoptera (caddis fly) larval cases	8	—

reduced amounts of *Ulmus* (elm) pollen and a great increase in records from plants of both grassland and cultivated land. The main apparent forest changes are the reduction in elm and ivy records—the oak/alder carr appears to have increased, if anything, but this may have been a fairly local vegetation type growing in wetter places such as the area of the peat bog, and hence very well represented in the pollen records. The main landscape change is the replacement of forest by grassland and arable fields. These have been divided up (as far as possible) on the pollen diagram.

Gramineae (grasses) are the most obvious sign of grassland on the diagram, probably because they spread so much pollen. The Compositae probably include plants like dandelions and hawkbits which grow mainly on grassland. *Trifolium repens* and *T. pratense* (white and red clover), *Vicia cracca* type (vetch) and *Lotus* (birdsfoot trefoil) are all grassland plants, as is *Plantago lanceolata* (ribwort plantain). *Potentilla* (cinquefoil), *Ranunculus* (buttercup), and *Rumex* (dock) are the other grassland plants whose increased presence at this stage show the change from forest to grassland. A very similar range of plants can be found growing today in meadows in Anglesey which have not been too exposed to modern farming practices.

The signs of arable land are less marked in this part of the diagram (25-32.5cm). There is a trace of Cerealia pollen, and scattered records from plants which could have been weeds of cultivated land. The Ericales pollen which appears at this stage shows that some heathland had formed, a sign of the acidification and depauperation of some of the soils.

The gorse which is now common on Anglesey is not evident on the pollen diagram, but this may be the result of low pollen distribution.

The soil pollen samples

The pollen records from the soils provide a direct link with the burial chambers, since those analysed were sealed by various phases of cairn construction. Samples 10(1) and 10(4) both appertain to Period I and come from the old ground surface sealed beneath the primary cairn. Period II is represented by three samples, 4b from the surface on which the second phase of the cairn was built and 1a and 1d from the equivalent surface below the third phase of the cairn: Sample 4b corresponds to the buried soil profile from Area B and samples 1a and 1d that from Area A, both discussed by Helen Keeley in Chapter 3. Pollen preservation in these samples was good, as can be seen from the large range of pollen types present. Like the peat bog samples, the soil samples have a biased record of pollen, in this case strongly showing up some of the plants which grew in the immediate locality, and to a lesser extent the regional vegetation. Forest vegetation is not apparent from the soil pollen, even in the earliest samples. There was only one possible record of *Ulmus* (elm) pollen, and one grain of *Carpinus* (hornbeam). *Quercus* (oak) pollen is present, decreasing in time, but this could have come from oak/alder carr growing on the peat bog, as would *Alnus* (alder) pollen which reaches nearly 400% on the peat bog, but only 1-2% in the soil, showing that it was not growing very near the megalith.

The signs of grassland, which were evident from the peat bog pollen, are also the dominant feature of the soil pollen records. Many of the same taxa are present, with similar representations. *Plantago lanceolata* (ribwort plantain) is much more abundant in the soil, reaching 42%. This very high pollen record is fairly easy to understand when looking at meadows on Anglesey which are almost black with plantain heads at the appropriate time of the year. Some of the Compositae (T) record, although grouped with weeds of arable land, is probably from *Bellis perennis* (daisy), another common meadow plant.

Arable land is indicated by the Cerealia pollen record, but it is hard to be sure what this might represent in terms of the past importance of cereal crops. Another indicator of arable land is the pollen of *Vicia faba* (broad bean, celtic bean), of which two pollen grains were found. The bean is a very interesting find because the small amounts of pollen which it liberates means that the pollen records from peat bogs, if any at all, are sketchy. The preservation of pollen in soils is not often good enough for the survival of the rather delicate pollen from this plant group. The grains were found by scanning the whole area of the pollen slide, after counting, to see whether any other taxa not seen during the actual count could be detected. Bean remains are not often preserved as macrofossils either, unlike the cereals which need heat during various treatment processes which can cause preservation from charring, or when chaff has been burnt. Thus there are practically no records of early bean cultivation although it is known from Bronze Age Danish deposits (Iversen 1973). It will be interesting to see whether this evidence for Neolithic bean growing can be confirmed by results from other sites.

Other types of vegetation indicated by the soil pollen record include wetland plants like Cyperaceae, although the pollen could have come from the boggy area or have been the result perhaps of wet patches developing in the fields as a result of gleying—the earlier samples lack Cyperaceae pollen. Heathland is also in evidence to a small extent, while the spore records show the presence of *Pteridium* (bracken), which is now widespread on poor land.

Upper peat; post-neolithic land use

The upper part of the peat profile, 0-25cm, differs from the part below it in stratigraphy and pollen assemblage. There are reductions in the pollen records from *Quercus* (oak), *Alnus* (alder), and Cyperaceae which may show that the boggy area was getting smaller. *Corylus* (hazel) also decreases, with a corresponding increase in Gramineae (grasses), Cerealia (cereals) and in records from a range of plants considered likely to have been weeds, like Chenopodiaceae (goosefoot), Cruciferae (crucifers), and *Urtica* (nettle). A record of *Centaurea cyanus* (cornflower) shows that this part of the deposit is likely to be medieval or later in date, as it is a cornfield weed. The amount of arable farming would appear to have increased in the area. The sediment is much richer in minerals, ranging from silty matter to small stones, so this increase in ploughing appears to have been local, and leading to increased erosion of soil which was washed into the bog. This upper part of the diagram may be a true record of events, or it could possibly have been truncated by peat-cutting at some time, and the peat could have re-grown. This is the risk when dealing with lowland peat deposits near centres of population. No sign has been detected of modern deposits at the top of the profile, which would be expected to contain pollen from exotic plants like *Picea abies* (Norway spruce, Christmas tree).

Comparison with other sites

These results cannot be readily compared with those from other sites because of the great differences in topography, for most of the other investigations have been done on sites high up and away from the coast. Professor Dimbleby's pollen analysis from the Dyffryn Ardudwy megaliths (in Powell 1973, 4-6) has far more signs of a wooded landscape at the time of building than at Trefignath (64% *Quercus* compared with 8% when calculated on the same basis, *Ulmus* present). This spectrum, from a buried soil, is much more like that from the peat at Trefignath, but without the alder and Cyperaceae.

Work near the megaliths at Carneddau Hengwm (Moore 1973) seems to represent a very different course of events, with upland peat growth apparently being encouraged by the effects of human activities such as forest clearance. There seems to have been many stages before the forest was cleared from the boggy area where the peat was growing although the evidence from the soil pollen suggests that the dry landscape, on the other hand, was substantially cleared early in the Neolithic.

The combination of peat and soil pollen studies can be seen to be extremely useful in trying to elucidate the landscape setting for a site like the Trefignath Burial Chambers. Macrofossil and other studies are also very valuable, especially if there is a gap in the pollen record at the crucial point where there is the first forest clearance. It would be interesting to see whether the beetle remains would provide information on landscape changes, for such a small bog could have received some representation from dry land fauna.

Erratum:

The reference to *Koenigia islandica* in Fig. 23 and in the text is incorrect. It should be *Sagittaria.*
Addendum: Peter Osborne has kindly identified remains of the following beetles from the 30-35cm peat sample; *Aphodius,* which is a dung beetle, and *Gyrinus, Helophorus, Xantholinus, Strophosomus, Plateumaris,* and *Agonum.*

Chapter 5—Radio-Carbon Dates

Radio-carbon dates were obtained from two contexts at Trefignath and details of these are provided in the following table:

Table 4—Radio-carbon dates

Context	Sample	Age in years bp (bc)		C^{14} half-life	Laboratory no.
12	8	5050 ± 70	(3100)	5570	HAR 3932
8	15	2210 ± 70	(260)	5570	HAR 3933

Following current practice (*Antiquity*, 1972, 265) no attempt has been made to convert these dates into true calendar years and they have not been corrected to the new half-life value of 5730 ± 40 years. Both dates were obtained from wood charcoal.

When these samples were submitted it was hoped that the radio-carbon dates obtained would provide a broad chronological framework for the development of the site. Sample 8 came from the old ground surface immediately below the primary cairn and sample 15 came from the portal of the final, eastern, chamber. In the event this hope was not realised for the latter sample gave a date over two millennia more recent than expected.

HAR 3932 is the first radio-carbon date associated with a megalithic tomb in North Wales. The precise context of the sample shows that it must antedate the construction of the earliest, western, chamber and strictly speaking provides only a *terminus post quem* for that event. However, sample 8 was directly sealed by cairn material and if it is assumed that HAR 3932 provides a date for the construction of the Simple Passage Grave this enables comparison with similar sites, all in Ireland, for which dates are also available. Table 5 provides a selection of radio-carbon dates from Passage Graves for comparison with Trefignath.

Table 5—Radio-carbon dates from Passage Graves

Site	Date in radio-carbon years bc	Laboratory no.
Carrowmore 4	3800 ± 85	LU1840
Carrowmore 7	3290 ± 80	LU1441
Trefignath	3100 ± 70	HAR3932
Carrowmore 27	3090 ± 60	LU1648
Knowth	2925 ± 150	UB318
Knowth (small tomb)	2845 ± 185	UB319
New Grange	2550 ± 45	GRN5462
New Grange	2465 ± 40	GRN5463

(sources: Burenhult 1980; *Antiquity*, 1981, 5-8).

HAR 3932 also provides a *terminus ante quem* for the settlement activity whch preceded the construction of the Simple Passage Grave, and further comparisons may be made with other dated Neolithic settlements in western Britain and Ireland.

Table 6—Radio-carbon dates from Neolithic settlements

Site	Date in radio-carbon years bc	Laboratory no.
Ballynagilly, Tyrone	3795 ± 90	UB305
Llandegai, Gwynedd	3290 ± 150	NPL223
Trefignath	3100 ± 70	HAR3932
Gwernvale, Powys	3100 ± 75	CAR113
Coygan Camp, Dyfed	3050 ± 95	NPL132
Ballynagilly, Tyrone	2960 ± 90	UB301
Townleyhall II, Louth	2730 ± 150	BM170

(sources: Lynch 1975, 65; Britnell 1980, 147).

Radio-carbon dates are conventionally quoted with a single standard deviation, in the case of HAR 3932 this is ± 70. This means that there is a two-thirds chance that the true radio-carbon date lies between 3170 and 3030 bc. If two standard deviations are used, i.e. ± 140 years there becomes a 95% probability that the date lies between 3240 and 2960 bc. However, the full impact of this date, and the others listed, only emerges when its implications in terms of calendar years are considered. In the absence of general agreement on the method of calibration to be employed (*Antiquity*, 1972, 265) I do not propose to suggest a specific date for HAR 3932 in calendar years. Nevertheless, it seems very likely that the Simple Passage Grave was constructed between the end of the fifth millennium BC and the middle of the fourth.

The calibration of radio-carbon dates from other Passage Graves (Burenhult, 1980 Fig. 31) has led to a revolution in the dating of these sites. Formerly regarded as a later Neolithic phenomenon (Megaw and Simpson 1979, 130-41) it was until recently possible to propose that Passage Graves dated from the middle of the third millennium BC and that great sites in the Boyne Valley, Ireland were among the earliest (Herity and Eogan 1977, Chapter 3). The calibration of radio-carbon dates has now changed all this (*Antiquity*, 1981, 82-84) and it appears that the earliest Passage Graves in the British Isles may date from the middle of the fifth millennium BC while the Boyne Graves seem to lie considerably later in the sequence. The date proposed for the Simple Passage Grave at Trefignath is in good accord with this and indicates that Passage Graves were among the first megalithic tombs to be built in Wales. The implications of HAR 3932 for the date of the pre-tomb settlement are less surprising, the dates from Llandegai and Coygan Camp having been available for some time. The Trefignath date, and the almost identical date obtained for the pre-tomb structures at Gwernvale provide interesting confirmation of the contemporaneity of early Neolithic settlement throughout Wales.

Sample 15 came from within the portal of the eastern chamber and was directly associated with sherds of two late Neolithic vessels (A and C). The radio-carbon date obtained (HAR 3933) is many centuries more recent than had been anticipated and requires special explanation. This date probably represents the earliest disturbance of the burial chambers of which we have record and suggests that at some time during the later first millennium BC the eastern chamber was entered and used as a temporary shelter, involving the disturbance of the burial deposits. Several finds of Iron Age and Romano-British date indicate that the site experienced a limited amount of squatter activity from this time on.

Chapter 6—Chipped Stone Tools

During the course of the three seasons' excavation 170 flint and 251 chert artifacts were found. The horizontal distribution of these pieces is illustrated in Figure 24 where they are distinguished according to raw materials, while details of each will be found in Appendix 2. Visual inspection of this data suggests that the flint and chert were not distributed randomly across the area excavated, but tended to be concentrated slightly towards the south west of its centre. If their distribution had occurred by chance the numbers of finds would have been approximately evenly distributed whereas the observed distribution departs markedly from such an even pattern. A simple Chi^2 Test (Gregory 1963, 163-70) was used to establish that there was about a one in ten likelihood of the actual distribution having occurred by chance. While this result is not statistically significant it is at least suggestive.

In order to pursue this analysis a little further similar tests were carried out on the flint and chert distributions separately. Here the results were more informative there being a less than one in twenty likelihood of the flint distribution having occurred by chance while the probability of chance accounting for the chert distribution was less than one in one hundred. Both these results are statistically significant.

The distribution of the flint artifacts was then compared, also by means of a Chi^2 Test, with the distribution of those made from chert. The result of this test was that, whatever the factors were that determined the distribution of the chert, the chance of them also having determined the flint distribution was about one in one thousand, a result implying that the two distributions are significantly different. Inspection of Figure 24 suggests that the greatest concentration of flint artifacts occurred somewhat to the north of the chert. Elizabeth Healey, who has considered the technological aspects of the assemblage, regards the industry as broadly homogeneous and we should not place too much emphasis on this difference in the distribution of flint and chert artifacts. However, it may have a functional basis and is worth recording for its own sake.

The total of 421 artifacts included fifty-six pieces with varying degrees of retouch. The distribution of these pieces is illustrated in Figure 25, in which the scrapers—the most common single type of

implement found—have been distinguished from the remainder. The numbers involved here are too small for a statistical analysis to be worthwhile but Figure 25 does seem to imply a fairly even distribution of retouched pieces across the site.

The stratigraphical limitations of the site were described in Chapter 1 and it will be recalled that material was recovered from three kinds of context; (i) the old ground surface from below the cairn (Period I), (ii) contexts that can be specifically associated with one or other of the phases in the development of the tomb (Period II), and (iii) unstratified material from within the surviving remnants of the cairn or from beyond its known limits. The distribution of flint and chert between these contexts is set out in Table 7.

Table 7—Stratigraphical context of flint and chert artifacts.

Artifacts category	Period		Unstratified[1]		Total
	I	II_3b	_?_	?	
FLINT					
Unretouched *débitage*	36	—	32	56	124
Utilized pieces	2	—	1	2	5
Retouched pieces	12	1	19	9	41
Total flint	50	1	52	67	170
CHERT					
Unretouched *débitage*	78	—	56	93	227
Indeterminate	—	—	1	4	5
Utilized pieces	1	—	1	2	4
Retouched pieces	2	—	2	11	15
Total chert	81	—	60	110	251

(note 1—_?_ unstratified within the cairn, ? unstratified beyond the limits of the cairn).

It can be seen from Table 7 that 131 items may be ascribed to Period I on the basis of having been found on or close to the old ground surface. The problems of assigning this material to a specific period of activity have been discussed in Chapter 2 and need not be repeated here. I believe most of it may be attributed to activity on site before the first of the burial chambers was erected, though some pieces may be considerably later. The distribution of the Period I finds is illustrated on Figure 8. An analysis, similar to that carried out for the total flint and chert assemblage, was also carried out for the lithic

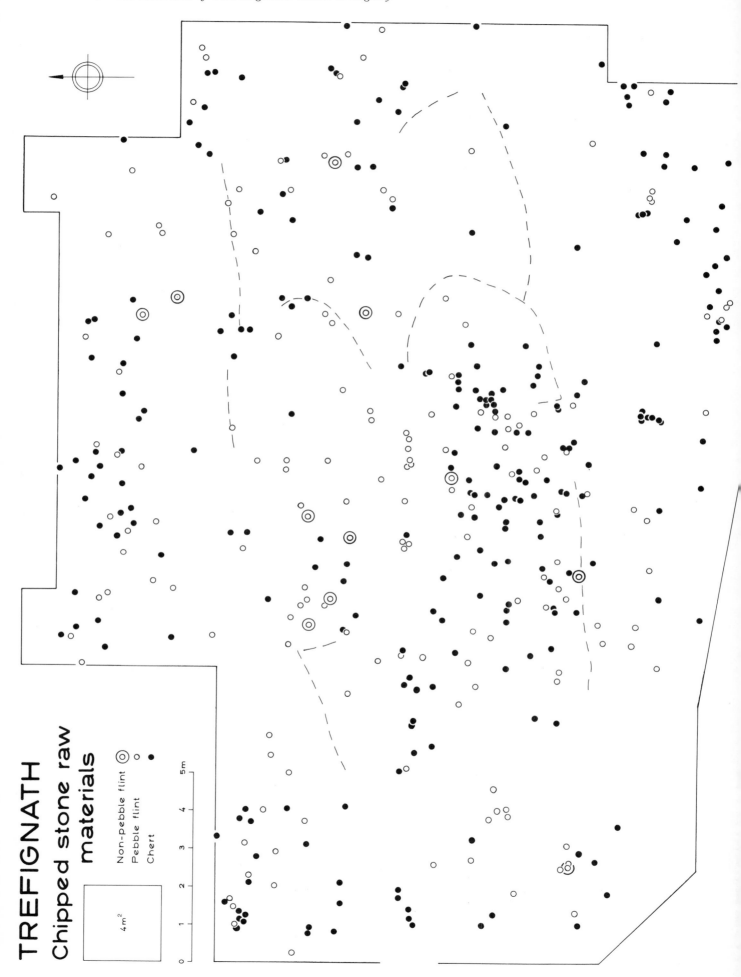

TREFIGNATH
Chipped stone raw
materials

Non-pebble flint ⊙
Pebble flint ○
Chert ●

4 m²

0 1 2 3 4 5 m

Fig. 25.   Flint and chert retouched pieces distribution.

component of the Period I assemblage. The result indicates that it is very unlikely (one chance in 1,000) that the observed distribution of stone tools attributed to Period I occurred by chance. In fact it appears in Figure 8 to be markedly concentrated and the significance of this for our understanding of the nature of the Period I activity has been discussed in Chapter 2.

The find spot for the one other stratified item (48) (Period II$_{3b}$) is shown in Figure 17. The distribution of the unstratified finds is illustrated in Figure 26. This distribution was not subjected to a statistical analysis.

LITHIC TECHNOLOGY
by
Elizabeth Healey

(i) *Raw Materials*

The raw materials selected for flaking are a black chert and flint, both of which could have been obtained locally, though there is some evidence to suggest that a few of the flint artifacts were imported. Chert is numerically more common than flint, but the difference is probably due to the more economical technology used for working the flint rather than a deliberate preference for chert, especially since there is a considerably higher proportion of retouched pieces of flint than chert. Chert may also have been brought to the site for cairn building material and some of this could have been accidentally flaked, thus artificially inflating the numbers of chert pieces.

Flint: The artifacts of flint are all in a fresh unrolled condition. Cortication (Shepherd 1972, 114-24) was noted on three pieces only, two of which had been burnt. Nearly all of the flint was obtained in the form of small pebbles, probably from the beach, but there are four pieces which are clearly of superior quality and are likely to come from the Irish Sea Drift (Greenly 1919, 717). A further six pieces may be from a similar source and seventeen others are indeterminate. The pebbles are mostly under 30mm in maximum dimension although larger pebbles were evidently available, as no. 35 and some of the larger flakes indicate. Cortex is usually thin and smooth or water worn; a few fragmentary pieces had rough, abraded areas and could have been struck from hammerstones or be the result of the use of the *écaillé* technique discussed below, but insufficient remains to be certain. The colour varies from light grey to orange-brown; some flakes are translucent but most are opaque. The non-pebble flint artifacts are grey in colour and translucent; the cortex on no. 48 is thick and unweathered.

Chert: All the chert is black. In texture it varies from fine grained to coarse and this affects its flaking predictability. Macroscopically it appears to be of carboniferous origin, similar to that occurring in the glacial deposits in the immediate vicinity (Greenly

1919, 715). As mentioned above, some of the nodules, particularly those found within the cairn (context ? in Table 7), could have been brought to the site as building material and flakes accidentally struck off, whereas other pieces seem to have been brought for the specific purpose of knapping.

(ii) *Technology*

Analysis of the *débitage* demonstrates that, with a few noteworthy exceptions, the chipped stone artifacts were manufactured on site. As will become clear, traditional classificatory schemes are inappropriate for the Trefignath material and it has been described simply by the method of flaking and raw material. Hammerstones, possibly used as flaking tools, are discussed in Chapter 8. It is likely that flint was struck on an anvil, using stone hammers and possibly also soft hammers (Norman 1977, 6), but the absence of data from controlled experimental replication makes difficult any assessment of wear on flaking tools and anvils used. Striking platforms on some of the chert flakes are lipped and some shattered, both typical of soft hammer flaking (Newcomer 1971, 88f.).

Flint: The nature of the raw material has already been alluded to. A large proportion of pebbles present seem to have been flaked or broken open using the *écaille* technique, that is they have been 'split' between a hammerstone and a fixed anvil (Jacobi 1980, 177; Norman 1977, 4-6). Item 113 (Figure 27) seems to have been an unsuccessful example, and many others have battered and splintered ends. Experimental splitting of pebbles suggests that not all will show splintered ends, and that they cannot always be distinguished from pieces struck using direct percussion methods, and once split some may have been subsequently struck with a soft hammer (Norman 1977, 6). Of these 'split' pebbles eighteen suitable halves were chosen for retouch as scrapers (Fig. 28). One (651) has had a further flake removed from its base after retouch. Others, though still flaked pebbles, seem to have been more regularly worked, occasionally from two directions (112, Fig. 27). Their small size however, makes it unlikely that they could have yielded many useful flakes and it may be that they were flaked for use in themselves.

Despite the virtual absence of formal cores or larger pebbles or other nodules a number of larger removals, and particularly those selected for retouch, must result from the flaking of larger raw material. Examples are provided by items 341 (Fig. 27), 55 (Fig. 29) and 397 (Fig. 29). The removals can be described as follows: thirty-nine flakes of which two flakes and a spall are trimming flakes; twenty-four spalls (flakes mostly under 20mm long, one of which may be a trimming flake); and nine chips and unidentifiable fragments (mostly burnt). The selection of different types of raw material for different purposes and its relation to technology and morphology of retouched pieces is set out in Table 8.

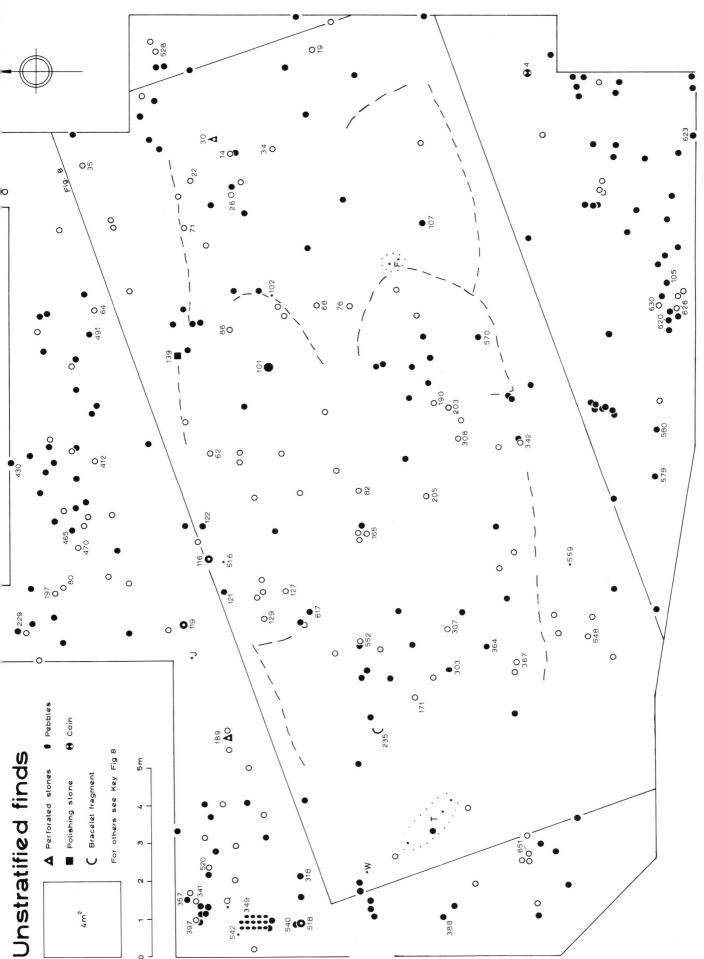

Fig. 26. Unstratified finds distribution.

Table 8—Utilization of flint

Categories	Un-retouched	Utilized	Retouched scrapers	others	Total
Split pebbles and cores	46	—	17	—	63
Flakes (pebble)	26	4	3	10	43
Flakes (prob. non-pebble)	3	—	—	3	6
Flakes (indeterminate)	12	1	1	3	17
Non-pebble	—	—	1	3	4
Spalls and chips	37	—	—	—	37
Totals	124	5	22	19	170

As Table 8 indicates pebbles were clearly being deliberately selected and split open for retouch as scrapers, whereas in some instances non-pebble flint was preferred (see also Table 10). It is concluded therefore that the apparently crude and haphazard nature of the flint working, though partly dictated by the type and quality of the raw materials available, nevertheless within these constraints shows deliberate selection of blanks for particular types of retouch.

Chert: The chert is flaked in a more usual manner, although the cores are not particularly systematically worked and there is a high number of chips and nodules with one or two random scars which cannot

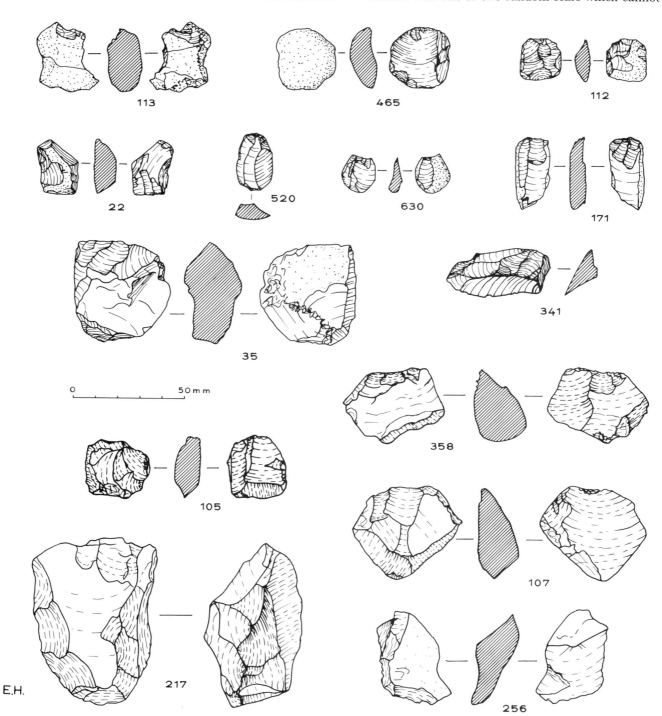

E.H.

Fig. 27.   Flint and chert cores and other *débitage*.

be further classified. The possibility of accidental fracture of nodules during cairn building has been referred to already.

Most of the nodules are quite large, up to 78mm but more usually between 50mm and 60mm in maximum dimension. There are also five small chert pebbles including items 37, 58, and 105 which have been struck on an anvil in a similar fashion to that employed for the flint pebbles, and at least four flakes show evidence for the use of the *écaillé* technique. Because of the seemingly *ad hoc* nature of the industry the cores have not been classified according to the system usually employed (Clark *et al* 1960, 216). The more regularly worked cores include four with a series of flakes detached from a single platform, but each one also shows random scars elsewhere on the core face, and two cores, 107 and 217 (Fig. 27), have a keeled or chopper-like edge. In fact 217 is not unlike a so-called chopper from Late Neolithic

contexts at Durrington Walls (Wainwright and Longworth 1971, F88, 176-79). The rest are randomly flaked or are fragmentary and include thirteen small fragments.

Table 9—Utilization of chert

Categories	Un-retouched	Utilized	Retouched	Total
Cores and struck nodules	73	—	2	75
Preparation flakes	27	—	2	29
Trimming flakes	5	—	—	5
Flakes	55	4	11	70
Spalls	38	—	—	38
Chips and in-determinate pieces	34	—	—	34
Totals	232	4	15	251

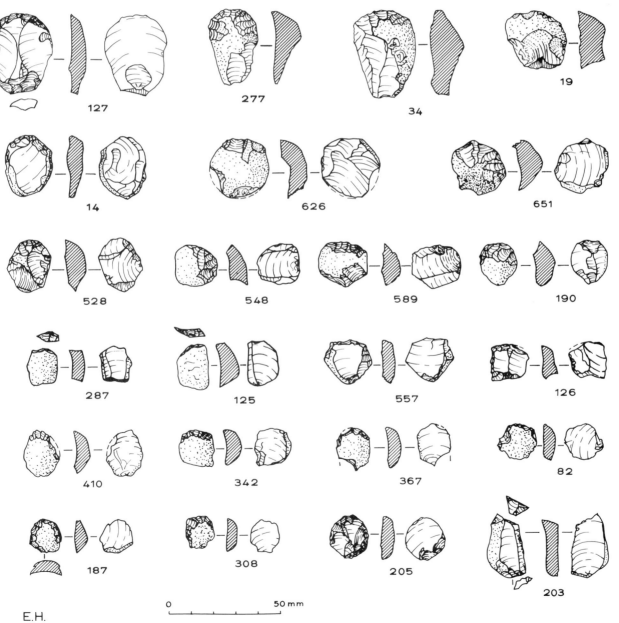

127 277 34 19
14 626 651
528 548 589 190
287 125 557 126
410 342 367 82
187 308 205 203

E.H.

0   50 mm

Fig. 28. Flint implements, mainly scrapers.

Preparation flakes are amongst the first flakes to be struck from a nodule to prepare it for use as a core, including the removal of awkward corners. The flakes are usually large and thick (over 16mm and up to 40mm thick). Some, including 256 (Fig. 27), are reminiscent of 'Clactonian flakes' with wide striking platforms and prominent bulbs of percussion.

As with the flint, trimming flakes are rare, probably because of the *ad hoc* manner in which the flakes were struck; only one attempts to remove an irregular striking platform, the others 'clean' the face of the core.

The flakes vary considerably in shape and size ranging between 18mm and 49mm in length and are normally between 4mm and 12mm thick. Striking platforms are mostly plain or occasionally dihedral, but there are also a few examples of linear platforms, some of which have a marked lip. There are also some shattered platforms.

Spalls are small flakes normally under 20mm in length; they tend to be squat in shape and seem to be accidental by-products of knapping rather than deliberate products in themselves. One fragment of fine grained chert appeared to have come from a bladelet, but apart from this there is no evidence for the deliberate manufacture of blades.

Table 10 provides metrical data for both flint and chert removals, amplifying the basic classification provided in Tables 8 and 9.

Table 10—Metrical data on removals (complete pieces)

(a) Flint

Length (mm)	Spalls (17)	Unretouched flakes (29)	Trimming flakes (1)	Scrapers (19)	Other retouched (5)
<9	6	—	—	—	—
10—19	11	5	—	9	—
20—29	—	23	—	7	1
30—39	—	1	—	2	2
40—49	—	—	1	1	—
50—59	—	—	—	—	1 (164)
60—69	—	—	—	—	—
70<	—	—	—	—	1 (48)
L/B index					
<0.5	—	—	—	—	—
0.6—1.0	11	8	—	5	1
1.1—1.5	2	13	—	12	2
1.6—2.0	2	1	1	2	—
2.1—2.5	2	6	—	—	1 (164)
2.6<	—	1	—	—	1 (48)
Thickness (mm)					
<2	6	—	—	—	—
3—4	8	4	—	—	—
5—6	2	8	—	4	1
7—8	—	7	—	6	1
9—10	—	6	—	5	2
11—12	1	3	1	1	—
13—14	—	—	—	2	—
15—16	—	—	—	1	—
......					
34<	—	1	—	—	—

(b) Chert

Length (mm)	Spalls (17)	Unretouched pieces (32)	Trimming flakes (3)	Preparation flakes (27)	Utilized (1)	Retouched (7)
<9	—	—	—	—	—	—
10—19	16	4	1	—	—	—
20—29	1	19	2	7	—	2
30—39	—	7	—	8	1	1
40—49	—	2	—	7	—	2
50—59	—	—	—	3	—	—
60—69	—	—	—	1	—	—
70—79	—	—	—	1	—	—
80—89	—	—	—	—	—	2
L/B index						
<0.5	—	—	2	—	—	—
0.6—1.0	8	11	—	16	—	1
1.1—1.5	5	12	1	8	1	4
1.6—2.0	3	8	—	3	—	2
2.1—2.5	—	1	—	—	—	—
2.6<	1	—	—	—	—	—
Thickness (mm)						
<2	1	—	—	—	—	—
3—4	10	5	—	—	—	—
5—6	4	10	—	—	1	1
7—8	2	7	1	—	—	1
9—10	—	7	2	—	—	2
11—12	—	3	—	4	—	1
13—14	—	—	—	5	—	1
15—16	—	—	—	5	—	1
17—18	—	—	—	5	—	—
19—20	—	—	—	1	—	—
21—22	—	—	—	1	—	—
23—24	—	—	—	2	—	—
25 +	—	—	—	1	—	—
35 +	—	—	—	3	—	—

(iii) *Retouched artifacts*

The unconventional nature of the industry also extends to the retouched pieces, especially those of chert. Most of the material is therefore illustrated in Figures 28, 29, and 30 in order to avoid lengthy descriptions, and traditional classification and terminology has been followed only where appropriate. The on-site distribution is illustrated in Figure 25. It should be noted that terms such as 'scraper', 'knife' etc., do not necessarily have any functional significance.

Flint implements

Scrapers There are twenty-two scrapers present, twenty-one of pebble or probably pebble flint and one (127, Fig. 28) of non-pebble flint. Their metrical data is summarised in Table 10a above. The flint scrapers are very small, all but three (34, 127, and 277) are under 30mm in length and these are all on flakes; eleven are 20mm or less. It is clear that the small size is dictated by the use of small split pebbles as blanks. However, as already mentioned, this selection seems to have been deliberate as other types of blank, though still largely of pebble flint, were used for other tool forms. The retouched area usually has a rounded contour (four are damaged), and is confined to a single edge. On four scrapers (187, 205, 308, and 589) it is more extensive and these are among the smallest present. Two (205 and 589) have retouch on

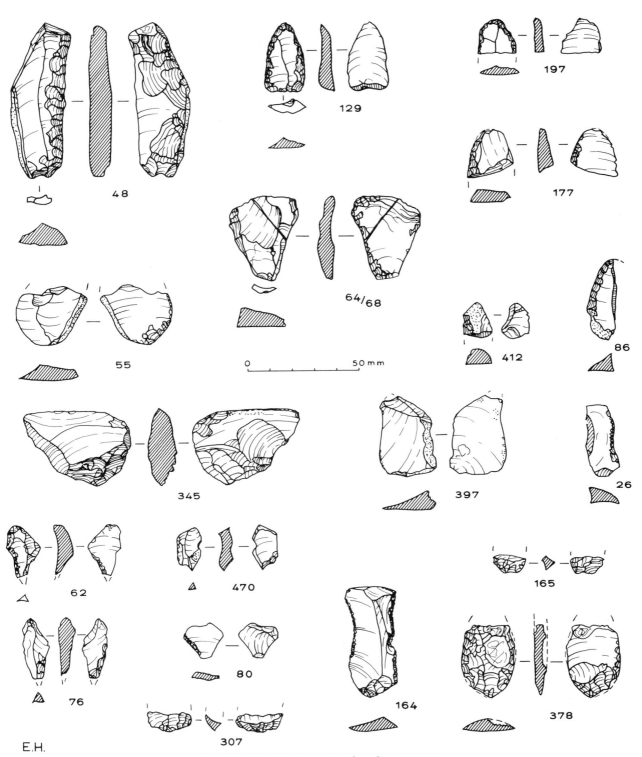

E.H.

Fig. 29. Flint implements other than scrapers.

two unconnected edges. The retouch is normally non-convergent and sometimes sub-parallel. It tends to be confined to the edge and is abrupt, but on 651, 528, 548, and 190 it clearly invades the surface of the pebble. Scraper 126 is worn smooth but subsequently broken so that it is not known whether the wear is localised or extended all round its edge. Small scrapers, especially scale-flaked examples, are usually considered to be characteristic of Beaker and Early Bronze Age tool kits (Smith 1965, 107; Wainwright 1972, 61-62) but they also occur in Late

Mesolithic techno-complexes in North Wales (Jacobi 1980, 177). However, in no case is the type of blank described, beyond noting the use of pebble flint. Freshwater West can no longer be used for comparison in dating as the assemblage is mixed (Jacobi 1980, 178).

Knives (Fig. 29) There are five knives and a fragment of a possible sixth present in the assemblage. A fine example, 48, was found in the portal to the eastern chamber. This knife is made of a long blade-like flake of light grey, non-pebble flint with cortex (fresh and unrolled) along part of the back. Whilst the flake edge has been retouched invasively, the other edge has been inversely flaked with flat, stepped retouch which continues around both ends. The other knives are less spectacular. Two (129 and 197) are sub-triangular in shape with retouch all round the edges. Another (177) appears to be morphologically similar but is bifacially flaked along one edge. The fifth knife comprises two conjoining fragments (64 and 68) found 6m apart (Fig. 26). It is a flaring flake with inverse retouch along the thinner edge. The fragment (412) is of pebble flint and has semi-abrupt retouch along one long edge. It may have come from a knife but it is too fragmentary to classify and has been counted with the unclassifiable retouch. The large knife (48) is morphologically very similar to knives from Late Neolithic contexts and at Trefignath it was found in association with pottery of that date (Vessels A and C). The other knives are less characteristic as they are of very simple form, but such knives are known from earlier Neolithic contexts onwards, as for example at Bishopstone (Bell 1977, nos. 93-94) and later at Durrington Walls (Wainwright and Longworth 1971, 174).

Saw (Fig. 29) A finely denticulated double-edge blade (164) was recovered from the old ground surface below the Neolithic cairn (Period I). It is made on a blade-like flake which ends in a hinge fracture and has a facetted butt. The teeth are made by the formation of minute notches by removing several small spalls. A narrow band of gloss can be observed on the edge of the teeth at the mid point on the ventral face. The method of manufacture and the relatively coarse denticulation suggest Later Neolithic affinities and may be compared and contrasted with examples of serrated flakes and saws from the primary levels at the Kennet Avenue (Smith 1965, 91, 239).

Arrowhead (Fig. 29) A single leaf-shaped arrowhead (378) was found. It has been heavily burnt but it is still possible to ascertain that it is made of non-pebble flint. Although it is incomplete a tentative reconstruction suggests that it is of Green's type 2b (Green 1980, Table II, 18). It was found on the old ground surface below the cairn but is otherwise not closely dateable. A bifacially flaked, but otherwise unclassifiable chip (165), may be a fragment of another arrowhead. It is from an unstratified context.

Piercers (Fig. 29) Three piercers (62, 76 and 470), all of pebble flint, were recovered from unstratified contexts. They have minimal retouch on a suitably pointed blank. The form, though not closely dateable would not be out of context in a Mesolithic or Neolithic tool-kit.

Truncated Blade (Fig. 28) One largish flake of pebble flint (203) has had its distal end obliquely truncated by abrupt retouch. It was found in an unstratified context within the body of the cairn. It is morphologically closer to the straight-ended scrapers from Freshwater West (Wainwright 1959, 200) than to Mesolithic truncated blades.

Notched piece (Fig. 29) A small flake of pebble flint (80) has a small semi-circular notch formed by abrupt retouch. It is from an unstratified context and is not a sufficiently distinctive form to be dated.

Sharpening flake (Fig. 29) Item 307 is a small triangular sectioned flake struck from a bifacially flaked object to remove a keeled edge. It was unstratified.

Other retouched pieces (Fig. 29) A large flake (345) shows bifacial flaking at its butt end, possibly an attempt to remove the striking platform and bulb of percussion and to make the piece thinner. The edges are utilized. Six fragments have areas of retouch on them but are otherwise unclassifiable. One (165) is from a thin bifacially flaked object and it has already been suggested that this may have been an arrowhead. Others show retouch on the edges and forming points.

Utilization Four flakes show signs of edge damage probably due to utilization and one (397) has gloss on the edge.

Chert implements

Comparatively few chert artifacts had been retouched and only some of these could be readily classified. A retouched nodule (357, Fig. 30) had a waisted edge and a rounded end somewhat like a plane. The retouch is partly bifacial on the end. Although not directly comparable this artifact is not unlike the 'waisted core-tools' from Late Neolithic contexts such as Arreton Down (Alexander and Ozanne 1960, 291 F36 and F38) and the Upper Levels at Windmill Hill (Smith 1965, 105 F148). A thermally fractured fragment (267, Fig. 30) with retouch on its nose end is possibly similar.

Pieces with edge retouch (Fig. 30) This group includes two preparation flakes and six others. One of the former (229) has crude flat flaking reducing the thickness of the side with traces of utilization on the opposite thinner edge, while the other (121) has retouch on the side of the flake and traces of utilization or irregular retouch from alternate faces along the long edge. The six flakes (29, 579, 318, 617, 620, and 430) have retouch on one or more edges of the blank. One (579) is concave and another (318) is notched, but this could be modern damage. Item 620 is of a fine quality chert and the retouch is abrupt and exceptionally regular.

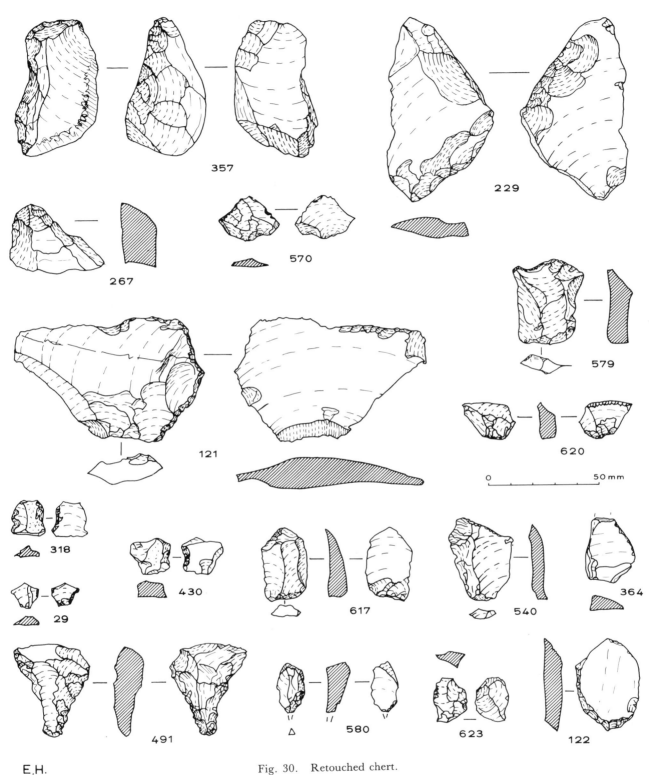

E.H.

Fig. 30. Retouched chert.

Points (Fig. 30) This group includes four pieces; 491 is the only clearly made point, 580 is retouched on converging edges but is broken at the tip, 623 is a small pointed flake with trimming on the edges, and 122 has only minimal irregular denticulated retouch forming a point, but it is not certainly deliberate.

Utilization Edge-damage was noted on a number of pieces which in four cases probably results from utilization. Two of the more certain examples (364 and 540) are illustrated in Figure 30.

The dating of the chert artifacts is difficult as none can be directly paralleled. The random flaking technology and the irregular non-conformist tools suggest a very *ad hoc* industry.

(iv) *Discussion*
The analysis of the chipped stone artifacts has demonstrated that the technology and typology

reflect the use of rather small and poor quality raw materials, especially the beach pebble flint. This limitation appears to have necessitated the importation of a few implements of superior quality flint.

On stratigraphical grounds, with the exception of 48, the assemblage has been divided into pre-cairn and unstratified contexts. This was summarised in Table 7 and is now set out in greater detail in Table 11. With a few exceptions, such as the piercers and the truncated blade, both groups appear to be technologically and typologically homogeneous, though the numbers are small and the relationship between the two contexts must remain speculative. This is also the case with the relationship between the flint and chert industries, which as we have seen, have a slightly different distribution pattern. However, it seems likely that they are contemporary and perhaps complementary, which could account for the small quantity of retouched chert.

The relatively high proportion of retouched pieces present in the flint assemblage, some 27%, calls for comment. For the most part this is likely to be due to the small size of the pebbles and the economy with which they were flaked, compared with the more usual core reduction process which produces a large amount of debris. No detailed information is available from other technologically similar industries, or even from other industries using beach pebble flint, but there is a mounting body of evidence to suggest that retouched pieces become proportionately more numerous when there is no source of good raw material in the immediate vicinity.

The only independently datable artifact is the flint knife (48) which was found in the portal to the eastern chamber in association with two Late Neolithic vessels (A and C), with which it is typologically consistent. This knife is non-pebble flint, similar to that used for a scraper (127), the serrated blade, or saw (164), and the leaf-shaped arrowhead (378). These three objects all came from pre-cairn contexts and, in the terms of the site sequence antedate the knife (48) by several phases. However, the serrated blade is also a very typically Late Neolithic product while the presence of finished objects of imported flint as well as the apparent trading of tool blanks is well documented in that period (Healey in Britnell 1982). It should not be forgotten, however, that potential trade objects of various types of stone are known from the Mesolithic (Jacobi 1980, 74) and quite apart from axes, are documented by the arrowheads in the Neolithic particularly in relation to chambered tombs (Green 1980, 62ff. and 98). The objects under discussion are likely to be of later Neolithic date which implies that they do not antedate the construction of the western chamber by more than a brief interval, if indeed they did not arrive on site as part of that activity.

The rest of the artifacts need not belong to such an horizon, but indications of date based on technology and typology are tenuous and contradictory. Technological considerations indicate that at least some of the pebbles have been flaked or split using the écaillé technique, but the evidence of battering or splintering on other pebbles is less clear. Some tentative replication experiments by the writer suggest that not all pieces would in fact show the battering and splintering usually considered indicative of the technique (cf Norman 1977, 6). It is also hard to see how the pebbles could have been held for flaking by direct percussion. It has been assumed, therefore, that apart from a few larger flakes the material has been flaked using the écaillé method.

Table 11—Technology and stratigraphy of flint and chert artifacts.

(a) Flint

Artifact category	Period I	II$_{3b}$	Unstratified[1] $\underline{?}$	?	Total
Unretouched pieces:					
Cores	13	—	15	18	46
Flakes	15	—	8	16	39
Trimming flakes	—	—	—	2	2
Spalls	7	—	6	10	23
Chips	1	—	3	10	14
Sub-totals	36	—	32	56	124
Retouched pieces:					
Scrapers	8	—	9	5	22
Truncated blade	—	—	1	—	1
Knives	1	1	2	1	5
Saw	1	—	—	—	1
Arrowhead	1	—	—	—	1
Piercers	—	—	2	1(?)	3
Misc. retouch	1	—	5	2	8
Utilized	2	—	1	2	5
Sub-totals	14	1	20	11	46

(note 1—$\underline{?}$ unstratified within the cairn, ? unstratified beyond the limits of the cairn).

(b) Chert

Artifact category	Period I	II$_{3b}$	Unstratified[1] $\underline{?}$	?	Total
Unretouched pieces:					
Cores	10	—	12	19	41
Struck nodules	9	—	6	17	32
Preparation flakes	7	—	10	10	27
Flakes	28	—	10	17	55
Trimming flakes	1	—	2	2	5
Spalls	15	—	9	14	38
Chips etc.,	8	—	8	18	
Sub-totals	78	—	57	97	232

Artifacts category	Period I	II$_{3b}$	Unstratified[1] $\underline{?}$	?	Total
Retouched pieces:					
Retouched	2	—	2	11	15
Utilized	1	—	1	2	4
Sub-totals	3	—	3	13	19

(note [1]—$\underline{?}$ unstratified within the cairn, ? unstratified beyond the limits of the cairn).

It has been argued that the *écaillé* technique is a technochronological phenomenon, rather than simply a response to raw material, and is likely to be Neolithic or later in date (Norman 1977, 8-9), though it could possibly occur at the very end of the Mesolithic and is likely to overlap with the Obanian. It is not used in the Mesolithic industries at Frainslake or Westward Ho! even though beach pebble flint was exploited there (Jacobi 1980, 174-75, 177-78). As the sizes of the available pebbles from these sites are not compared to those where the *écaillé* technique is practised the dating of the technique to the Neolithic is not conclusive, as it could still be a size related phenomenon. At Trefignath the use of the technique seems deliberate and is confined to the manufacture of scrapers. The larger pieces are more normally struck and could, of course, be of a different date.

Although the use of beach pebble flint is recorded elsewhere in Anglesey and North Wales no comment is made on the technology used. It may be significant that the coastal Obanian industries, with which Trefignath could be broadly contemporary, are also quite different from other Mesolithic Scottish industries, but the relationship between the two is not understood (Norman 1977, 8).

The chert industry is also unlikely to be Mesolithic in date because at all other sites in North Wales where chert is exploited it is systematically flaked and a typical Mesolithic tool kit present, as for example at Hendre, Rhuddlan (Healey in Manley and Healy 1982) and the Brenig (Healey in preparation). A preliminary examination of material from the Ty Mawr site on Holyhead Mountain also supports this statement.

Of the retouched pieces of pebble flint little can be positively said. Artifacts which could have Mesolithic affinities include the truncated blade (203) and the piercers (62 and 76) which are superficially like the *mèche de forêt* from Nab Head, though they lack the characteristic abrupt retouch (Jacobi 1980, 154 and Fig. 158). It has also been argued that small scrapers could be Mesolithic (Jacobi 1980, 177). They are also very similar to the predominant type at Freshwater West though it is not certain from the published information whether these belong to the Mesolithic or Neolithic facies on the site (Wainwright 1959 or Jacobi 1980, 178). Whatever their date it is likely that their form was dictated by the raw material, even though this was deliberately chosen.

Discussion of the chipped stone artifacts has so far concentrated on their date and on general technological and typological comparanda. Specific reference to lithic material from other tombs can only be made in the case of one of the knives (48) as this was the only item found in a funerary context. However, this is without close parallel in such a context in Wales, although knives are known from other tombs (Lynch 1969, 150). Pre-tomb settlement is difficult to document because of the uneven nature of the evidence and the small areas generally excavated. In Wales the clearest evidence for pre-tomb activity comes from Gwernvale, which had lithic evidence for activity on site since the Upper Palaeolithic and through the Mesolithic and Neolithic (Healey and Green in Britnell 1984). Comparable evidence comes from Bryn yr Hen Bobl where the pre-tomb activity seems to be Neolithic in date, though this evidence is not without ambiguity. The problem of the interpretation of the relationship of artifacts from pre-tomb contexts to those belonging to the use of the tomb is clearly analogous to that of pre-barrow and barrow finds discussed by Saville (1980, 21-22) and requires a similar programme of research.

Chapter 7—Pottery

The top soil at Trefignath contained a large quantity of Nineteenth and Twentieth Century pottery dating from the time when the site was used as a dump by the occupants of Trefignath farm. This material was not recorded in detail and has now been discarded. Detailed records were kept of all other ceramic finds. The total assemblage comprises 1.6kg of prehistoric pottery recovered from sixty different locations on site, a small group of Romano-British and medieval sherds and five stratified sherds of post-medieval date. The prehistoric pottery, comprising the bulk of the assemblage is considered first.

Prehistoric Pottery

By a careful consideration of fabric, surface treatment, and find spot it has been possible to divide the 1.6kg of prehistoric pottery found at Trefignath into twenty-one vessels, with a residue of eight sherds that are insufficiently distinctive for them to be attributed to any specific vessel or given vessel status in their own right. The twenty-one vessels are labelled alphabetically (letters I and O being omitted) and details of the sherd groups of which each is composed are given in appendix two. The distribution of this material is illustrated in Figures 8, 9, 13, 17, and 26 while the material itself is illustrated in Figures 35 and 36. It must be remembered that no complete vessels were found at Trefignath and in several cases vessels are represented by a few sherds only. Indeed, Vessels J, Q, and W were each represented by a single sherd.

Material from seventeen vessels, and three sherds from Din Dryfol, was subjected to detailed petrographic analysis by David Jenkins of the Department of Biochemistry and Soil Science, University College of North Wales, Bangor. Dr Jenkins' report is reproduced here in full before discussion of the stratigraphical context of the Trefignath vessels or their cultural affinities.

The remains of Vessel P were found to be heterogeneous and may not represent a single pot. Vessels T, U, V, and W were not identified as distinct vessels as opposed to residue until after the analytical project was complete. From the archaeological point of view it was hoped that the petrographic analysis would provide information on the provenance of the material used, and in particular whether the vessels considered were likely to have been made locally, i.e. on Ynys Gybi, or farther afield.

PETROGRAPHIC ANALYSIS

by
David Jenkins

1. INTRODUCTION

Ynys Gybi, like adjacent Ynys Môn, presents a varied and distinctive solid geology. Outcrops include localised masses of serpentinite/gabbro and both Palaeozoic and Tertiary dolerite dykes within a range of metamorphic rocks. There is therefore a strong possibility that some of the distinctive rock types among such an assemblage might be identifiable within the temper used in the manufacture of the potsherds found at Trefignath, and consequently that the provenance of the temper might be established as being either local to Ynys Gybi or extraneous. This potential has been investigated by the preparation and petrographic analysis of thin-sections from seventeen selected vessels as well as from local rock outcrops and sediments. Such analytical data simultaneously provide an alternative basis for the classification of the potsherds. For four sherds, where sufficient material was available and where—in one case—clasts are virtually absent from the fabric, petrographic data have been supplemented by heavy mineral analysis. These heavy mineral analyses relate more to the provenance of matrix material than to that of the temper, and, again comparative analyses have been made of the local superficial deposits. Three sherds from the contemporaneous site at Din Dryfol have also been examined and, since they show affinities with certain of the sherds from Trefignath, the results from both sites are presented and discussed together. First, however, a brief description of the petrographic background to the area will be given. This is illustrated together with sampling sites in Figure 31.

The geology of Ynys Gybi is dominated by metamorphosed sedimentary rocks of late Precambrian age. The rocks in the vicinity of Trefignath have been mapped by Greenly (1919) as belonging to the Celyn Beds of the semi-pelitic New Harbour Group in the Monian succession. At the north west end of the Island these Beds pass down into more psammitic rocks of the South Stack Group which include the Holyhead Quartzite. The Celyn Beds are green mica schists which have been extensively reconstituted: they contain secondary quartz, albite,

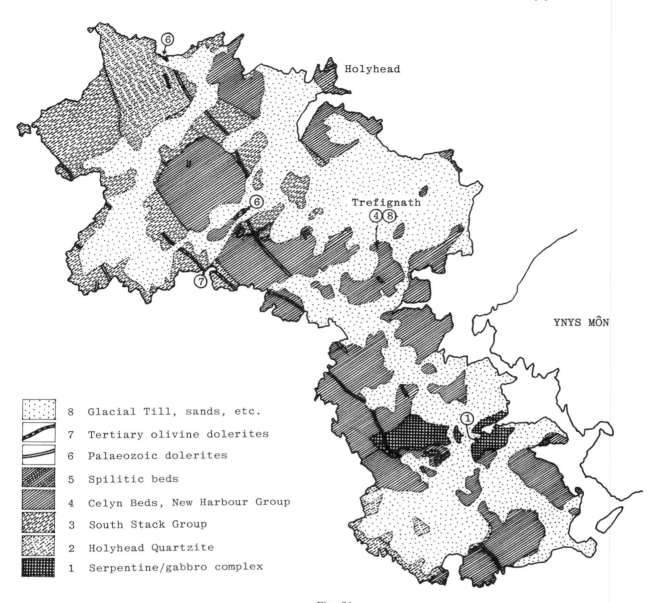

Fig. 31.

epidote, clinozoisite, titanite, apatite, chlorite, and muscovite, although original clastic quartz is still recognisable. A green biotite which was found to be common elsewhere in these Beds by Greenly (1919) was not seen in the outcrops, stones, gravel, or sand fraction at Trefignath itself. At other localities on the island, these strata also include purplish-red jaspers, pigmented by haematite, and pale grey-green massive spilitic beds containing albite, chlorite, epidote and actinolite. Recently a reinterpretation of the stratigraphic and structural position of these rocks has been presented by Barber and Max (1979).

A suite of ultramafic rock outcrops in amongst these green mica schists a few miles to the south east of Trefignath. It is dominated by pale to dark green serpentinites in which olivine and orthopyroxene have been wholly replaced (e.g. by lizardite and/or antigorite), whilst large pale green plates of a striated diallagic clinopyroxene (diopside/pigeonite) survive, sometimes carrying a rim of tremolite. Small granules of magnetite, chromite and picotite also

occur together with ilmenite/leucoxene, and the rocks show a variety of microfabrics which have been described in detail by Maltman (1978). Associated with these serpentinites are intrusive "altered gabbroic rocks" containing some original plagioclase felspar (An_{30}) and green clinopyroxene (diallage), but much altered to chlorites, tremolite, epidote and, rarely, fine granular garnet and anthophyllite. Peripheral to this igneous complex the green mica schists show increasing development of epidote to produce what are interpreted as epidote hornfelses. Elsewhere, metasomatic alteration has produced secondary talc, diopside, and small areas of carbonate rocks, chlorite/magnetite, and tremolite schists.

Intruded into these Precambrian rocks are two distinct generations of dolerite dykes, the major examples of which form distinctive features in the landscape of the island. The earlier Palaeozoic dolerites are dull, green, massive rocks containing altered plagioclase and pale brown ophitic augite. In addition there are often original broad prisms of brown hornblende with secondary blue green, green and colourless amphibole as prismatic/fibrous extensions, small flakes of brown biotite, chlorites, slender prisms of apatite, calcite, magnetite, and ilmenite/leucoxene. The fresh spheroidal cores of the later Tertiary dolerites are darker, rougher, and often altered marginally to softer brown material. They differ mineralogically in carrying, in addition to zoned, strongly twinned, plagioclase and ophitic brown augite, fresh and pseudomorphed grains of olivine and rare secondary prehnite, whilst hornblende and biotite are rare or absent, and apatite less abundant.

Apart from the solid rock outcrops in Ynys Gybi described above, another potential source of material for use as temper could have been the extensive superficial deposits of the island (Fig. 31). These are dominated by a stony glacial till which, to the east in Anglesey, is found to contain foreign rocks which imply that the till was deposited by ice that had traversed the floor of the present Irish Sea to the North. However, the stone fraction at Trefignath was found to be dominated by the local schists with occasional quartzites and only rare dolerites, microdiorites, and felsites. Similarly, petrographic analysis showed the 2.0-0.6mm fraction to be derived exclusively from local rock types—i.e. quartzites (46%), quartz/muscovite/chlorite schists (44%) and vein quartz (10%). The effect of extraneous material can, however, be detected in the ''heavy mineralogy'' of the sand fraction of deposits at Trefignath, as will be described in a later section.

2. PETROGRAPHIC METHODS EMPLOYED

Wherever possible sherds were subjected to a standard procedure of analysis. If available, floating undecorated fragments of the order of 2.5 × 2.5cm were selected and their macroscopic features—as seen under a stereozoom binocular microscope—noted (e.g.: colour, texture, and fabric in terms of clast and pore density, shape and distribution). The sherd was then sawn into two roughly equal halves with a dental diamond saw, and one half ignited overnight at 500°C in an electric muffle furnace in an oxidising environment. Original and re-ignited fragments were then placed side by side in a suitable glass tube, together with a label, and impregnated with a polystyrene resin system (e.g. ''Autoplax'' + 2% 28C hardener) either under vacuum (0.1mm Hg) or using a system diluted 1:1 with acetone: in the latter case the tube was kept corked for several days to allow thorough penetration by the resin, and then uncorked to allow the acetone to evaporate and the resin to polymerise, a process which generally takes a further four to eight days by either method. Once hardened, the glass tube was removed and a 5mm slice cut off with a diamond saw to provide a transverse section through the two sherd fragments. One surface was ground with corundum (50μm) and then automatically polished with

diamond paste (6, 3 & 1μm) before being attached to a glass slide (48 × 28mm) from which a 25-30μm thin-section was prepared in the normal way. For this a Logitech Precision Lapping machine was used to take sections down to 50μm, the final grinding being done by hand, followed again by diamond polishing.

Thin-sections were made of rocks from outcrops at the site in the normal manner, whilst the superficial geology was sampled in the form of the 2.0-0.63mm fraction, separated by wet-sieving from soil material. This coarse sand fraction was impregnated with resin and then sectioned in the same way as described above for the sherds.

Prior to microscopic examination a magnified (× 15) negative photographic print was made of the section by projecting it from a Leitz 35mm projector. A 1cm grid was superimposed during production of the print which subsequently allowed features to be readily located by means of a grid reference. Under the microscope, the composition of the sherd was recorded quantitatively (vol.%) using a Swift Automatic Point Counter: the components distinguished being ''void'', ''matrix'', ''grains'', ''grog'', and ''clasts''. The distinction between matrix, grain, and clast is to some extent arbitrary, the intention being to provide some parameter of the ''clay'' texture, and to attempt to distinguish material (''clasts'') added as temper. For this former purpose it was convenient microscopically to separate sand-sized material (''grains'') from silt and clay (''matrix'') according to the current soil limit of 63μm, although these values have not been used in the following discussion: for the latter clasts have been identified as polymineralic fragments generally greater than 630μm, but extrapolating petrographically down to 200μm for recognisable clast components.

The following features were described and recorded:

Clasts: petrographic types and their abundance (frequency %) within the section and also their shape—i.e. rounded (detrital) or angular (clastic). Their position was individually recorded by annotating the enlarged photographic print.

Grains: shape, sorting, and mineralogical composition (e.g. occurrence and abundance of orthoclase, microcline, plagioclase, muscovite, biotite, amphiboles, pyroxenes, etc.). Any other distinctive components were also noted (e.g. charcoal, phytoliths, spicules, diatoms, etc.).

Matrix: general texture (i.e. silt/clay) and fabric (degree of clay orientation; homogeneity, etc.).

Grog: shape, colour, fabric, texture, clasts etc., in contrast to the host sherd.

Voids: shape (e.g. irregular linear cracks; geometrically regular ''casts'' etc.) distribution, and contents—especially within the unignited sample (e.g. orientated linings of clay, Fe-oxides; spores, faecal pellets, etc.).

These data can then be assessed for their significance in terms of the classification of the sherds as well of the provenance of their components. For the former it is convenient to resolve the variety of data through some such procedure as Principal Component or Cluster Analysis. The latter assessment depends on the recognition of distinctive rock types among the clasts or assemblages of minerals among the grains.

3. RESULTS.

Introduction

In all some thirty-seven thin-sections have been prepared from twenty sherd fragments, seventeen from Trefignath and three small isolated pieces from Din Dryfol. Replicate sections of both ignited and unignited portions were made where the volume of sherd available allowed: the corresponding laboratory section numbers are listed in Appendix 1. The Trefignath samples were selected from floating fragments that had been macroscopically assigned to individual vessels (A-S). In the case of Vessel P, however, the four fragments sectioned were found to be heterogenous in their petrography, and this sample has therefore been omitted from this discussion. Conversely, sherds 431 and 498 have subsequently been linked as deriving from a single vessel (S)—they have been designated S and S^1 where necessary. Four vessels (T-W) have also been recognised subsequent to the petrographic study, and they have been assigned to petrographic groups on the basis of macroscopic examination only.

Apart from providing a lead to provenance, the petrographic data can be used as a set of intrinsic properties by which the sherds may be grouped or classified. The different properties vary in significance and could be weighted accordingly, but since the simplest empirical and statistical treatments provide sensible and meaningful results, these alone will be presented. Empirically, the sherds may be grouped both according to the nature of their fabric and also according to the petrography of their clasts, where present. With respect to fabric, three groups can be readily distinguished:

GROUP 1: Ten vessels in which clasts are relatively abundant (16-38%).

GROUP 2: Four vessels in which clasts are sparse (2-3%) but which are generally devoid of biolith fragments and which contain large irregular to tabular voids.

GROUP 3: Five vessels in which clasts are effectively absent (<1%) but which are distinguished by their high content of biolith fragments and by the presence of small rhomb-shaped voids.

Those groups of vessels containing clasts (i.e. Group 1 and, less easily, Group 2) can then be sub-divided according to their petrography, and here a different further four groups can be recognised:

GROUP A: Seven vessels containing fragments of metamorphic rocks, including various schists, metaquartzites, and fragments of vein quartz.

GROUP B: Five vessels containing ultramafic rock fragments (serpentinites).

GROUP C: Two vessels containing mafic rock fragments (dolerites).

GROUP D: Other rock fragments, including coarse and fine grained silicic igneous material and unrecognised rock types.

These last four groups are not mutually exclusive in that clasts of A may be found in sherds dominated by clasts of group B or C, B in those dominated by A, but they are nevertheless well defined. Thus, combining fabric and clast composition, six groups may be recognised overall, i.e. GROUPS 1A, 1C, 1B, 2A, 2A/B and 3. Conveniently, five of these six groups (all but Group 3) are contained within two separate 3-component (clast petrography) systems, and the relative compositions of the individual vessels can therefore be depicted quantitatively on triangular diagrams (Fig. 32). Upon more detailed study, to be discussed later, it was found convenient to further subdivide two of these groups—i.e. 1C(i) and 1C(ii), and 3(i) and 3(ii).

3b: Group 1A—Vessels A, B, C and G

This group of four vessels consists of thick (15mm) rough-surfaced dense sherds, coarsely gritted with common large (5-8mm) angular clasts including numerous conspicuous fragments of white quartz. The sherds are generally reddish-brown (Munsell colour: 5YR4/4-5/4) with patchy development of dark grey to black areas within the interior, and show an irregular fracture.

In thin-section the matrix is seen to be a silty clay, uniform in most cases but occasionally showing a banding between darker/lighter and more or less silty material: the degree of orientation of the clay fraction as expressed in aggregate birefringence is generally moderate to weak, but occasional patches of strongly oriented matrix occur. Grains lie mostly within the fine sand to silt range and are dominated by angular to subangular quartz, with rarer plagioclase, muscovite, clinozoisite, tourmaline, and chlorite: in sherds of Vessels C and G rare grains of a chert-like material were also noted. Voids (5-9%) are irregular linear, lenticular, or ovoid in shape. Clasts (16-27%) are mostly large angular fragments of vein quartz (37-73%), typically made up of subparallel anhedral prisms showing strained extinction and traversed by trains of inclusions, sometimes carrying rouleaux of chlorite, and often with metaquartzite or schist attachments. Individual fragments of metaquartzite (occasionally containing fresh euhedral plagioclase), chlorite, muscovite, biotite, and epidote schist are generally smaller and often subrounded. In thin-sections of Vessel A rare fragments of a fine grained mosaic of quartz occur with granules of haematite outlining angular shapes, probably corresponding to a jasper-like rock. Grog fragments are mostly sparse (0.5-7%) and generally consist of rounded fragments of darker pigmentation.

3c: Group 1B—Vessels H, J, R, and S

These four vessels comprise rough surfaced dense sherds, 8-10mm thick, with common large (6-9mm) angular rock clasts, some of which (e.g. in S) show lustrous silvery planar surfaces; occasional fragments of milky white quartz are also visible (e.g. in H). The sherds are mostly a dark reddish-brown (5YR3/4) throughout, except for superimposed staining by Mn oxides, although Vessel H is a darker grey (5YR2.5/2) with only a thin patchy dark reddish-grey oxidised surface.

In thin-section the matrix is a relatively uniform silty clay varying to clayey silt in parts. It contains abundant silt-sized angular quartz but larger angular grains are rare: occasional grains of muscovite together with rare grains of felspar, tourmaline, hornblende, clinopyroxene, rutile, and epidote are present. The matrix is distinguished by the common occurrence of sponge spicules, mostly composed of style fragments with rarer tylostyle, acanthostyle and tetract fragments (e.g. Plate XIX*d*), together with occasional rectangular pitted phytoliths. Other distinctive opaline silica bodies of unknown origin were noted, particularly in thin-sections of Vessel S which also carried distinctive diatoms tentatively identified as *Diploneis interrupta* (Plate XIX*g*). Diatoms were absent from the other sherds, or present only as rare small fragments. Voids (4-20%) are essentially irregular linear and ovoid features.

The clasts (22-38%) are very distinctive, being dominated by serpentinite, the only other rock types identified being small fragments of metaquartzite and muscovite schist (Vessel H) and vein quartz (Vessel R). The serpentinite clasts range from 8mm down to 50μm in size and illustrate the full range of textures described by Maltman (1978) for the Holyhead serpentinites. The material ranges from colourless to grey brown in the original sherd, often darkening towards the margins presumably due to oxidation, and to orange brown in the re-ignited samples where features generally are greatly clarified: original pale green serpentine is rarely present, suggesting oxidation in the original firing. The textures observed include "meshes" resulting from multiple, transversely fibrous "cords" enclosing fine mosaic cores, the latter containing isotropic "serpophyte" and length-fast "α-serpentine", conforming with Maltman's record of the less common "Fensterstruktur" in the Holyhead serpentinites (Plate XIX*b*); "ribbon" texture is also represented, and there are developments of the "bladed mat" texture resulting from both small and large colourless blades of antigorite. Dark brown to opaque cubic granules of magnetite, and possibly also chromite and picotite, are common, often outlining the margins of a pre-serpentinisation granular structure. An associated clinopyroxene is present in one sherd section only (S-431) as common large striated colourless grains showing high relief, low birefringence, and $\gamma \wedge c$ of 40°—i.e. diopside/diallage. This mineral is absent from the otherwise very similar sherd (S-498) which on macroscopic grounds was considered to derive from the same vessel (S): it would seem improbable, but not impossible, that such divergence in mineralogy

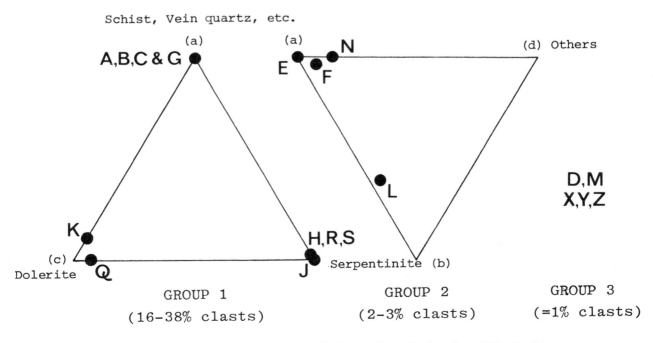

Fig. 32.   Petrographic classification of sherds from Trefignath and Din Dryfol.

would occur within the clasts in the same vessel. Rounded grog fragments are variable within sherds of this group (0.2-10%) and may be either darker or paler.

3d: Group 1C(i)—Vessel Q

This comprises a thick (11mm) dense sherd with numerous small (3mm) angular clasts of grey rock and rare vein quartz, imparting a rough surface. A thin (1mm) surface skin of the sherd is pale reddish-brown (5YR5/3) whilst the interior is a very dark grey (5YR3/2). In thin-section it shows marked similarities to Group 1B sherds in terms of composition and nature of the matrix, and in particular in its biolith content i.e. spicules and rare *Diploneis interrupta*. In terms of clast content (38%) the link with Group 1B persists in the presence of minor amounts (7%) of serpentinite, but the dominant component is a dolerite (93%). The latter is a coarse granular rock with prisms of plagioclase and colourless clinopyroxene (augite), with only rare development of ophitic texture. The zoned plagioclase is patchily much altered to chlorite and mica, whilst the pyroxene is accompanied by—and even mantled by—a heavily iron-stained green or brown amphibole. In parts the whole rock fabric is heavily impregnated with iron-rich material; apatite prisms occur rarely. Grog fragments (2%) are inconspicuous.

3e: Group 1C (ii)—Vessel K

The sherd of this vessel is thick (13mm) and dense, with smoothed surfaces and numerous small (<3mm) angular grey-white rock fragments. The colour is mostly a uniform reddish-brown (5YR4/3) although in places the surface is slightly greyer (5YR4/2). In thin-section the matrix is a dense fine textured clay showing strong orientation over small areas, and carrying a small number of silt-sized angular quartz and occasional larger grains of quartz, mostly angular but occasionally well rounded, and rare plagioclase clinopyroxene, clinozoisite, and a chert-like material: no bioliths are detectable. The clasts are common (23%) and consist mainly (89%) of a coarse dolerite of similar nature to that in Group 1C(i), described above. In addition there are occasional small clasts of muscovite, chlorite and epidote schists, metaquartzite, jaspery quartzite, and what appears to be a mylonite. Grog fragments are conspicuous, (12%) often having a darker and coarser-textured matrix, though still devoid of bioliths, and on occasions showing two successive generations of reuse. They carry clasts of schist and in one instance a clast of an unusual perthitic biotite granite (Plate 000c).

3f: Group 2A—Vessels E, F, and N

The sherds of these vessels are 8-10mm thick with smoothed surfaces often showing a pattern of fine sub-parallel striations. The group is distinguished by the presence of numerous angular pores (2-5mm in size) pitting the surface, often tabular/platy in shape and some appearing to have been impressed into the surface: the flat surfaces of some of the larger pores show a vague ribbing. Occasional small (3mm) angular dark grey rock and rare white quartz fragments can be seen. The colour of the sherds is mostly a dark reddish-brown or grey (5YR3/2-4/2) with or without a thin (1-2mm) surface zone which is darker or browner (5YR3/3-3/1).

In thin-section the matrix of this group is variable, ranging from silty clay with weak orientation (E, N) to more clay rich with moderate to strong orientation (F). Grains are dominated by angular quartz, but rare, larger, rounded quartz with orientated overgrowths are also present in E and F. Other minerals noted include rare grains of amphibole, clinopyroxene, felspar, muscovite, and clinozoisite/epidote. The matrix appears to be devoid of diatoms and spicules but carries corroded prismatic phyoliths—occasional in E and N but common in parts of F. Clasts are sparse (1.6-3.4%) but include schists, metaquartzites and, in E and F, epidote-rich rock fragments; in N there is a granular aggregate of quartz, microcline, and plagioclase, which could be either a metasandstone or granite; rare small chert-like fragments were seen in F. Grog fragments are sparse (3-6%) and are usually darker and less silty in texture. Voids (8-10%) include irregular linear cracks, but there are also distinctive voids tending to be trapezohedral or even rectangular in outline: these are best developed in F, where the larger (e.g. 8 × 2mm) is seen to be slightly curved with some faint corrugation evident on the convex surfaces. In sherds of Vessel E there are also oval voids, some infilled with organic debris and presumably originating from its oxidation.

3g: Group 2B/A—Vessel L

This vessel is represented by a smooth surfaced sherd 8mm thick showing the same general characteristics in terms of its pitted surface as these of the preceding Group (2A). However, the occasional small angular rock clasts also include rare lustrous silvery fragments, and the colour is brown (7.5YR5/2) with a slightly darker interior. In thin-section the matrix is seen to be a silty clay with weak to moderate orientation, larger grains being mostly angular quartz but including occasional well-rounded grains and some which display oriented overgrowths. Rare grains of plagioclase, clinopyroxene, clinozoisite, and a chert-like material were also noted. No bioliths were detected other than rare corroded phytoliths. The sparse small clasts (2%, <0.5mm) are dominated by serpentinite, similar to that seen in clasts in Group 1B sherds, and are accompanied by muscovite, chlorite, and epidote schist fragments, one carrying prismatic tremolite. Grog fragments are inconspicuous (3%) but the voids are again distinctive, including—in addition to irregular linear and oval voids—some which are tabular/angular in nature similar to, though not so regular as, those in Group 2A.

3h: **Group 3(i)—Vessels D and M**

These two vessels are represented by relatively thin sherds (7-8mm). They are again distinguished by a smooth surface pitted by numerous small (1mm) angular and occasional larger (3mm) tabular pores, but clasts are very rare, only one small (20mm) fragment of quartz being seen. The sherds have dark reddish-brown interiors (5YR4/2) with thin (1mm) slightly redder surfaces (5YR4/3).

In thin-section the matrix comprises a silty clay showing impersistent banding due to small changes in texture and colour and moderate to strong orientation of the clay fraction. The grains are mostly small (2μm) angular quartz with occasional larger rounded grains, and there are occasional flakes of muscovite and grains of felspar, clinozoisite/epidote, and green tourmaline, and rare grains of zircon and clinopyroxene. The matrix is distinguished by the common occurrence of fragments of pinnate diatoms (Plate XIX*e/f*) phytoliths and less common spicules, as well as by an abundance of small (10-20μm) irregular spherical bodies presumed to be some form of spore; these bioliths are often concentrated in seams. Clasts are small and sparse (0.2mm; 0.7%) and appear to consist of chlorite, muscovite, and epidote schists, metaquartzites, a fine grained silicic igneous rock, and possibly serpentinite, although positive identification of such small fragments is not always possible. The most distinctive feature of these sherds is the presence (nominally 3-4%) of small (100-500μm) voids with sharp linear margins defining part or all of a regular rhomboid shape, but lacking any internal contents (Plate XIX*a*). Irregular linear voids also occur as do ovoid cavities containing organic debris: grog fragments are relatively common (8%) and conspicuous, comprising small subrounded fragments which are generally a darker red-brown and more clay rich; they carry rare clasts of what may be chlorite schist and have the same distinctive rhomb voids as the host sherd (Plate XIX*a*) but appear to lack the bioliths and other distinctive organic components.

3i: **Group 3(ii)—Din Dryfol pots X, Y, and Z**

Sherds of these pots from Din Dryfol are relatively thin (6-9mm) with smooth surfaces pitted with numerous small (1-2mm), and occasional larger (5mm) angular voids, but lacking detectable clasts. The surfaces are generally brown (10YR5/3) but the bulk of the interiors are a very dark grey (10YR3/1). In thin-section the matrix of these sherds is a very silty clay showing weak to moderate orientation of the clay fraction. The silt sized grains are dominated by angular quartz, but with common to occasional plagioclase and muscovite and rare grains of microline, perthite, zircon, rutile, green tourmaline, garnet, green amphibole, clinopyroxene, and clinozoisite. Bioliths are common but patchy in distribution, even within the same sherd where they may be concentrated in seams; they are less common in X. They comprise fragments of pinnate diatoms,

common corroded phytoliths and occasional spicules, together with small (∼10μm) spherical bodies presumed to be spores. Clasts are sparse to absent (<0.1%), only single small rounded fragments of quartzite and chert-like material being seen in X and Y respectively. Similarly grog is rare (<0.4%) comprising small rounded darker fragments in X and Y. Apart from the bioliths, the distinguishing feature of these sherds is the common occurrence of small rhomb-shaped voids (nominally 5-10%) similar to those in group (i), in addition to the irregular linear and oval voids, some of which show evidence of an original organic content.

3j: **Vessels T, U, V and W**

No thin-sections were made from sherds of these four vessels and suggestions as to which group they may belong rests on visual inspection only.

Vessel T: Thin (6mm) smooth sherds, the surfaces pitted with small (1mm) angular and occasional large (5mm) pores. Dark reddish-brown surface (5YR3/2) with a darker grey interior: no clasts visible. These sherds show affinities to those of group 3(i) or possibly 2A.

Vessel U: Smooth sherds 8mm thick with brown surfaces (7.5YR5/2) and darker interiors (7.5YR4/2), the surface pitted with regular shaped tabular pores (3-5mm): rare small (2mm) grey rock clasts present. These show affinity to Group 2A.

Vessel V: Thick (10mm +) coarse textured sherds with numerous large (5mm) angular white quartz and grey rock clasts giving a rough surface reddish-brown in colour (5YR4/3) grading to very dark grey inside (5YR3/1). These match closely the sherds of Group 1A.

Vessel W: A 10mm thick sherd, reddish-brown on the surface (5YR4/3) grading to a darker shade (5YR3/2) inside, and containing numerous small (1-2mm) whitish irregular rock fragments. In this it shows similarities to Vessel K (or possibly Q) of Group 1C.

4. **DISCUSSION OF RESULTS**

The results of the petrographic analyses of sherd thin-sections, detailed in the previous section, can be used to validate the grouping of sherds proposed initially (Fig. 32) and to interpret the provenance of the materials used for both clay and temper in the manufacture of the vessels. A discussion of these two aspects will now be presented followed by comments on the voids and grog contents generally, and concluded by the results of further mineralogical analyses aimed at elucidating the provenance of material used in the clast-free sherds of Group 3.

4a: Further comments on the grouping of the sherds

The petrographic data, both quantitative and qualitative, can be used to test the proposed groupings by means of such standard statistical procedures as Principal Component Analysis and Link Cluster Analysis (Williams and Jenkins 1976). For this purpose the quantitative data in Table 1, with the clast compositions reduced to a proportion of the total sherd via the %-clast, can be supplemented by other features given in the table, such as texture of the matrix (1-silt rich; 2-silty clay; 3-clay rich), the degree of clay orientation (1-weak; 2-moderate; 3-strong) and the abundance of the various siliceous bioliths (phytoliths, spicules and diatoms; 0-absent; 1-occasional; 2-common). Some of these categories merge (e.g. voids—rhombic voids) whilst others are discrete (e.g. % serpentinite). Most reflect the composition of the materials used, although some (e.g. fabric orientation, % voids) are influenced by production techniques.

The results of subjecting these data to principal Component Analysis (UCNW programme DFACT) and to Link Cluster Analysis (programme CLUST: FOR Dr J. Conway) are presented in Figs. 33 and 34. It will be seen that at least four of the six groups originally proposed are clearly distinguishable. However there is no separation of Groups 2A and 2B which are divided petrographically by the high proportion of serpentinite in 2B (sherd L). Principal Component Analysis also fails to divide Groups 1B and 1C and displaces one member (K) juxtaposing it to Group 2A. It would seem that the petrographic distinction between dolerite and serpentinite is not of sufficient weighting, whilst the void, schist, and grog contents outweigh the dominance of the dolerite amongst the more abundant clasts of sherd K: the significance of the differences in detailed petrography and biolith content between sherds K and Q will be discussed further below, but already a possible weakness in the petrographic linkage between these two sherds in group 1C is evident. Similarly Cluster Analysis divides the sherds of group 3, interposing Group 2A between the Trefignath sherds (Group 3(i):D, M) and the Din Dryfol sherds (Group 3(ii): X, Y, and Z). In this case the significance of rhombic voids and bioliths apparently counts for less than the traces (0.7%) of clast material in the Trefignath sherds. Such anomalies could probably be removed by appropriate weighting of the data, but it is felt that, with the possible exception of Group 1C, the two relatively unbiased treatments presented in Figs. 33-34, already provide adequate justification for the original subjective grouping proposed in Fig. 32.

4b: Petrographic evidence for provenance

As was suggested in the introduction, the presence of distinctive rock types in the vicinity of Tefignath offered the potential of establishing whether or not local material had been used in the manufacture of the vessels. This potential has to a large degree been realised in the petrographic analysis of the clast components. The rock types represented amongst the clasts have been grouped into four categories, namely: metamorphic rocks, dolerites, serpentinites, and "others". The relevance of these groups to provenance will now be summarised together with that of additional information from the biolith content and other features.

Metamorphic rocks dominate the rock clasts of seven sherds in Groups 1A (A, B, C, and G) and 2A (E, F, and N) and are common in those of Group 2B (L); there are possible traces in Group 3(i) (M and D). They encompass a range of schists dominated by quartz-muscovite or brown biotite, together with metaquartzites, and are generally associated with abundant vein quartz to which fragments are sometimes attached: the latter dominates in the one sherd (B) and chlorite schists are also common in two sherds (F and L). Such rock types are hardly distinctive and are to be found in many low grade metamorphic terrains other than the Monian of Anglesey. However, the clasts also include more distinctive epidote/tremolite-rich rocks in four sherds (A, C, E, and G; and possibly also in D) and, in one sherd (A), rare haematite-rich rock fragments which correspond with the spilites, hornefelses, and jaspers respectively of the Monian. This increases the probability of these clasts being derived from NW Anglesey generally, if not Ynys Gybi itself. The small yet distinct differences within this group (A-C-E-G; B; N; F-L) indicate different specific sites of origin, but these could all be encountered within a relatively small distance from Trefignath.

"Doleritic" clasts dominate the two sherds of Group 1C(K and Q). However, insofar as it is possible to establish from the material present in thin-sections, these two sherds are similar in that both gave doleritic clasts which carry amphiboles and apatite. Such rocks occur widely, if sparsely, in North Wales and elsewhere, but they could be matched on Ynys Gybi by the Palaeozoic (as distinct from Tertiary) dolerite dykes, such as that forming a feature to the west of Trefignath (Site 6, Fig. 31), or possibly by parts of the "altered gabbroic rocks" in the serpentinite complex to the South (Site 1, Fig. 31). Apart from the clasts, detrital grains of pyroxenes and amphiboles were also noted in the dolerite-free sherds N, F (Group 2A), and M (Group 3) suggesting a possible link with dolerite material in the clay, if not in the temper.

The serpentinites are the most distinctive of the rock types represented among the clasts and these dominate the four sherds of Group 1B (H, J, R, and S) and are the major constituent of the sherd (L) in Group 2B/A: small traces may also be present in Group 3(i) (D and M). Outcrops of this rock-type are rare, small, and localised, and the proximity of one such site to Trefignath, with its matching distinctive "Fensterstruktur" and, in one sherd (S) diopsidic pyroxene, makes it most probable that this outcrop (see Fig. 1) was the source for the serpentinite clasts.

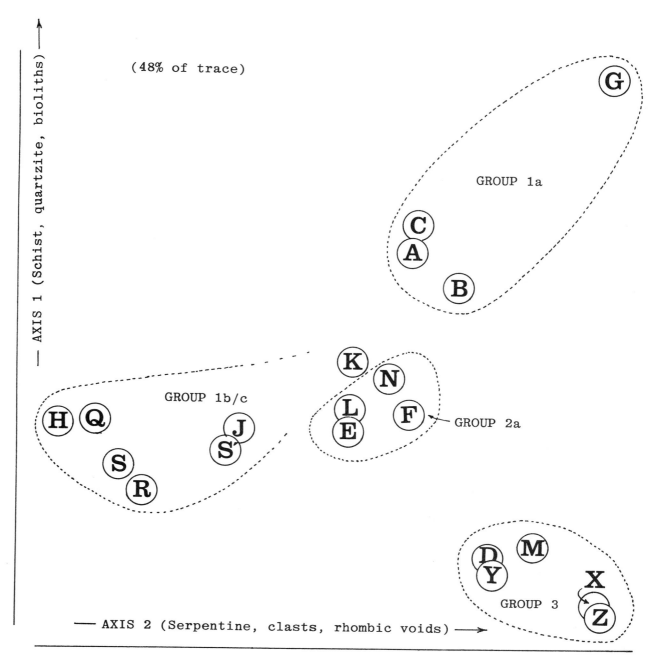

Fig. 33.   Classification of Sherds by Principal Component Analysis.

The "other" rock types occur sporadically in minor amounts among the clasts of all groups, especially 2A. Unfortunately they are less informative petrographically and thus of less value in terms of provenance. They include rare small fragments of what could be cherty or rhyolitic material (M, L, and F), felspathic sandstone (?N), and mylonite (?K).

Of the four groups, the serpentinites are thus the most useful diagnostically. Although present exclusively in one sherd (J), in others serpentinite clasts occur together with a dolerite (Q) and with metamorphic rocks (L and F) whose provenances is thus, by escavation, likely to be local. Such a local provenance could then be extended, again by association, to the other exclusively metamorphic clast assemblages, especially those with spilite/hornfels contents; this would encompass the remaining sherds of Groups 1 and 2, including K if its dolerite were to be the same as that of Q. The conclusion from the petrography of the clast contents is therefore that the material used to temper Group 1B and 2B sherds was locally derived from the vicinity of Trefignath, and that this is probably true for the sherds of Groups 1A, 1C, and 2A: the sparse clasts of Group 3(i) also suggest a local origin, but the evidence is too meagre for a definite conclusion.

Another lead to provenance is the siliceous biolith content (phytoliths, spicules, diatoms), although this relates to clay rather than temper, and to sediment environment rather than solid geology. As described in section 3, bioliths have not been detected in sherds of Groups 1A, 2A, or 2B/A, but were characteristic of those of Groups 1B, 3, and Vessel Q (Group 1C).

Group 3 differs from Groups 1B and 1C (Q) however, in that phytoliths and pinnate diatoms (*Pinnularia ssp.?*) are abundant and spicules rare in the former, whilst spicules are abundant in the latter and diatoms are either absent or, if present, of a different species (*Diploneis interrupta?*). Spicule types and diatom species in Group 1B are all indicative of a marine sediment, whilst the evidence for Group 3 is inconclusive and could relate to either fresh or saline water environments, although the abundance of phytoliths and spores suggests proximity to a terrestrial environment. There are thus three distinct environmental sources for the materials used for the clays. These are (i) a biolith-free source which was presumably a terrestrial deposit such as glacial till (Groups 1A, 2A, and 2B/A), (ii) fine grained marine sediments (Groups 1B and 1C) and (iii) unresolved fresh/saline aqueous deposits such as marsh or estuarine clays (Group 3). All such environments would have been available on Ynys Gybi within close proximity to Trefignath, but possible sites could only be identified by a detailed study of past and present biolith contents of sediments.

There remains the other sherd, K, of petrographic Group 1C. It differs sharply from Q in that it is devoid of bioliths suggestive of terrestrial deposits (till?) whilst Q contains bioliths comparable to those in Group 1B. This accentuates the small petrographic differences already noted between these two sherds and suggests that the general petrographic similarity between their clasts may be incidental and

that they should indeed be placed in separate groups as suggested by Principal Components Analysis.

4c: Voids

The abundance of voids varies from 4-22% (by volume: Table 12). There is little correlation with the petrographic groupings recognised other than Trefignath groups 2A and 3 showing slightly higher (7-10%) and the Din Dryfol Group 3 markedly higher values (17-22%). This and other minor differences in fabric favours the subdivision of the sherds in Group 3 into those from Trefignath (Group 3(i)—D, M) and those from Din Dryfol (Group 3(ii)—X, Y, Z), a schism already hinted at by Cluster Analysis (Fig. 34). Most of the voids are irregular linear features, the product of manufacturing techniques, but they may also arise as artefacts of the thin-sectioning procedure, where clasts of soft rock material such as serpentinite (groups 1B and 2B/A) are particularly vulnerable. Voids may also result from the natural loss of components during manufacture; for example organic material—incorporated incidentally or added specifically as a temper—may be destroyed on ignition as seems to have been the case in sherds of Vessel E. Such voids can be large, of a size sometimes comparable to that of the sherd section, and this is likely to result in sampling errors which could explain the large variations within individual groups.

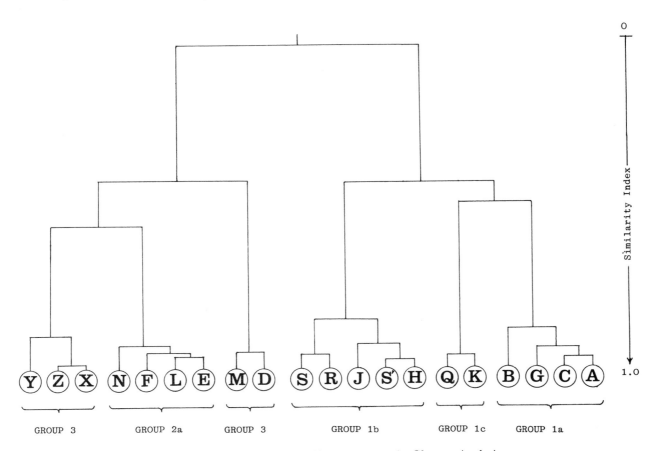

Fig. 34. Classification of Sherds by Link Cluster Analysis.

TABLE 12: SUMMARY OF PETROGRAPHIC DATA FOR SHERDS FROM TREFIGNATH (Trf: A-S) AND DIN DRYFOL (DD)

		Vol. %				Clasts—Frequency %						Fabric Z—silt C—clay	Orient^n S—strong W—weak	Diatoms	Spicules	Phytoliths
		Voids	Rhomb Voids	Grogs	Clasts	Schists	Quartzite	Vein Quartz	Dolerite	Serpentine	Others					
Trf.	A.	6.7	0.0	7.0	18.6	19	36	45	—	—	—	Z/C	W	—	—	r
	B	9.3	0.0	0.5	16.3	13	14	73	—	—	—	Z/C	WS	—	—	—
	C	4.7	0.0	6.2	22.1	17	30	52	—	—	—	Z/C	W	—	—	r
	D	4.5	4.4	7.7	0.7	—	75	25	—	—	—	C	W/S	c	—	c
	E	10.3	0.0	3.8	1.6	18	24	58	—	—	—	Z/C	W	—	—	r
	F	10.1	0.0	6.4	2.4	42	26	22	—	4	6	C	W/S	—	—	r
	G	7.2	0.0	1.5	26.6	27	30	37	—	—	6	Z	W/S	—	—	—
	H	6.6	0.0	0.6	38.3	1	1	—	—	98	—	Z/C	W	—	c	r
	J	20.6	0.0	0.2	27.6	—	—	—	—	98	2	Z/C	W/S	—	c	r
	K	8.6	0.0	2.4	22.6	6	4	—	89	—	1	C	S	—	—	—
	L	7.4	0.0	3.1	1.9	33	2	2	—	59	4	Z/C	W	—	—	—
	M	3.5	3.4	9.1	0.7	60	—	—	—	—	40	Z/C	S	c	—	c
	N	8.4	0.0	3.0	3.4	11	36	39	—	—	14	Z	W	—	—	—
	Q	4.9	0.0	1.8	38.3	—	—	—	93	7	—	Z	W	—	c	c
	R	3.8	0.0	10.1	25.5	—	—	2	—	98	—	Z	W	—	c	c
	S	6.1	0.0	7.9	21.5	—	1	—	—	99	—	Z	W	—	c	r
D.D.	W4	9.0	10.0	0.0	0.0	—	—	—	—	—	—	X	W/S	c	—	c
	AW9	11.1	10.7	0.4	0.0	—	—	—	—	—	—	X	W/S	c	—	c
	D30	12.2	5.1	0.0	0.0	—	—	—	—	—	—	Z	W	c	—	c

r—rare
c—common

Voids in both groups 2 and 3, however, are particularly interesting being very distinctive though different. In Groups 2A and 2B/A large angular tabular voids are evident to the naked eye, sometimes showing a faint corrugation; in thin-section they are seen as parallel-sided voids up to 8 × 2mm in size, occasionally showing a slight curvature with a weak corrugation detectable in one or two cases on the convex surface. These characteristics all suggest that the voids are the casts of some specific material although no trace of it is now detectable. The most probable material would be provided by fragments of ribbed lamellibranch shells composed of calcite (= and/or aragonite—$CaCO_3$) and calcite-gritted ware has been described previously (e.g. Peacock 1977). The smaller voids in Group 3 sherds are also sharply defined shapes but differ in that in around half of them the linear margins define a rhombic shape (Plate XIX*a*). In this case the only commonly available material which could result in such casts would be coarsely crystalline calcite (or dolomite) which produces rhomb-shaped cleavage fragments when crushed. Suitable calcite could be obtained from certain limestones and vein deposits, and also from the shells of some marine organisms; in this context it is of relevance that the biolith content of Group 3 sherds (though not of those from Group 2) suggests derivation of "clay" from a coastal environment, as discussed above.

The complete disappearance of calcite from the sherds of both groups 2 and 3 could occur in several ways. It could arise through thermal decomposition upon firing (>800°C) and subsequent dissolution of the calcium oxide, but this is a process which is known to result in expansion upon initial hydration, leading to spalling from the surface (i.e. "lime blowing"). Alternatively, calcite could have been leached out under acidic conditions, either artificially, or naturally during burial in the acid soild environment (pH <6), although it would then be surprising that no calcite should have survived protected by enclosure within more impermeable sherd fabric. Thus, whilst different calcite tempers are the most likely explanations for the tabular and rhomb-shaped voids characteristic of Groups 2 and 3, the problem of these distinctive "corky" sherd fabrics needs more detailed analysis and experimentation for a satisfactory understanding of their genesis.

4d: Grog

Grog fragments vary according to the ease with which they can be distinguished from the fabric of the host sherd. In many instances they stand out clearly by virtue of small differences in colour, texture, or orientation of their fabric, but in certain cases they merge imperceptibly and the values in Table 12 may therefore be underestimates. The values range from <0.1-16% by volume, but again show no obvious distribution pattern within the petrographic groupings recognised other than to re-confirm the subdivision of Group 3 sherds (i.e.—Group 3(i)

Trefignath Vessels D and M 7-9%; Group 3(ii) Din Dryfol pots X, Y, and Z <0·4%). However, it is interesting to note that the grog fragments in Group 3(i) sherds whilst containing the same distinctive rhomb-shaped voids as the host sherds (Plate XIX*a*), appear to be devoid of bioliths suggesting use of a different source for the clay yet a continuity of production technique.

In most instances, grog fragments are similar in composition to their host sherds, differing only in pigmentation or orientation of fabric, indicating successive phases of similar pottery manufacture. In sherd K two generations of grog can on occasions be distinguished and this sherd also carries the most interesting of the grog fragments. The fragment in question is illustrated in (Plate XIX*c*) and is distinctive in containing a small clast of perthitic biotite granite, the only rock type encountered which is definitely alien to Trefignath and North West Wales generally, but which could perhaps be matched by outcrops in Ireland, Scotland, or Cornwall. It is possible, but unlikely, that the clast came from a chance fragment of an erratic within the local till; it is more likely that the grog was derived from a broken pot of foreign manufacture. Vessel K could have been manufactured locally, incorporating the foreign grog from an imported vessel or could itself have been imported, but this is unlikely since the provenance of the dolerite and schists which comprise the clasts could well be local to Trefignath although it cannot be proved to be so. However, these considerations are based on the chance inclusion of a 0.5mm clast in a grog fragment within one of the three thin-sections analysed from the vessel, and any conclusion would be difficult to verify.

4e: Heavy Mineral Analyses: further evidence in the provenance of Group 3

It will have been noted that Group 3 of the Trefignath sherds lacks useful clasts and thus any conclusive petrographic evidence as to the provenance of the material used in its manufacture. Furthermore, this group is distinguished by its siliceous biolith content and rhomb-shaped voids, features shared with the three sherds examined from Din Dryfol. It was therefore particularly desirable to establish provenance for this group, and as an alternative means to this end the diagnostic minerals in the "heavy fraction" of the fine sand were isolated and identified, occasional grains of such minerals as tourmaline, amphiboles, pyroxenes, zircon etc., having already been noted in thin-sections. This was achieved by gentle (minimal) crushing of sherd fragments and wet-sieving through nylon meshes to isolate the 60-200μm fraction which comprises the more easily identifiable monomineralic grains. Heavy minerals were then separated by centrifugation in tetrabromoethane (SG>2.95) and identified under methyl salicylate by polarised light

microscopy. This technique, however, is more demanding of material than thin-section petrography, and sufficient amounts (10g) were available from only four vessels, one (D) fortunately being that from the enigmatic Group 3. The other three (B and C—Group 1A; E—Group 2A) were included to corroborate the petrographic evidence and for comparative purposes, as also were samples of superficial deposits from both Trefignath and Din Dryfol. The results are presented in Table 13.

Considering first the three Trefignath vessels whose provenance has been established as local from petrographic analysis of their clasts, it should be noted that heavy mineral analysis will relate to matrix as well as to clasts and that the provenance of the former could conceivably differ from that of the latter. It will be seen from Table 13 that there are general similarities in the heavy mineralogies of Vessels B, C, and E and of the deposit from Trefignath, although the former differ from the latter in their relative paucity of apatite, clinopyroxene, and chlorite. Minor differences also exist between the three sherds, as in the presence of common colourless amphibole (E), occasional brown amphibole (B), hypersthene (E) and andalusite (B); rare grains of anatase (C) and staurolite (B, E) were also observed. Such assemblages may all be interpreted as representing provenances dominated by local Precambrian schists and dolerites, and diluted by small amounts of extraneous material (anatase, brookite, staurolite, kyanite, andalusite, hypersthene, glaucophane, etc.) which elsewhere in North Wales are associated with Northern Glacial Drift.

TABLE 13: HEAVY MINERAL (SG>2.96) ANALYSES OF THE 60-200μM FRACTIONS

(Visual assessment of abundances: 0—absent; 1—rare; 2—occasional; 3—common; 4—abundant).

	Sherds/(Group)				Superficial Deposits	
	B(1A)	C(1A)	E(2A)	D(3)	Trefignath	Din Dryfol
Zircon	2	3	2	2	2	1
Rutile	2	2	1	1	1	0
Anatase	0	1	0	0	1	0
Brookite	0	0	0	1	1	0
Titanite	0	0	0	0	0	1
Tourmaline	2	3	2	2	3	0
Apatite	2	0	2	0	3	1
Garnet	2	2	3	2	2	3
Staurolite	1	0	1	1	0	1
Kyanite	0	0	0	1	1	0
Andalusite	2	0	1	0	0	0
Hypersthene	0	0	2	0	0	2
Diopside	0	0	0	2	0	0
Augite	2	3	3	3	3	4
Colourless ⎱ amph.	0	0	2	2	0	2
Green ⎰ amph.	2	3	2	2	2	3
Brown amph.	1	0	0	0	1	2
Glaucophane	0	0	0	1	0	1
Clinozoisite	3	3	2	2	2	2
Epidote	3	2	3	2	2	2
Pale chlorite	0	0	1	0	2	2
Dark chlorite	2	3	2	2	3	2
Titan/epid. grains	3	3	3	3	3	0

All these assemblages could therefore, readily be matched with local superficial deposits within, for example, Ynys Gybi. However, the precise individual locations obviously vary· for each sherd, and none of the assemblages matches exactly that of the mineralogy of the deposits at Trefignath itself.

Turning to the problematical Vessel D, it will be seen from Table 2 that its heavy mineralogy is again generally similar to those of the other three sherds. There are minor differences in the presence of occasional thin plates of a colourless pyroxene (diopside?) and of rare grains of brookite, kyanite, and glaucophane, but the same general conclusions may be drawn about the local provenance of the material used in its manufacture. Diopside has been recorded in the ultramafic suite on Ynys Gybi and, indeed, in the thin-section of sherd S-431. By contrast the mineralogy of the deposits at Din Dryfol differs markedly. Tourmaline, rutile, apatite, zircon and composite granular epidote/sphene are sparse or absent; conversely, the relative abundances of clino- (and ortho) pyroxenes and of pale green, blue-green, and brown amphiboles reflect the local outcrops at Din Dryfol of Gwna green schists and spilitic beds carrying numerous Palaeozoic and one major Tertiary dolerite dyke. The assemblage is also characterised by a distinctive etched yellow garnet. It is therefore possible to exclude Din Dryfol as a source for the material used for sherd D and presumably the other Group 3 pot, (M); the same possibility is raised for the Din Dryfol sherds themselves, but unfortunately there is insufficient sherd material to be able to confirm this by analysis.

5. CONCLUSIONS

This analytical study of pottery from Trefignath has been based on the microscopic examination of some forty thin-sections prepared from twenty sherd fragments and also from local sediments and rocks. From these it has been possible to group the sherds according to their fabric (% clasts, void types, etc.), clast composition (petrography), and other matrix features (biolith contents, etc.), and to attempt an interpretation of these observations in terms of the provenance of the clay and temper used in the manufacture of the original pots. For four sherds it proved possible to supplement this information with heavy mineral analyses. Groupings of sherds and conclusions concerning provenance vary in their certainty according to the diagnostic significance of the components involved; this is because some groups contain readily identifiable rare rock types (e.g. serpentinites) or matrix features (e.g. diatoms) whilst others lack distinctive features: in the latter case provenance can only be established tenuously through association. One sherd collection proved to be heterogeneous and has therefore been omitted from this discussion (i.e. Vessel 'P') whilst in another case microscopic examination partially supports the likely association of particular sherds as deriving from the same vessel (e.g. S-S¹). A few sherds have

subsequently been assigned to specific groups by macroscopic examination only (i.e. T, U, V, W).

The groupings proposed, their distinctive features and their interpretation in terms of a local provenance, are summarised in Table 14 and from this it is evident that some minor reassessment of the groupings proposed on the basis of clast petrography may be necessary. Thus there is now a clear distinction between Groups 1C(i) and 1C(ii), their initial juxtaposition on the basis of their common dolerite clast content possibly being incidental; rather, Group 1C(i) shows some affinities to Group 1B. Conversely, the divisions between Groups 3(i) and 3(ii) now appear to be of less significance, as perhaps are those between Groups 2A and 2B/A.

With regard to provenance it will be seen that the probability of a local source for their constituent materials is very high for the six sherds of Groups 1B, 1C(i), and 2B(A) which contain serpentinite clasts, and is reasonably high for another nine sherds in Groups 1A and 2A. Sherd K (Group 1C(ii)) poses an interesting problem due to its combination of possible local dolerite (containing amphiboles: Palaeozoic?) and schist clasts with a distinctly alien granite clast within a grog fragment. This problem is one which could only be resolved by further petrographic analyses producing more diagnostic information, or by heavy mineral or trace element analysis for which sufficient material is unfortunately unavailable. An equally interesting if different problem is posed by the remaining sherds of Group 3(i) (Trefignath) and 3(ii) (Din Dryfol) due to their lack of useful clast components: the two sub-groups differ in such details as matrix texture, void and grog content, but show sufficiently close affinities through their distinctive contents of pinnate diatoms and rhombic voids to justify their association within Group 3. As to the provenance of the material used in this group, apart from the environmental implications of the diatoms, the only evidence comes from the heavy mineral analysis of one member of Group 3(i) and, tantalisingly, from the rare, very small, clasts in this same Group. The former analysis is comparable to those of three other sherds from Groups 1A and 2A and both are consistent with an origin for the clay from a marshy/estuarine site within the vicinity of Trefignath, though not of Din Dryfol. However, this evidence is not conclusive and its extrapolation to Group 3(ii) is even less so.

The information extracted by this analytical study has thus provided a useful basis for grouping the various vessels recovered from Trefignath. It has also provided strong support for a local origin for the temper used in all the vessels, excepting K, D, M, X, and Z where the evidence is more tenuous, a conclusion made possible by the distinctive petrography of the geology of Ynys Gybi. The delicacy of this petrographic analysis is illustrated by recognition of an exotic rock clast within a grog fragment in a sherd of Vessel K, with its implication for the history of that vessel. Additional clues to

TABLE 14: PETROLOGY AND PROVENANCE.

Proposed groups	Pots/ vessels	% clasts	Metamorphics	Dolerite	Serpentinite	Spicules	Diploneis diatom	Pinnate diatom	Tabular voids	Rhombic voids	Other features	Local (Trefignath) Provenance Clasts	"Clay"
1A	A, B, C, G, (V)[a]	>16	*	—	—	—	—	—	—	—		Probable	glacial? (B, C)[b]
1B	H, J, R, S	>16	+	—	*	*	+	—	—	—	(Diploneis in S only)	v. probable	marine?
1C(i)	Q (W?)[a]	>16	—	*	+	*	+	—	—	—		v. probable	marine?
1C(ii)	K	>16	+	*	—	—	—	—	—	—	Exotic clast in grog	possible	glacial?
2A	E, F, N, (U?)[a]	2-3	*	—	—	—	—	—	*	—		probable	glacial? (E)[b]
2B/A	L	2-3	+	—	*	—	—	—	*	—		v. probable	glacial?
3(i)	D, M, (T?)[a]	0.7	+	—	?	+	—	*	—	*	7-9% Grog, <9% Voids	—	Estuarine? (D)[b]
(ii)	X, Y, Z	<0.1	—	—	—	+	—	*	—	*	<0.4% Grog, >17% Voids		

Symbols: * abundant; + occasional; — absent

(V etc.)[a]—grouped by visual inspection only, no microscopic data.

(B etc.)[b]—probable local provenance of sherd clay as indicated by heavy mineral analysis.

possible local environment sources of the clay used in some vessels are provided by the interesting and diverse biolith content. Thus it has been possible to relate the Neolithic sherds from Trefignath to the local geological context.

6. ACKNOWLEDGEMENTS

Assistance in the preparation and examination of thin-sections by Mr Mark Webster, B.Sc., is gratefully acknowledged, as is guidance on the nature of the bioliths by Dr W. C. Jones, School of Animal Biology, U.C.N.W. and help in Cluster Analysis by Dr J. Conway, Dept. Biochemistry and Soil Science, U.C.N.W. Bangor.

Stratigraphical Analysis

The sub-division of the assemblage into a number of vessels provided the first stage in its analysis. The second stage was provided by the petrographic study which gives a basis for grouping the vessels according to fabric type and provenance of raw materials, as summarised in Table 14. Consideration of the stratigraphical position of the vessels, within the site as a whole, takes the study a stage further and provides a basis for some chronological sub-division. The stratigraphical context of the Trefignath pottery is set out in Table 15. The stratigraphical periods used were described in Chapter 2.

TABLE 15: STRATIGRAPHY OF TREFIGNATH PREHISTORIC POTTERY

Period	Vessels	% of total by number	% of total by weight	Residue
Unstratified	F,J,Q,T,W	23.8	3.4	542,516
II_{3c}	B	4.8	17.8	
II_{3b}	A,C,G	14.3	43.6	
II_{3a}				
II_{2b}	K	4.8	3.3	332,249
II_{2a}	E	4.8	11.3	
II_{1b}	P,V	9.5	1.3	
II_{1a}				
I	D,H,L,M,N,R,S,U	38.0	15.6	145,200 265,439

Whereas the petrographic analysis established that all the Trefignath pottery could have been made within the vicinity of the site this was shown to be more likely in some cases than others. In Table 14 this is expressed in terms of three levels of probability: very probable, probable, and possible.

The distinction between probable and very probable lies in the fact that vessels in the former category include materials of widespread provenance, not confined exclusively to Ynys Gybi. The converse is the case with vessels in the 'very probable' category. These include materials such as the serpentinites which are virtually confined to Ynys Gybi and make local manufacture a near certainty. Vessels in the 'possible' category could have been made outside the area altogether. Table 14 also distinguishes those vessels which, lacking clasts, give little petrological guide to provenance, but on the basis of heavy mineral analyses appear to have been manufactured in an estuarine environment. Although Trefignath would have been close to such an environment in the fourth and third millennia this was not necessarily the one involved. This information on provenance is combined with that on stratigraphy in Table 16.

TABLE 16: STRATIGRAPHY AND PROVENANCE OF TREFIGNATH PREHISTORIC POTTERY

Period	Local provenance			Estuarine
	very probable	probable	possible	
Unstrat.	J,Q,?W	F	?W	T
II$_3$	A,B,C,G			
II$_2$		E	K	
II$_1$		V		
I	H,L,R,S	N,U		D,M

The earliest activity at the site is that represented by the pre-tomb settlement (Period I) and the pottery attributed to this period was found either in contexts sealed by the later cairn or within 0.1m of the estimated old ground surface on which the cairn was built. Its distribution is shown in Figure 8. This Period I pottery has a homogeneous appearance being fired to a grey brown colour and making no use of decoration. Surfaces, where they survive, can be seen to be carefully smoothed but not actually burnished. Unfortunately no complete profiles can be reconstructed. Those vessels that can be illustrated (H,L,M,N, and U) (Fig. 35) suggest that more than one variety is present. Vessels H,L, and M appear to have been simple, rather globular, bowls with plain vertical rims. The curving everted rim of Vessel N implies a rather different type of bowl as does the carination on the body sherd of Vessel U. These two may both have been carinated bowls of the type exemplified at Trefignath by Vessel E, to be considered below. The fragmentary nature of the vessels in this group (Table 15) reflects their status as domestic refuse. The radio-carbon date HAR3932 (5050 ± 70 bp) provides a probable *terminus ante quem* for their deposition.

No pottery was found in contexts associated with Period II$_{1a}$—the construction of the western burial

chamber and primary cairn—but fragments of at least two vessels, 'P' and V, appear to belong to Period II$_{1b}$ when that chamber was in use (Fig. 9). The fragments attributed to Vessel 'P' were found in the stone hole of orthostat XVI and have been shown to be petrographically heterogeneous, and may accordingly derive from more than a single vessel. Those of Vessel V lay amid the disturbed material lying in the entrance to the chamber. Its fabric is heavily gritted and resembles most closely the vessels attributed to Period II$_3$ which are discussed below. Vessel 'P' is particularly interesting in that some of its tiny fragments bear clear traces of decoration by finger nail impression. The stratigraphical position of this material is equivocal as it could derive from the pre-tomb assemblage and be residual in the later burial chamber. However, no distinctly Period I type pottery was found within the chamber and Vessels 'P' and V are of a rather different type. I prefer to attribute them to the use of the chamber to which they could have been introduced at any time up to its final closure in Period II$_{3a}$.

No pottery was found in contexts associated with either the closure of the central and western chambers, Period II$_{3a}$, or the construction of the eastern chamber, Period II$_{3a}$. The next group to be considered is associated with the use of the eastern chamber in Period II$_{3b}$, and consists of the remains of three vessels; Vessel G being found within the chamber itself and Vessels A and C in the portal area (Fig. 17). The stratigraphical position of none of these vessels is entirely secure for one sherd of Vessel G was found within one of the late disturbances of the chamber and Vessels A and C appear to have been disturbed when the chamber was entered late in the first millennium BC. All three vessels have heavily gritted fabrics and A and C are extensively decorated with a combination of finger nail incisions, feint horizontal striations, and impressed whipped cord 'maggots' (Fig. 36, Plate XX). The two vessels can be seen to be very similar though they can be distinguished by the greater use of decoration on the exterior of Vessel C and by the use of horizontal striations in addition to whipped cord on the inner surface of the rim of Vessel A. A flat base was found among the sherds of Vessel A making possible a tentative reconstruction of the complete profile. Vessel G was represented by two sherds only, one of which was sacrificed for petrographical analysis. The surviving rim fragment, although of a similar fabric to Vessels A and C is of a rather different shape and appears to have been decorated only along its flat, top edge with rather short impressions of whipped cord.

Vessel B is similar in fabric to Vessels A and C but was found intermingled with the disturbed blocking in the forecourt of the eastern chamber (Fig. 17). In Chapter 2 it was suggested that Vessel B may originally have held a secondary interment within pit 11 but had been disturbed when the blocking had been removed to gain access to the chamber.

Although superficially similar to Vessels A and C the decoration of Vessel B is really quite distinctive. The 'maggots' appear to have been made with impressions of twisted, rather than whipped, cord and the interior face of the rim is decorated with parallel lines of twisted cord (Fig. 36, Plate XX). This latter decoration seems to have been executed by a cord tied around a cylindrical object which was then used as a roulette. Each line was done individually and the starting and finishing points of the middle and lower circuits do not coincide exactly.

The remainder of the assemblage is strictly speaking unstratified (Fig. 26). Vessel F was found lying on top of the remains of the cairn immediately to the south of the eastern chamber. It was at too high a level to be associated with the Period I activity and probably originated in either the central or eastern chambers, arriving at its find spot when those

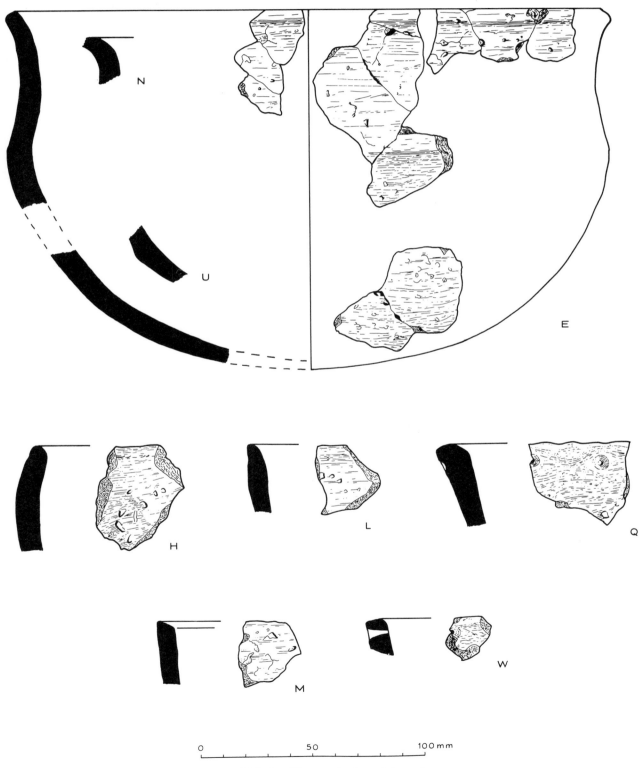

Fig. 35. Irish Sea Ware and other plain pottery.

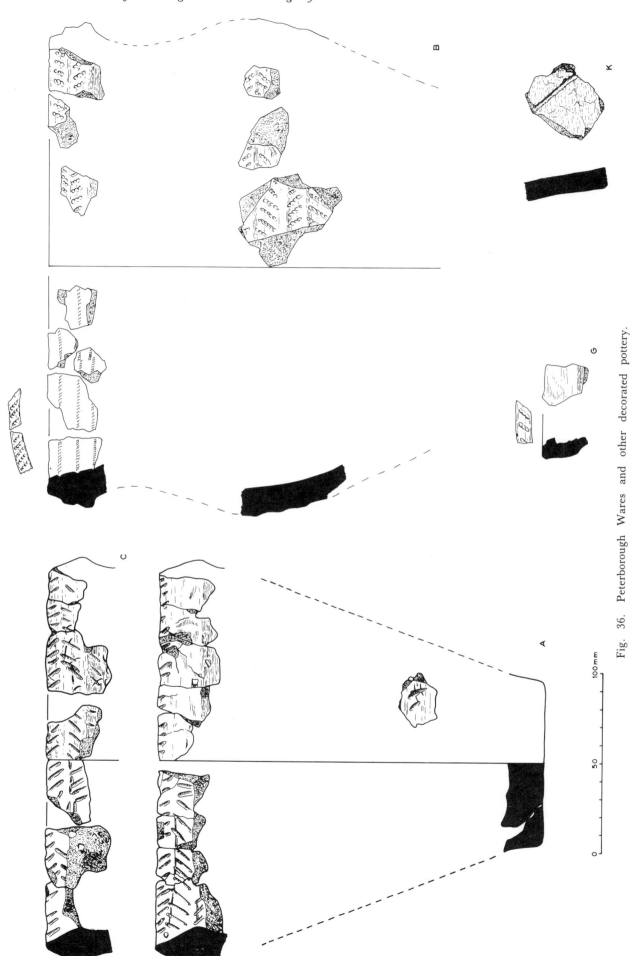

Fig. 36. Peterborough Wares and other decorated pottery.

chambers were disturbed. Vessel T is similar to Vessel F. Both are dark grey-brown in colour and devoid of all trace of decoration, although smearing on the inner surface of Vessel F may have been caused by grass wiping. Unfortunately both are represented by body sherds only and little can be said about the shape of the vessels except that they appear to have had a rather gentle 'S' shaped profile.

Vessel E comes from a context believed to belong to Period II_{2a}, the construction of the central chamber and the wedge-shaped long cairn. Its sherds were found lying on one of the artificial ledges in the quarry at the western end of the site. This quarry provided stone for the retaining walls of the wedge-shaped long cairn and Vessel E can only have been deposited there after the quarrying had taken place. This vessel is the most complete in the whole assemblage and is unlikely to have been lying around the site for long before its deposition. It may, accordingly, be associated with the use of the quarry. Sufficient remains of this vessel for its complete profile to be reconstructed (Fig. 35, Plate XX). It may be described as a carinated bowl with a rather weak carination and gently curving neck. The rim is plain. The vessel is undecorated but both the inner and outer surfaces have been carefully smoothed.

Vessel K and the residual sherds 332 and 249 are associated with the use of the central burial chamber during Period II_{2b} having been found within the chamber itself or, in the case of the residual sherds, on the surface of the cairn in the immediate vicinity. Their positions are marked on Figure 13. The fabric of Vessel K is unlike the rest of the Trefignath assemblage in that it includes grog fragments of distinctly foreign origin. This means that Vessel K either incorporated as grog material from a discarded imported vessel or had been imported itself. The latter is the more economic explanation and is consistent with the other petrographic evidence which establishes the likelihood of local manufacture as no more than a possibility (Tables 14 and 16). Although represented by body sherds only Vessel K is very distinctive being thick and dark brown in colour with a smoothed interior and burnished exterior. It is also distinguished by having a clear groove running diagonally across the exterior surface (Fig. 36, Plate XX). The two unattributed sherds, 332 and 249, may both have come from a single vessel. They are heavily gritted and resemble the fragments of Vessel V described above and the larger group of heavily gritted vessels attributed to Period II_{3b}.

Vessels J, Q, and W and residual sherds 242 and 516 were all found beyond the limits of the cairn (Fig. 26). Vessel J was represented by a single sherd, part of a simple, upright and flattened rim similar to several vessels belonging to Period I. Vessels Q and W are both represented by single rim sherds (Fig. 35). Vessel Q is distinguished by its coarse unsmoothed surfaces, slightly indented rim and shallow hollows immediately below the rim. Vessel

W, of which only a small fragment survives, appears similar except that in this case the shallow hollow has become a perforation through the entire thickness of the sherd. These three vessels have interesting petrologies. Both J and Q include fragments of serpentinite and were very probably made nearby. This enables them to be tentatively linked with the other vessels which incorporate this material (H, L, R, and S) all of which are attributed to Period I. The position of Vessel W is somewhat equivocal. It was not examined in thin-section but appears to have similarities with both Vessels K and Q. In the former case this might imply importation, in the latter almost certain local manufacture.

The foregoing consideration of the stratigraphical position of the various vessels in the Trefignath assemblage provides the basis for a relative chronology of Neolithic pottery in Anglesey. Trefignath is the first of the Anglesey megalithic tombs to be totally excavated and the only comparable ceramic assemblage from the area, that from the Bryn yr Hen Bobl megalith, is without stratigraphic record. Much of the pottery recovered during the excavations at Dyffryn Ardudwy was found in well-stratified contexts but these were of more limited chronological range than those at Trefignath, and the assemblage from the latter site provides an outline sequence for North Wales as a whole. For this reason the discussion has so far proceeded without reference to the cultural affinities of the material. It was felt desirable that the sequence should be clearly established first. The time has now come to turn to the wider connexions of the Trefignath assemblage.

Cultural Affinities

To begin with it will be recalled that the Trefignath material may be divided into two main groups. The first of these is mainly associated with pre-tomb activity and consists of a series of plain bowls, some with distinct carinations. The second group is associated with use of the burial chambers and is characterised by heavily decorated vessels with a markedly gritty fabric. All the pottery from Trefignath is of types known from other assemblages and it may now be reviewed in these wider terms.

The bulk of the undecorated pottery may be regarded as belonging to the type known as Irish Sea Ware, a variety of Western Neolithic pottery with connexions to the south and west (Lynch 1976, 63-65, Fig. 1). Pottery of this kind is typified by plain open bowls, often with a distinct shoulder or carination and made in what has been described as a 'corky' fabric. The type also includes simple hemispherical bowls made in a similar fabric. Vessel E (Fig. 35) is the best example of a carinated bowl from Trefignath and can be closely paralleled by vessels found at Llandegai, Caernarfonshire (Gwynedd), while the hemispherical bowls H and L should be compared with a vessel from Clegyr Boia,

Pembrokeshire (Dyfed) (Lynch 1976, 64, Fig. 1). Radio-carbon dates for sites using Irish Sea Ware establish that it was in widespread use by the middle of the fourth millennium and the date of 3100 ± 70 bc (HAR3932) associated with its use at Trefignath is in good agreement with this. Throughout the area of its distribution Irish Sea Ware is usually the earliest pottery found, although it does appear to have remained in use for a long time. Vessel E at Trefignath, being found in the quarry associated with the construction of the central chamber and cairn (Period II$_{2a}$) may be several centuries later in date than most of the rest of the material in this group which is attributed to the pre-tomb activity (Period I).

Vessel Q closely resembles pots F and G from the eastern chamber at Dyffryn Ardudwy (Powell 1973, 27, Figs. 9.2 and 9.3, 46) which were in turn compared with the large coarse jars of Lough Gur Class II (O'Riordáin, 1954). Powell preferred to regard both pots F and G as broadly contemporary with the fine Irish Sea Ware from the site and the same is probably the case with Vessel Q from Trefignath.

Vessels 'P' and V were found within the western chamber and are believed to be associated with its use for funerary purposes. It was argued in Chapter 2 that such use, having begun in Period II$_{1b}$, may have continued down to Period II$_{3a}$ when the entrance to the western chamber is thought to have been blocked for the last time. It follows from this time that Vessels 'P' and V may be broadly contemporary with both the Irish Sea Bowl, Vessel E, of Period 22$_{2a}$ and the Grooved Ware Vessel K (described below) of Period II$_{2b}$. Unfortunately both Vessels 'P' and V were represented by only a few sherds. However, some of the former were decorated with finger nail incisions suggesting comparison with the heavily decorated Peterborough Ware vessels described below while the latter had a very coarse fabric which is also characteristic of that type. Vessel K, possibly contemporary with Vessels 'P' and V, was represented by three sherds only, two of which were sacrificed for petrographic analysis. It is, nevertheless, one of the most distinctive vessels in the whole assemblage and its dark brown colour, burnished exterior, and grooved decoration suggest that it may be identified as an example of Grooved Ware, until recently a great rarity in Wales. Before the discoveries at Gaerwen, Anglesey (White 1981, 19) and Trelystan, Montgomeryshire (Britnell 1981, 201-02) the only parallel for Vessel K would have been provided by three sherds found in the Lligwy Burial Chamber, Anglesey (Baynes 1909, 224; Lynch 1970, 52-54). These are made of a light coloured fabric, have rather shallow unemphatic grooves and are less like the classic Grooved Ware known from Southern England than Vessel K. Grooved Ware is currently regarded as a middle to late Neolithic type and radio-carbon dates from Gaerwen and Trelystan confirm its use in

Northern Wales during the second half of the third millennium BC. The deposition of Vessel K in the central chamber provides a very approximate *terminus ante quem* for the construction of that chamber during Period II$_{2a}$, and a *terminus post quem* for its final blocking in Period II$_{3a}$ with the construction of the eastern chamber.

Vessels A, B, and C comprise the bulk of the heavily decorated group. The character and extent of the decoration employed on Vessels A and C enables them to be classified as belonging to the Peterborough Ware group, and the flat base of Vessel A suggests its Fengate subdivision (Smith 1974, 112). With the exception of the material found at Bryn yr Hen Bobl, which provides close parallels for the decoration on Vessels A and C, Peterborough Ware is, on the whole, rare in North Wales and has not previously been found definitely associated with the use of a megalithic tomb. It is conventionally regarded as a late Neolithic type and would appear to have been deposited within the eastern chamber towards the end of the third millennium. Vessel G is also associated with the use of that chamber and although less extensively decorated probably belongs to the same group.

The remains of Vessel B were found in the forecourt of the eastern chamber. In terms of fabric it is indistinguishable from Vessels A and C, but the decoration and rim profile are quite distinctive and cannot be easily paralleled among the late Neolithic vessels found at Bryn yr Hen Bobl. The distinctive decorative elements of Vessel B are the use of lines of twisted cord impressions on the inside of the rim, the use of twisted, as opposed to whipped, cord 'maggots' on the body of the vessel, and their grouping in zig-zags separated by shallow corrugations. These features can be paralleled among the Food Vessels and Collared Urns of Anglesey (Lynch 1970, 109-72; and in White 1981, Plate 2 pp. 22-23) but the remains of Vessel B are insufficient for it to be ascribed to either of those classes with any certainty. Taking its fabric into account it may be no more than a rather unusual example of Peterborough Ware.

Vessels F and T are undecorated but appear to belong to a relatively late period in the development of the site. Their remains are insufficiently distinctive for detailed comparisons to be possible but Frances Lynch has drawn my attention to similarities between these vessels and a grass-wiped vessel found in the blocking of one of the chambers at Gwernvale. Here a relatively late date is also implied, compared with other undecorated pottery from that site.

The two main groups into which the Trefignath pottery has been divided can be seen to be valid in cultural terms also. The undecorated bowls, found mainly associated with the pre-tomb activity, belong to the category of Irish Sea Wares of the early and middle Neolithic while the heavily decorated vessels associated with the use of the chambers are mostly identifiable as examples of Peterborough Ware of later Neolithic date. Several vessels are sufficiently distinctive petrographically for local manufacture to be very probable. It is noticeable that the probability of local manufacture is somewhat stronger among the Irish Sea Wares and other plain vessels at Trefignath than it is among the more heavily decorated wares. But this may not be significant.

Trefignath was the first megalithic tomb in North Wales to be fully excavated and the wide range of pottery recovered has enabled a sequence to be established which may be tentatively applied to the region as a whole. The disturbed nature of the site means that the stratigraphical basis of this sequence is not as firm as it should be and it is to be hoped that further discoveries at other sites will refine and eventually supersede it.

Romano-British and Medieval Pottery

Three anomalous sherds (102, 411, and 559) do not appear to belong to either the prehistoric assemblage or the large collection of post-medieval pottery recovered during the excavation. Sherds 102 and 559 come from wheel-made vessels with thin oxidized fabrics and have been tentatively identified by Richard Brewer of the National Museum of Wales as examples of Romano-British coarse ware. They may be seen as part of the small group of finds indicating interest in the site during the early years of the present era. There find-spots are shown on Figure 26. Sherd 411 is also very thin but has a brittle, reduced fabric. It is too small to allow for a certain identification but could be part of a medieval cooking pot.

Post-Medieval Pottery

A large amount of post-medieval pottery was recovered during the course of the excavation but it almost all came from the surface of the cairn immediately below the turf and dates from the period during which the site was used as a refuse dump by the occupants of Trefignath farm. None of this superficial material has been retained. The only post-medieval pottery for which detailed records were kept is a small group of sherds from stratified contexts and documenting the disturbance of the site. Sherd 243 is a piece of Buckley Ware and was found within the disturbed stone hole for the southern portal of the central chamber. Another sherd of Buckley Ware and fragments of white and blue china (553 and 554) were found within the western chamber.

Chapter 8—Other Finds

In this chapter limited consideration is given to finds other than flint, chert, and pottery. The find-spots of those associated with Period I are indicated in Figure 8 while unstratified pre-medieval finds appear in Figure 26.

Utilized stone

The excavation recovered a number of artifacts best described as utilized stones. With the exception of three recent objects, a slate pencil (337), a sharpening slate (17), and a hone (347, Fig. 37), the remainder can be divided according to whether they may be associated with the pre-tomb activity of Period I or the later squatter activity of Period III.

The finds which are stratigraphically part of the Period I assemblage consist of a sandstone disc (264, Fig. 37), one complete but broken hammerstone (495, Fig. 38), and a fragment of another (266). The disc is too small to be a spindle whorl and although of crude appearance was probably a button or bead. Perforated stone beads are known from a number of sites in Wales dating from the Mesolithic period (e.g. Linney Burrows, Freshwater East, and Nab Head (Jacobi 1980, 137 and 158)), but these are usually rather smaller than the Trefignath example, do not have biconical perforations and are basically disc-shaped pebbles. Beads of a similar size but sometimes with a biconical perforation are recorded from Passage Graves in Brittany (e.g. Ile Carn and Ile Gaignog (L'Helgouach 1965, Figs. 35.6 and 36.9)), but the best parallels for the Trefignath object are the small perforated sandstone discs found at the Ty Isaf long cairn (Grimes 1939) and the Gwaenysgor settlement (Glenn 1914, 265-66).

The complete hammerstone (495, Fig. 38) is a waisted pebble of banded chert broken along one of the bands. Wear on the edges of the break suggests that this may have occurred in antiquity. Overall the piece measures 92 × 60 × 43mm and weighs approximately 270 grammes. The smaller end is abraded all over and has battering on one side associated with heavy percussion which has also caused one largish flake and several spalls to flake off. The wider end has a band or strip of abrasion on the end and both sides near the end are heavily abraded with some accidental flaking on one side. There is light, sporadic abrasion on the waist, perhaps caused

from use as an anvil and this could have caused the stone to break. There are also four grooves as though something has been rubbed or sharpened on it. Item 266 is a fragment of a chert pebble with abrasion on the end suggesting use as a hammerstone.

The remaining items of utilized stone, although unstratified, may by analogy with material found elsewhere be associated with the pre-tomb activity at Trefignath.

Item 524 (Fig. 37) is an elongated pebble with traces of abrasion at both ends and damage at one in the form of a flake scar, presumably caused by striking the pebble against a harder stone. This implement is too small and light to have been serviceable as a hammerstone and does have features in common with the bevelled pebbles discussed by Jacobi 1980, 188-89). These implements are thought by some to be associated with the exploitation of shellfish resources and experience has shown that the wear and damage on the Trefignath specimen could have been caused by using it to detach limpets, which requires a sharp lateral blow. Jacobi regards bevelled pebbles as belonging to the later Mesolithic period.

Number 139 (Fig. 37) is a tabular piece of chert approximately 45mm square and quite indistinctive except for the fact that both of its main surfaces are very finely polished. The quality of this polishing is similar to that noted on the axe polishing stones found at Bryn yr Hen Bobl and Gwernvale, both in the National Museum of Wales. These stones are associated with pre-tomb activity as also appears to be the case at Trefignath. But the Trefignath stone is tiny by comparison and can only have been used for re-polishing or sharpening already finished implements.

The remaining finds in this group that may be associated with the pre-tomb activity are a further hammerstone fragment (101) and fourteen egg-shaped pebbles of chert (349) between 19 and 25mm long and weighing on average about 7.5 grammes. They were all found within a few centimetres of each other to the north west of the entrance to the western burial chamber and clearly need to be considered as a group. Their function is purely a matter of conjecture but they are too small for use as sling stones and could have been gaming pieces. The possibility that they may be attributed to Neolithic activity at Trefignath is suggested by similar finds from Passage Graves in Ireland such as cairns H and

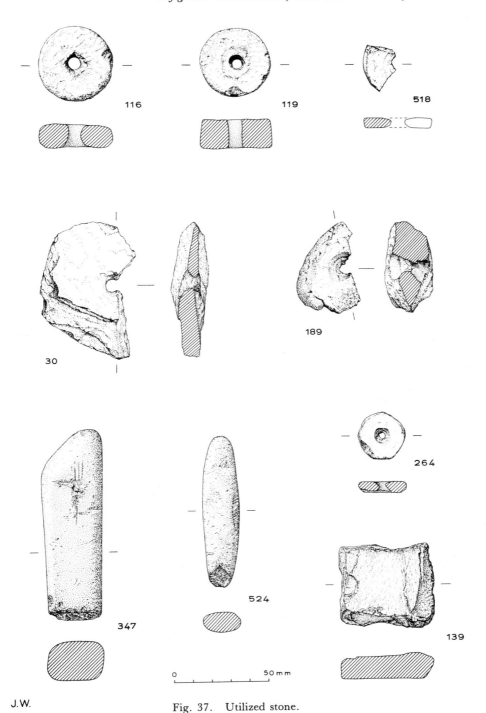

J.W.

Fig. 37. Utilized stone.

R2 at Loughcrew and cairn G at Carrowkeel (Herity 1974, 237, 241, and 275).

The remaining finds are all examples of objects commonly found at Iron Age and Romano-British settlements within the area and are most appropriately attributed to the phase of squatter activity dated by radio-carbon date HAR 3933, *viz* c. 260 bc. They comprise two spindle whorls (116 and 119) and part of a third (518), parts of two perforated stones (30 and 189), and a dolerite pebble (303).

Spindle whorls (Fig. 37) are common finds on settlements of the later prehistoric period and Savory illustrates a selection from throughout Wales (Savory

1976, 104, Fig. 39(a)). The two perforated stones both have biconical perforations and were probably weights, although 189 is much lighter than 30. Perforated pieces of slate are reported from the Romano-British enclosed homesteads of Hafoty-Wernlas and Caerau (Williams 1923, 90-91; O'Neil 1936, 316). Apart from slight battering at one end, which could be natural, there is no sign that the dolerite pebble was utilized in any way. However, it is not a natural find on the site and must have been brought there with some end in view. Such pebbles have been a recurring find in the excavations at the Ty Mawr homestead on Holyhead Mountain where they appear to have been used as pot boilers a

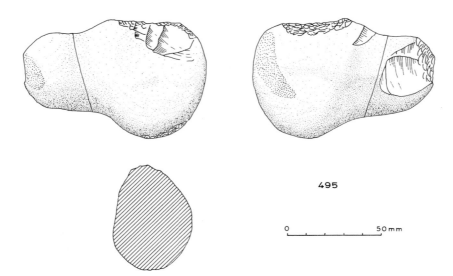

Fig. 38.   Chert hammerstone number 495.

function to which dolerite seems to have been particularly well suited. Such a find could be of almost any date.

Coins and Metalwork

Eight coins were found in the top soil and these are listed in Appendix 2. The only one of particular interest (4) may be Roman and with the two sherds of Romano-British pottery may be taken as evidence of interest in the site during the early centuries of the present era. The remaining coins are all of Eighteenth Century or later date.

A variety of highly corroded iron fragments were found in the topsoil but none of these were recorded in detail. Ten objects on non-ferrous metal were also found and these are listed in Appendix 2. Of these five may be described as small articles of dress, such as 561 a fastening from a suspender belt, dating from Victorian or more recent times. The remaining five comprise two copper nails (11 and 33) of types used in ship building, a washer from a mortice lock (44), a fragment of casting waste (425), and a length of copper wire (10). None of these finds is in any way exceptional and they may be attributed to the period when the site was used as a dump.

Bone

Fifteen fragments of very poorly preserved bone (54) were recovered from the pit (58) excavated for the concrete pad *c.* 1911. These were at first thought to be human (Smith 1981, 136) but a subsequent more detailed consideration by Rosemary Powers, whose list appears in Appendix 2, has failed to confirm this identification. If not part of an original interment within the eastern chamber these bones may have been introduced when the chamber was entered in the late first millennium BC and subsequently redeposited when the timber prop and its concrete pads were put in place.

During her 1977 visit to the site Helen Keeley tested the soils both inside and outside the eastern chamber for phosphate (Keeley 1977). Although the values inside the chamber were no more than weak-trace they are nevertheless contrasted with the situation outside where phosphate appeared to be absent. This distinction could arise from the funerary use of the chamber but equally be attributed to its subsequent use as a shelter by farm animals, as witnessed by John Aubrey (Chapter 1).

Finally, in 1855 H. Longuevile Jones recorded a tradition that 'urns and bones' had been found when the chambers had been disturbed. This probably occurred *c.* 1790 and attests that at least one chamber had contained an inhumation. The facts that the eastern chamber had been disturbed many centuries earlier and that Passage Graves usually contain cremations rather imply that the bones in question had been found in the central chamber.

Cannel coal bracelet
by
Pauline Beswick

Find number 235 consists of nearly half of a circular ring (Fig. 39), 'D'-shaped in cross-section with a slight central ridge on the internal face. Roughly

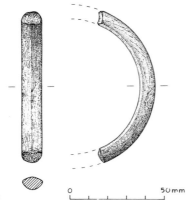

235

Fig. 39.   Cannel coal bracelet number 235.

concentric coarse abrasion marks are visible on the inner face and partially visible on the outer face, indicating that final polishing was incomplete. Slight vertical cuts and scratches on the outer surface are probably wear damage. It has an internal diameter of 76mm, a maximum thickness of 7.5mm and a depth of 10.5mm. It is black with a dull gloss surface. XRF analysis by G. D. Bussell and A. M. Pollard of The Research Laboratory, Oxford, provides the following data:

> "Spectra shows a large amount of Fe plus some Mn and Ti, and very little K and Ca. These results are fairly characteristic of cannel coal and the large amount of Fe precludes it being a jet."

The object is part of a simple bracelet or armlet, a long-lived type of ornament made from jet-like substances and found throughout Britain in Prehistoric and Romano-British contexts.

The earliest workshop so far recorded is at Swine Sty, Derbyshire and is of Early Bronze Age date (Beswick 1977). Widespread Later Bronze Age and Iron Age ring production is well attested, for example from sites such as Eldon's Seat, Dorset (Cunliffe 1968) and Staple Howe, Yorkshire (Brewster 1963), and by the increasing numbers of finished rings excavated on settlement sites, including hillforts.

For well over a millennium manufacturing techniques changed little. They were based on a 'Stone Age' technology using hammerstones for flaking and pecking, flint tools for cutting, drilling, and gouging and polishing stones for finishing. Lathe turning appears to have been introduced by the first century AD (Calkin 1953).

The slight ridge on the internal face of the Trefignath ring indicates that the central core was cut from both surfaces equally. There is no evidence to show whether this was done by hand or on a simple lathe. The abrasion marks are typical of marks produced at the final stages of shaping and polishing by hand, using stone rubbers. Dating, therefore, on technological or stylistic grounds is not possible.

The raw material used agrees well with previous analyses based largely on prehistoric material (Pollard, Bussell, and Baird 1981). Simple crude objects such as rings have been found to be made from non-jet substances such as shales, cannel coals, and lignites, all widely available raw materials. In contrast jet was used for more complex high status objects such as Bronze Age beaded necklaces. Rings, therefore, appear to have been locally produced items of low status value.

Appendix I—Index of Contexts

During the excavation each archaeological context recognised was numbered in a simple running sequence, 59 being the highest number allocated. As work progressed it became possible to delete some numbers as they were found to be parts of contexts already identified, and in the text of this report only the original numbers have been used. In the index

the additional numbers appear in brackets after the main one. Details of each main context are recorded on Context Report Forms which have been retained in the unpublished excavation archive.

Number	Period	Description	Figures
1 (37, 41)	III	Superficial rubble	—
2 (3)	II_{3c}	Eastern forecourt blocking	6
4	$II_{3a/b}$	Eastern cairn extension	6, 17, 18
5	$II_{3a/b}$	Eastern chamber	6, 17, 18, 19
6 (17)	$II_{3a/b}$	Eastern retaining walls	6, 17, 18
7	II_{3c}	Eastern extra-revetment	6, 18
8	II_{3b}	Deposit within the eastern portal	19
9 (15, 18, 19, 22, 39)	$II_{2a/b}$	Central retaining walls	6, 13, 14
10 (21)	$II_{2a/b}$	Central cairn	6, 13, 14
11	$II_{3a/b}$	Pit in eastern forecourt	17
12 (24, 47)	I	Old ground surface below cairn	6, 9, 10, 13, 14, 17, 18
13	$II_{3a/b}$	Septal wall in eastern portal	6, 17, 19
14	$II_{2a/b}$	Central chamber	6, 13, 14, 15
16	II_{3a}	Central forecourt blocking	6, 13
20	$II_{1a/b}$	Western chamber	6, 9, 10
23	III	Robbers' pit in central forecourt	6, 15
25	$II_{2a/b}$	Stone hole for south portal of central chamber	13, 15
26	$II_{3a/b}$	Stake hole in eastern forecourt	17
27	$II_{3a/b}$	Stake hole in eastern forecourt	17
28	$II_{3a/b}$	Stake hole in eastern forecourt	17
29	$II_{3a/b}$	Stake hole in eastern forecourt	17
30	$II_{2a/b}$	Stone hole for the south side slab of the central chamber	15
31 (56)	I	Post Hole	7
32	I	Post hole	7
33	I	Post hole	7
34	$II_{2a/b}$	Retaining wall on the west side of the entrance to the western chamber	6, 10, 13
35	II_{3a}	Blocking in entrance to the western chamber	6, 13
36	$II_{1a/b}$	Stone hole for orthostat XVIII	9, 10
38	$II_{1a/b}$	Western cairn	6, 9, 10
40		(deleted as natural)	
42	$II_{1a/b}$	Stone hole for orthostat XVII	9, 10
43 (44)	$II_{1a/b}$	Stone hole for orthostat XVI	9
45		(unsubstantiated, deleted)	
46	$II_{1a/b}$	Entrance to western chamber	6, 9, 10
48	$II_{2a/b}$	Lateral wall in central cairn	13
49	$II_{1a/b}$	Stone hole for orthostat XIX	9, 10
50	$II_{1a/b}$	Cleft in entrance to western chamber	9, 10
51	$II_{2a/b}$	Inner retaining wall of the central cairn	13
52	II_{2b}	Keying stone for the blocking of the central chamber	15
53	II_{2a}	Quarry	6, 13
54	$II_{1a/b}$	Levelled bedrock in western chamber	9, 10

Number	Period	Description	Figures
55	I	Post hole	7
57	III	Robbers' pit in eastern chamber	19
58	III	Robbers' pit in eastern chamber	19
59	II$_{2a/b}$	Rubble fill between 9 and 51	13

Appendix II—Index of Finds

Each registered find was allocated a number and recorded three-dimensionally. Topsoil finds other than recent pottery and corroded iron fragments were also numbered individually. The highest number allocated was 666 but 140 items were subsequently discarded being of recent date or natural in origin. The remainder comprises 422 chipped stone artifacts (List 1), sixty-eight pottery sherds or sherd groups (List 2), seventeen utilized stone objects (List 3), eight coins (List 4), ten items of non-ferrous metal (List 5), and one bone group.

The horizontal distribution of most of these finds is illustrated in Figures 8, 9, 13, 17, 24, 25 and 26. The problems concerning their stratigraphical position were discussed in Chapter 2. Where possible the finds are ascribed to one of the periods identified in the history of the site. Full details of each find have been kept on record cards and these are retained along with the other excavation records as part of the unpublished archive.

List 1—Chipped stone artifacts

This list provides details of 422 artifacts of chipped flint and chert. This exceeds by one the number of pieces discussed in Chapter 6, finds 64 and 68, although recorded separately, being found to be part of the same implement. The distribution on site of 415 of these artifacts is shown in Figures 8, 17, 24, and 26, pieces of special interest being indicated individually by their numbers (Figs. 8, 17 and 26). The remaining seven pieces cannot be plotted because insufficient records were kept at the time of their discovery.

Number	Context	Period[1]	Description[2]	Figures
13	1	?	Chert *débitage*	
14	1	?	Flint scraper	26, 28
15	1	?	Chert *débitage*	
16	1	?	Flint *débitage*	
18	1	?	Chert *débitage*	
19	1	?	Flint scraper	26, 28
20	1	?	Flint *débitage*	
22	1	?	Flint core	26, 27
			Chert flake	
23	1	?	Flint *débitage*	
25	1	?	Flint *débitage*	
26	1	?	Flint thermal flake, possibly utilized	26, 29
27	1	?	Chert *débitage*	
29	12	I	Chert blade, utilized	8, 30
31	1	?	Chert *débitage*	

Number	Context	Period[1]	Description[2]	Figures
34	1	?	Flint scraper	26, 28
35	1	?	Flint core	26, 27
36	1	?	Chert *débitage*	
37	1	?	Chert *débitage*	
42	1	?	Chert *débitage*	
43	1	?	Chert *débitage*	
48	8	II$_{3b}$	Flint knife, non-pebble	17, 29
52	12	I	Chert *débitage*	
53	12	I	Flint *débitage*	
55	12	I	Flint *débitage* with retouch	8, 29
61	12	I	Chert *débitage*	
62	1	?	Flint piercer	26, 29
64	1	?	Flint knife, part; joins 68	26, 29
65	1	?	Flint *débitage*	
66	1	?	Flint *débitage*	
67	1	?	Flint *débitage*	
68	1	?	Flint knife, part; joins 64	26, 29
70	1	?	Chert *débitage*	
71	1	?	Flint *débitage*	
72	1	?	Chert preparation flake	
73	1	?	Chert preparation flake	
75	1	?	Flint *débitage*, possibly utilized	
76	1	?	Flint piercer	26, 29
77	1	?	Chert preparation flake	
78	1	?	Flint *débitage*	
79	1	?	Chert *débitage*	
			Chert *débitage*	
80	1	?	Flint, with retouch	26, 29
81	1	?	Flint *débitage*	
82	1	?	Flint scraper	26, 28
84	1	?	Chert *débitage*	
85	1	?	Flint *débitage*	
86	1	?	Flint, with retouch	26, 29
87	1	?	Flint *débitage*	
88	1	?	Flint *débitage*	
89	1	?	Flint *débitage*	
90	1	?	Chert *débitage*	
92	1	?	Flint *débitage*	
93	1	?	Chert *débitage*, utilized	
94	1	?	Flint *débitage*	
95	1	?	Flint *débitage*	
96	1	?	Flint *débitage*	
97	1	?	Chert *débitage*	
98	1	?	Chert *débitage*	
99	1	?	Chert *débitage*	
105	1	?	Chert core	26, 27
106	12	I	Flint *débitage*	
107	1	?	Chert core	26, 27
108	1	?	Flint *débitage*	
112	12	I	Flint core	8, 27
113	12	I	Flint core	8, 27
114	1	?	Flint *débitage*	
115	1	?	Flint *débitage*	
117	1	?	Flint *débitage*	
120	1	?	Flint *débitage*	
121	1	?	Chert, with retouch	26, 30
122	1	?	Chert (?) point	26, 30
123	1	?	Chert *débitage*	
124	12	I	Flint *débitage*	
125	12	I	Flint scraper	8, 28
126	12	I	Flint scraper	8, 28
127	1	?	Flint scraper	26, 28
128	12	I	Flint *débitage*	
129	1	?	Flint knife	26, 29
130	1	?	Chert *débitage*	
131	1	?	Flint, (?) with retouch	
132	12	I	Flint *débitage*	
133	1	?	Chert *débitage*	
135	12	I	Chert *débitage*	
136	1	?	Chert *débitage*	
138	12	I	Flint *débitage*	
140	1	?	Chert *débitage*	
147	1	?	Chert *débitage*	
150	1	?	Flint *débitage*	
159	1	?	Flint *débitage*	
162	1	?	Flint *débitage*	
163	1	?	Chert *débitage*	
164	12	I	Flint, serrated blade	8, 29
165	1	?	Flint, bifacially flaked fragment	26, 29
166	1	?	Chert *débitage*	
167	1	?	Chert *débitage*	
168	1	?	Flint *débitage*	
169	1	?	Flint *débitage*	
170	1	?	Flint *débitage*	
171	1	?	Flint core	26, 27
175	1	?	Chert *débitage*	
176	12	I	Chert *débitage*	
177	12	I	Flint knife	8, 29

Number	Context	Period[1]	Description[2]	Figures
178	1	?	Flint *débitage*	
180	1	?	Flint *débitage*	
181	1	?	Chert *débitage*	
182	1	?	Chert *débitage*	
183	12	I	Flint *débitage*	
184	12	I	Flint *débitage*	
185	12	I	Flint *débitage*	
187	12	I	Flint scraper	8, 28
190	1	?	Flint scraper	26, 28
192	1	?	Flint *débitage*	
194	12	I	Flint *débitage*	
196	1	?	Flint *débitage*	
197	1	?	Flint knife	26, 29
198	12	I	Flint *débitage*	
199	1	?	Chert *débitage*	
203	1	?	Flint, truncated blade	26, 28
204	12	I	Chert *débitage*, utilized	
205	1	?	Flint scraper	26, 28
208	1	?	Chert preparation flake	
209	12	I	Chert *débitage*	
210	1	?	Chert *débitage*	
212	1	?	Chert *débitage*	
214	12	I	Chert *débitage*	
216	12	I	Flint *débitage*	
217	12	I	Chert core 'chopper'	8, 27
219	12	I	Flint *débitage*	
220	1	?	Chert *débitage*	
223	12	I	Chert *débitage*	
227	1	?	Flint *débitage*	
228	1	?	Chert *débitage*	
229	1	?	Chert, with retouch	26, 30
230	12	I	Chert *débitage*	
232	1	?	Chert *débitage*	
233	12	I	Flint *débitage*	
234	12	I	Chert *débitage*	
236	12	I	Chert *débitage*	
237	12	I	Chert *débitage*	
238	12	I	Chert *débitage*	
239	12	I	Chert *débitage*	
240	12	I	Chert *débitage*	
244	12	I	Chert *débitage*	
245	1	?	Chert *débitage*	
247	1	?	Chert *débitage*	
248	12	I	Chert *débitage*	
250	1	?	Chert *débitage*	
252	1	?	Flint *débitage*	
253	12	I	Chert *débitage*	
254	12	I	Chert *débitage*	
255	12	I	Flint *débitage*	
256	12	I	Chert prepration flake	26, 27
258	12	I	Chert *débitage*	
261	1	?	Chert *débitage*	
263	12	I	Flint *débitage*	
267	12	I	Chert, with retouch	8, 30
270	1	?	Chert *débitage*	
271	1	?	Chert preparation flake	
272	1	?	Chert *débitage*	
276	1	?	Chert *débitage*	
277	12	I	Flint scraper	8, 28
278	12	I	Flint *débitage*	
279	1	?	Flint *débitage*	
280	1	?	Chert *débitage*	
281	12	I	Flint *débitage*	
282	1	?	Chert *débitage*	
283	12	I	Flint *débitage*	
284	1	?	Flint *débitage*	
286	1	?	Flint *débitage*	
287	12	I	Flint scraper	8, 28
302	1	?	Chert *débitage*	
304	1	?	Flint *débitage*	
305	1	?	Chert *débitage*	
307	1	?	Flint, bifacially flaked	26, 29
308	1	?	Flint scraper	26, 28
310	1	?	Flint *débitage*	
314	1	?	Flint with retouch	
316	1	?	Flint *débitage*	
317	12	I	Flint *débitage*	
318	1	?	Chert with retouch	26, 30
319	1	?	Flint *débitage*	
323	1	?	Chert *débitage*	
325	1	?	Flint *débitage*	
327	1	?	Chert *débitage*	
328	1	?	Chert *débitage*	
330	1	?	Chert *débitage*	
331	1	?	Chert *débitage*	
333	1	?	Chert *débitage*	
334	1	?	Chert *débitage*	
336	12	I	Chert *débitage*	
338	1	?	Flint *débitage*	
341	1	?	Flint core-rejuvenation flake	26, 27
342	1	?	Flint scraper	26, 28
343	1	?	Chert *débitage*	
344	1	?	Chert *débitage*	
345	12	I	Flint *débitage*, utilized	8, 29
346	1	?	Chert *débitage*	
350	1	?	Flint *débitage*	
351	12	I	Chert *débitage*	
352	12	I	Chert *débitage*	
355	12	I	Flint *débitage*	
356	1	?	Flint *débitage*	
357	1	?	Chert with retouch	26, 30
360	12	I	Chert *débitage*	
361	1	?	Chert *débitage*	
363	12	I	Chert *débitage*	
364	1	?	Chert *débitage*, utilized	26, 30
365	12	I	Chert *débitage*	
366	12	I	Chert *débitage*	
367	1	?	Flint scraper	26, 28
371	1	?	Flint *débitage*	
372	12	I	Chert *débitage*	
374	1	?	Flint *débitage*	
376	1	?	Flint *débitage*	
377	1	?	Flint *débitage*	
378	12	I	Flint leaf-shaped arrowhead	8, 29
379	1	?	Chert *débitage*	
380	1	?	Chert *débitage*	
381	1	?	Chert *débitage*	
382	12	I	Chert *débitage*	
383	12	I	Chert preparation flake	
384	12	I	Flint *débitage*	
386	12	I	Chert *débitage*	
387	1	?	Chert *débitage*	
388	1	?	Chert core	26, 27
391	12	I	Chert *débitage*	
392	12	I	Chert *débitage*	
393	12	I	Flint *débitage*	
394	12	I	Flint *débitage*	
395	12	I	Chert *débitage*	
397	1	?	Flint *débitage*, utilized and with gloss	26, 29
398	1	?	Chert *débitage*	
399	1	?	Chert *débitage*	
400	12	I	Chert *débitage*	
401	1	?	Chert *débitage*	
402	12	I	Flint *débitage*	
403	1	?	Chert *débitage*	
404	12	I	Flint *débitage*	
405	12	I	Chert *débitage*	
406	12	I	Chert *débitage*	
408	12	I	Chert *débitage*	
409	12	I	Chert preparation flake	
410	12	I	Flint scraper	8, 28
412	1	?	Flint with retouch	26, 29
413	1	?	Chert *débitage*	
415	12	I	Chert *débitage*	
416	12	I	Chert *débitage*	
417	12	I	Chert *débitage*	
418	12	I	Flint *débitage*	
419	1	?	Flint *débitage*	
420	12	I	Chert *débitage*	
421	12	I	Chert *débitage*	
422	1	?	Chert preparation flake	
423	1	?	Flint *débitage*	
424	1	?	Chert *débitage*	
426	12	I	Flint *débitage*	
427	12	I	Chert *débitage*	
428	1	?	Chert *débitage*	
429	12	I	Chert *débitage*	
430	1	?	Chert with retouch	26, 30
432	12	I	Chert *débitage*	
433	12	I	Chert *débitage*	
434	1	?	Flint *débitage*	
436	12	I	Flint *débitage*	
437	12	I	Flint *débitage*	
438	12	I	Chert *débitage*	
440	1	?	Flint *débitage*	
441	12	I	Chert *débitage*	
442	1	?	Flint *débitage*	
443	1	?	Flint *débitage*	
444	12	I	Chert *débitage*	
445	1	?	Flint *débitage*	
446	12	I	Chert *débitage*	
449	12	I	Chert *débitage*	
450	12	I	Chert *débitage*	
452	1	?	Chert *débitage*	
453	1	?	Chert *débitage*	

Number	Context	Period[1]	Description[2]	Figures
455	12	I	Chert *débitage*	
456	12	I	Chert *débitage*	
458	12	I	Chert *débitage*	
459	1	?	Chert *débitage*	
460	12	I	Chert *débitage*	
462	1	?	Flint *débitage*	
464	1	?	Flint *débitage*	
465	1	?	Flint core	26, 27
466	1	?	Flint *débitage*	
467	1	?	Chert *débitage*	
468	1	?	Flint, an unworked pebble	
470	1	?	Flint (?) piercer	26, 29
471	1	?	Chert *débitage*	
473	1	?	Chert *débitage*	
481	1	?	Chert *débitage*	
482	1	?	Chert *débitage*	
486	1	?	Chert *débitage*	
487	1	?	Chert *débitage*	
488	1	?	Chert *débitage*	
489	1	?	Chert *débitage*	
490	1	?	Chert *débitage*	
491	1	?	Chert point	26, 30
492	1	?	Chert *débitage*	
493	1	?	Chert *débitage*	
494	1	?	Chert *débitage*	
496	12	I	Chert *débitage*	
497	1	?	Chert *débitage*	
499	1	?	Chert *débitage*	
501	1	?	Flint *débitage*	
503	12	I	Chert *débitage*	
504	12	I	Chert *débitage*	
507	12	I	Chert *débitage*	
508	12	I	Chert *débitage*	
510	1	?	Chert *débitage*	
512	1	?	Flint *débitage*	
513	1	?	Flint *débitage*	
515	12	I	Chert *débitage*	
517	1	?	Chert *débitage*	
520	1	?	Flint core	26, 27
521	1	?	Chert *débitage*	
522	1	?	Chert *débitage*	
525	1	?	Chert *débitage*	
526	1	?	Flint *débitage*	
527	1	?	Flint *débitage*	
528	1	?	Flint scraper	26, 28
529	1	?	Flint *débitage*	
533	1	?	Chert *débitage*	
534	1	?	Chert *débitage*	
535	1	?	Chert *débitage*	
536	1	?	Chert *débitage*	
537	1	?	Chert *débitage*	
538	1	?	Chert *débitage*	
540	1	?	Chert *débitage*, utilized	26, 30
541	1	?	Chert *débitage*	
543	1	?	Chert preparation flake	
544	1	?	Flint *débitage*	
545	1	?	Flint *débitage*	
546	1	?	Flint *débitage*	
548	1	?	Flint scraper	26, 28
550	1	?	Flint *débitage*	
551	1	?	Chert *débitage*	
552	1	?	Chert *débitage*	
555	1	?	Chert *débitage*	
556	12	I	Chert *débitage*	
557	12	I	Flint scraper	8, 28
558	12	I	Chert, with 'chopper edge'	
560	1	?	Chert *débitage*	
562	1	?	Chert *débitage*	
563	1	?	Chert *débitage*	
568	1	?	Flint *débitage*	
569	1	?	Chert *débitage*	
570	1	?	Chert with retouch	26, 30
572	1	?	Chert *débitage*	
573	1	?	Chert *débitage*	
574	1	?	Chert *débitage*	
575	1	?	Chert *débitage*	
577	1	?	Chert *débitage*	
579	1	?	Chert with retouch	26, 30
580	1	?	Chert point	26, 30
581	12	I	Flint *débitage*	
583	1	?	Chert preparation flake	
584	1	?	Chert *débitage*	
585	12	I	Flint *débitage*	
587	12	I	Chert *débitage*	
588	12	I	Chert *débitage*	
589	12	I	Flint scraper	8, 28
590	1	?	Chert *débitage*	
592	12	I	Chert *débitage*	

Number	Context	Period[1]	Description[2]	Figures
593	1	?	Chert *débitage*	
594	12	I	Flint *débitage*	
596	12	I	Chert *débitage*	
597	1	?	Chert preparation flake	
598	1	?	Chert *débitage*	
600	1	?	Chert *débitage*	
603	1	?	Flint *débitage*	
604	12	I	Chert *débitage*	
605	1	?	Chert *débitage*	
606	1	?	Chert *débitage*	
607	1	?	Chert *débitage*	
609	1	?	Chert *débitage*	
611	1	?	Chert preparation flake	
614	1	?	Chert preparation flake	
615	1	?	Chert *débitage*	
617	1	?	Chert with retouch	26, 30
618	1	?	Chert *débitage*	
619	1	?	Flint *débitage*	
620	1	?	Chert with retouch	26, 30
621	1	?	Chert *débitage*	
622	1	?	Chert *débitage*	
623	1	?	Chert with retouch	26, 30
624	1	?	Chert *débitage*	
625	1	?	Flint *débitage*	
626	1	?	Flint scraper	26, 28
627	1	?	Chert *débitage*	
628	1	?	Chert *débitage*	
629	1	?	Chert *débitage*	
630	1	?	Flint core	26, 27
631	1	?	Chert *débitage*	
633	1	?	Chert *débitage*	
634	1	?	Chert *débitage*	
635	1	?	Chert *débitage*	
636	1	?	Chert *débitage*	
637	1	?	Chert *débitage*	
638	1	?	Chert *débitage*	
639	1	?	Flint, burnt	
641	1	?	Flint core-rejuvenation flake	
642	1	?	Chert *débitage*	
643	1	?	Chert *débitage*	
644	1	?	Chert preparation flake	
645	1	?	Flint *débitage*	
646	12	I	Chert *débitage*	
648	1	?	Chert *débitage*	
649	1	?	Flint *débitage*	
651	1	?	Flint scraper	26, 28
652	1	?	Flint *débitage*	
654	12	I	Chert *débitage*	
659	12	I	Chert *débitage*	
660	1	?	Flint *débitage*	
661	12	I	Flint *débitage*	
662	1	?	Flint *débitage*	
664	1	?	Chert *débitage*	
665	1	?	Chert *débitage*, joins 666	
666	1	?	Chert *débitage*, joins 665	

(notes: 1 unstratified finds are distinguished as *?* found on or within the cairn, and ? found beyond the limits of the cairn.

2 identifications have been provided by Elizabeth Healey.)

List 2—Pottery

Part (i) Sherd groups by find number

Number	No. of sherds	Weight in gms	Context	Period[1]	Vessel	Figures
2a	57	200	2	II_{3c}	B	17, 36
2b	4	10	8	II_{3b}	A	17, 36
3	2	60	2	II_{3c}	B	17, 36
5	9	50	8	II_{3b}	A	17, 36
7	2	20	8	II_{3b}	A	17, 36
24	6	25	2	II_{3c}	B	17, 36
28	4	10	8	II_{3b}	C	17, 36
32	3	5	8	II_{3b}	C	17, 36
39	2	18	8	II_{3b}	A	17, 36
40	13	70	8	II_{3b}	A	17, 36
41	3	5	8	II_{3b}	C	17, 36
46	1	10	8	II_{3b}	A	17, 36
47	3	25	8	II_{3b}	A	17, 36

Number	No. of sherds	Weight in gms	Context	Period[1]	Vessel	Figures
49	1	10	8	II_{3b}	C	17, 36
50	1	15	8	II_{3b}	C	17, 36
51	1	5	8	II_{3b}	A	17, 36
54	1	10	58	III	G	17, 36
56	1	5	8	II_{3b}	G	17, 36
58	6	430	8	II_{3b}	C	17, 36
102	1	5	1	III	—	26
109	1	5	1	?	F	26
145	1	5	12	I	—	8
146	1	5	12	I	H	8, 35
149	1	5	12	I	H	8, 35
151	1	15	12	I	H	8, 35
152	3	5	12	I	H	8, 35
153	2	10	12	I	H	8, 35
154	1	5	12	I	H	8, 35
158	1	5	1	?	J	26
186	3	50	14	II_{2b}	K	13, 36
188	3	10	1	?	F	26
200	1	5	12	I	—	8
241	1	5	1	?	T	26
242	1	5	1	?	T	26
243	1	5	35	III	—	
249	1	10	10	II_{2b}	—	13
259	1	10	12	I	U	8, 35
262	1	5	12	I	U	8, 35
265	3	10	12	I	—	8
273	1	5	1	?	T	26
275	1	5	1	?	W	26, 35
329	2	5	46	II_{1b}	V	9
332	1	5	10	II_{2b}	—	13
335	1	5	46	II_{1b}	V	9
368	1	10	12	I	R	8
407	1	5	12	I	N	8, 35
411	1	5	1	III	—	26
431	3	5	12	I	S	8
435	2	5	12	I	R	8
439	1	5	12	I	—	8
472	34	75	12	I	D	8
474	3	10	12	I	L	8, 35
480	1	5	12	I	L	8, 35
483	2	10	12	I	M	8, 35
484	1	30	12	I	N	8, 35
485	4	25	12	I	N	8, 35
498	1	10	12	I	S	8
502	1	5	46	II_{1b}	V	9
505	16	5	43	II_{1b}	'P'	9
514	1	20	20	III	—	
516	1	5	1	?	—	
531	1	15	1	?	Q	26, 35
532	2	5	12	I	N	8, 35
542	1	5	1	?	—	26
553	2	5	20	III	—	
554	1	5	20	III	—	
559	1	5	1	III	—	26
656	57	180	53	II_{2a}	E	13, 35

(note 1 the convention used for unstratified finds is the same as in list 1).

Part (ii) Sherd groups according to vessel attribution.

Vessel	Sherd groups	Weight in gms	Figures
A	2b, 5, 7, 39, 40, 46, 47, 51	208	36
B	2a, 3, 24	285	36
C	28, 32, 41, 49, 50, 58	475	36
D	472	75	
E	656	180	35
F	109, 188	15	
G	54, 56	15	36
H	146, 149, 151, 152, 153, 154	45	35
J	158	5	
K	186	50	36
L	474, 480	15	35

Vessel	Sherd groups	Weight in gms	Figures
M	483	10	35
N	407, 484, 485, 532	65	35
P	505	5	
Q	531	15	35
R	368, 435	15	
S	431, 498	15	
T	241, 242, 273	15	
U	259, 262	15	35
V	329, 335, 502	15	
W	275	5	35

Part (iii) Pottery samples analysed.

Vessel	Sherd(s) selected	Laboratory numbers at UCNW	
		Thin sections	Heavy mineral
A	5, 47	1573-4	—
B	3	1589-90, 1598-9	632
C	49, 58	1575-6	639
D	472	1577-8	638
E	656	1591-2	633
F	188	1579, 1593	—
G	54	1580	—
H	154, 153	1581, 1585	—
J	158 (total sample used)	1611	
K	186	1582-3, 1594	—
L	474	1586, 1595	—
M	483	1601	—
N	532	1596, 1600	—
P	505 (heterogeneous)	1612	—
Q	531	1597	—
R	435	1587-8	—
S	431, 498	1584, 1613	—
T	241, 272, 273	—	—
U	259, 262	—	—
V	329, 335, 502	—	—
Comparative samples from Din Dryfol			
X	DD.W4—A	1603	—
Y	DD.AW9—B	1609	—
Z	DD.D30—D	1610	
Till (2—0.6mm)			
Trefignath		1604-5	631
Din Dryfol		—	641

List 3—Utilized stone.

Number	Context	Period	Description	Figure
17	1	III	Smoothed fragment of slate	
30	1	III	Perforated fragment of schist	37
101	1	?	Fragment of a chert hammerstone	
116	1	III	Stone spindle whorl	37
119	1	III	Stone spindle whorl	
139	1	?	Polishing stone	37
189	1	III	Perforated stone	37
226	12	I	Fragment of a chert hammerstone	
235	1	III	Cannel coal bracelet	39
264	12	I	Perforated sandstone disc	37
303	1	?	Dolerite pebble	
337	1	III	Slate pencil	
347	1	III	Hone	37
349	1	?	Fourteen chert pebbles	
495	12	I	Chert hammerstone	38
518	1	III	Stone spindle whorl fragment	37
524	1	?	Elongated pebble tool	37

List 4—Coins, all from context 1 and ascribed to Period III

Number	Description
4	A bronze disc 22mm across, much corroded but possibly Roman
6	A copper half-penny dated 1930
38	A copper Irish half-penny token dated 1792
74	A copper disc 25mm across, much corroded but possibly a counterfeit half-penny of eighteenth century date
288	A copper half-penny dated 1938
300	A brass Spade Guinea counter; very worn but inscribed GEORGIVS .II DEI GRATIA /G.Y.I. ET .G REX .. .UF . ST. DS.T. . SET. 1701. Probably a product of George Iliffe and Frederick Gardner of Suffolk St. and likely to date from the second half of the nineteenth century, the inscribed date being entirely arbitrary
301	A copper penny dated 1954
547	A three-penny bit dated 1937

(Identification of 4, 38, and 74 by G. C. Boon and 300 by J. M. Lewis).

List 5—Non-ferrous metal, all from context 1 and ascribed to Period III

Number	Description
8	A bronze button, 12mm across, very corroded but with a cast-on eyelet; probably eighteenth century or later
10	A 185mm length of copper wire, with a point at one end and a loop at the other, bent
11	A copper planking nail from a wooden ship, probably nineteenth century
12	Fragments of a bronze chain, about 30mm overall, each link 3mm across
33	A copper sheathing nail from a wooden ship, probably nineteenth century
60	A bronze buckle spike, 31mm long and tapering—10mm at the hinge end, 2mm at the point; possibly eighteenth century
414	A copper washer from a door lock, recent
425	A piece of bronze casting waste weighing 10 gms
561	A bronze eyelet fastening, probably from a ladies suspender belt, recent
582	Part of a mass-produced, stamped dress fitting; Victorian or Edwardian

(Identifications of 8, 11, 33, 60, 414 and 582 by J. M. Lewis; for parallels for 11 and 33 cf. Peterson 1965, Plate 56)

Bone group, find number 54 from context 58, ascribed to Period III.

54.1	Fragment, possibly of a metapodial but not human
54.2	Fragment, possibly the head of a metatarsal
54.3	Fragment, showing cancellar tissue as on pelvis
54.4	Six small flakes of long-bone or mandible
54.5	Possibly the distal end of a human fibula but too deteriorated for certainty
54.6	Possibly part of 54.5, badly deteriorated
54.7	Probably either long-bone, clavicle or mandible, but not identifiable as human
54.8	Possibly a pelvic fragment but no indication that it is human
54.9	Two pieces 125mm long overall of a triangular sectioned long bone incomplete at both ends. Neither texture nor curvature indicate that it was human

(Identification by Rosemary Powers).

Appendix III—Samples

A series of samples was collected during the course of the excavation for soil pollen identification and radio-carbon dating. These were numbered in a simple running sequence from 1 to 15 but as many were duplicates the numbering of the samples actually analysed is not continuous. The sampling positions are indicated in Figure 8.

(a) Soil Pollen

Number	Context	Period	Sealed by context
1.a	12 (00-25mm)	I	6 (Period II$_{3a}$)
1.d	12 (75-100mm)	I	6 (Period II$_{3a}$)
4.b	12 (25mm plus)	I	9 (Period II$_{2a}$)
10.1	12 (00-20mm)	I	38 (Period II$_{1a}$)
10.4	12 (60-80mm)	I	38 (Period II$_{1a}$)

(b) Charcoal for radio-carbon dating

Number	Context	Period	Sealed by context
8	12	I	38 (Period II$_{1a}$)
15	8	III	unstratified

Plate I

W. O. Stanley's water colour drawing of Trefignath *c.* 1867, reproduced as an engraving in *Archaeologia Cambrensis* 1867, 234 (reproduced here by permission of Lord Stanley of Alderley).

Plate II

W. O. Stanley's water colour drawing of Trefignath *c.* 1874, reproduced as an engraving in *Archaeological Journal* 31 (1874), 2 (reproduced here by permission of Lord Stanley of Alderley).

Plate III

The western chamber in 1976, looking south east.

Plate IV

The central chamber in 1976, looking east.

Plate V

The eastern chamber in 1976, looking south.

Plate VI

The eastern chamber in 1977, during excavation, looking north west.

Plate VII

The excavation in 1978, seen from the photographic tower, looking west with the eastern chamber in the central foreground. The stepped masonry support was removed shortly after.

Plate VIII

The excavation in 1979, seen from the photographic tower, looking east with the western end of the long cairn in the foreground.

Plate IX

The western chamber in 1979, looking south, with the orthostats removed and the Period II$_2$ retaining walls and blocking in the foreground.

Plate X

The junction of the Period II$_2$ retaining walls at the entrance to the western chamber, looking west.

Plate XI

The quarry, looking east.

Plate XII

The retaining wall on the south side of the central forecourt.

Plate XIII

The outer and inner retaining walls on the north side of the central forecourt.

Plate XIV

Vertical view of the abuttment of the eastern and central retaining walls.

Plate XV

The south side of the cairn in 1978 showing the retaining walls of the original wedge-shaped long cairn in the background and in the centre and foreground its subsequent eastwards extension. Soil Pit B can be seen in the baulk.

Plate XVI

A section through the extra-revetment to the south of the eastern chamber.

Plate XVII

The putative extra-revetment in the eastern forecourt.

Plate XVIII

Detail of extra-revetment immediately in front of the retaining wall on the south side of the eastern forecourt.

Plate XIX

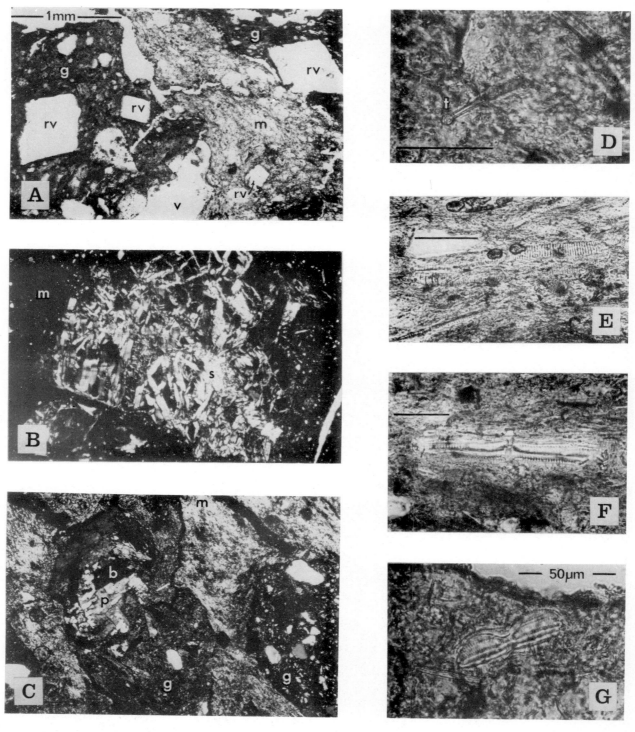

Petrographic thin-sections.

A—Fabric of sherd from Vessel M (TS.1601) showing the distinctive rhombic voids (rv) both in the matrix (m) and in grog (g). (Scale as shown; plane polarised light).

B—Serpentine clast (s) showing characteristic "Fensterstruktur" in sherd of Vessel S (TS.1584) (Scale as in A; crossed polars).

C—Granitic clast with perthite (p) and biotite (b) within a grog fragment (g; matrix m) in a sherd from Vessel K (TS.1594). (Scale as in A; crossed polars).

D—Sponge tylostyle (t) in a sherd from Vessel S' (TS.1613) (Scale bar 50μm).

E—Diatom (*Pinnularia ssp?*) in a sherd from Vessel D (TS.1578) (Scale bar 50μm).

F—Diatom (*Pinnularia ssp?*) in a sherd from Vessel D (TS.1578) (Scale bar 50μm).

G—Diatom (*Diploneis interrupta?*) in a sherd from Vessel S' (TS.1613) (Scale as shown).

Plate XX

i (E) × ½

iv (C) × ⅔

ii (A) × ⅔

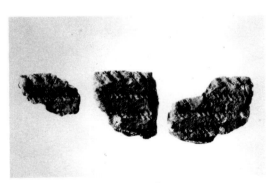

iii (B) × ⅔

v (B) × ⅔

vi (K) × ⅔

Neolithic pottery.

PART 2

The Excavation of the Din Dryfol Chambered Cairn —1969-1970 and 1980

by Frances Lynch

WITH CONTRIBUTIONS FROM
J. S. Conway, M. P. Denne, D. A. Jenkins and T. P. O'Connor

List of Figures (Din Dryfol)

List of Plates (Din Dryfol)

(Following page 136)

Din Dryfol—Chapter 1: Introduction

Din Dryfol tomb (SH 396 725) stands on a narrow ledge projecting from the north side of Dinas, a massive boss of rock which rises sharply from the floor of the wide shallow valley of the river Gwna. This valley on the south west side of the island is one of several which divide Anglesey's rocky plateau into a series of parallel troughs and ridges. The Gwna flows between the narrow ridge of Llangristiolus and the broader plateau of Heneglwys; it runs into Llyn Coron and from there to the sea at Aberffraw. The tomb is four miles from the coast and is situated in the parish of Aberffraw.

The underlying rock of the area is chloritic schist, the Gwna schists of the Mona Complex (Greenly 1919, 67, 352-54), some of the oldest and most resistant rocks in Anglesey. Right across the island these rocks form a stream of knolls and outcrops and in the Gwna valley in particular they create a landscape which is at the same time both intimate and wild. The scenery around the tomb can still be described in the words of Hugh Prichard writing over a hundred years ago. ''The meadow lies in the hollow of a natural basin, the receding sides of which are studded with picturesque rocks; some of them protruding their grey summits, in pleasing contrast, above the hawthorns and furze with which they are partially clothed; while others start up abruptly from surrounding pasture, adding to the interest of the

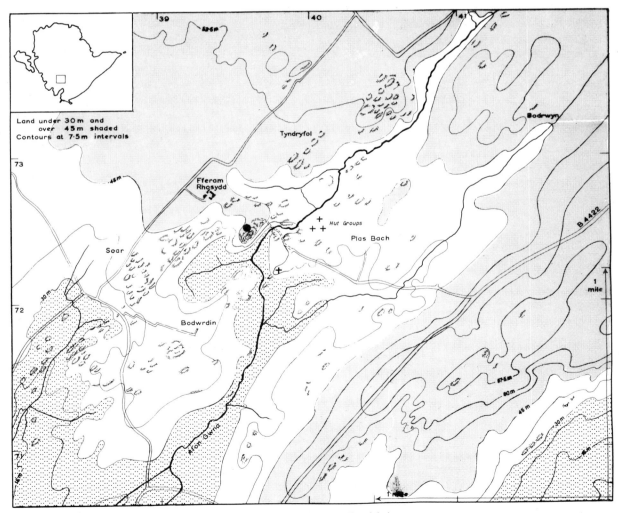

Fig. 40. Map of the Din Dryfol Area.

spot and contributing to its snugness and seclusion.'' (Prichard 1871, 300).

The soils are brown earths and gleys formed on a glacial drift derived from the Mona Complex. They belong to the Trisant, Gaerwen, and Gesail series (Roberts 1958) and for the most part are light and well drained, though close to the river there are problems of drainage (Grimes 1945). This light soil in the valley may explain the predominately low lying distribution of early settlement. However it must be admitted that there is no concentration of Neolithic material in the area (Lynch 1970, Map 2); there are no stone axes or other chance finds to indicate the site of occupation contemporary with the monument, a situation which is true of most other tombs in Anglesey and elsewhere. The distribution of megalithic tombs in the island is a scattered one; there are no close concentrations and the pattern would seem to reflect settlement by independent communities each maintaining a single tomb within its own lands. The impression is reinforced by the intermingling of architectural styles, no one tradition becoming predominant in a district. There are several tombs in this corner of Anglesey, all about two to four miles apart and belonging to different traditions. Nearer the coast are Ty Newydd, an early Passage Grave, and Barclodiad y Gawres, a later one of Irish type. Din Dryfol, their nearest neighbour, obviously belongs to a different group, but further inland at the head of Malltraeth Marsh there may have been another Cruciform Passage Grave (Lynch 1970, 40-43).

The presence of the tomb at Din Dryfol must indicate occupation in the Gwna valley and this was maintained in the Bronze Age. The round barrow just south west of Dinas (RCAHM 1937, 214) may be discounted (it is a solid boss of rock), but the famous Bodwrdin mould for Early Bronze Age spearheads was found in the river to the south and a palstave has come from Bodrwyn to the north (Lynch 1970, 195). It is however in the first few centuries AD that there is evidence for intense occupation, with the establishment of several enclosed hut groups in the centre of the valley not far from Din Dryfol (Prichard 1871 and RCAHM 1937, 2). The excavation results have suggested that this large Romano-British population did a great deal of damage to the Neolithic tomb. Nevertheless, it has survived, at least in part, while the remains of their houses were swept away during the late eighteenth and nineteenth centuries when a period of intensified agriculture began.

''Dindryfwl'' was the centre of a mediaeval township and the existence of a mill a short way up the river from the tomb and of a chapel-of-ease about a quarter of a mile away suggests that quite a large community flourished here in the thirteenth to fifteenth centuries (Carr 1982). With the sixteenth century consolidation of estates and the eventual closure of the mill the population subsequently declined towards its present level (Tomos Roberts, *pers. comm.*).

Early References to Din Dryfol

Although Henry Rowlands mentions ''Dindryfal'' he speaks of it in terms of battles and fortifications and is obviously referring to Dinas (which is not fortified) or Cadmarth on the other side of the river (which was enclosed) (Rowlands 1766, 25 and supplement, 32). He does not appear to know of the existence of the tomb which, even more surprisingly, is not shown on either of the two very detailed mid-eighteenth century estate maps which cover this area (UCNW Bodorgan 1579 and Penrhos II.773), nor is it among those visited or commented upon by early writers or tourists such as the Reverend John Skinner. The earliest reference is in a brief list of antiquities published by the Reverend H. Longueville Jones in which the two surviving parts of the monument, the fallen chamber at the west end and the tall portal at the east, are considered as separate monuments, a chamber and and independent *maenhir* or standing stone (Longueville Jones 1855, 24, 25). This view was maintained until the 1920s.

In 1870 and 1871 the tomb was again mentioned in passing in lists of Anglesey monuments published by W. O. Stanley (who owned the site) and Albert Way (Stanley 1870, 58; Way 1871, 105). 1871 also saw the publication of a more important article, the factual description of the remains by Hugh Prichard, a description which was accompanied by a competent plan and an engraved view (Prichard 1871, 310-12). Prichard follows Longueville Jones in regarding the remains as two separate monuments. He interprets the western group (which consisted of Stones 2, 4, 5, 7 and the capstones in their present position, with Stone 3 standing to the east) as part of a chamber extending to the south west. He was influenced in this view by the presence of two large holes, 3.25m apart, then visible some distance to the south west. He was told that these holes had formerly held uprights supporting a capstone 4.5m long. The 1980 excavation was designed to cut across the site of these holes, but nothing was found there. Since Prichard saw the holes they must have existed somewhere; the trilithon may be more fanciful. Prichard envisages the chamber as transepted in plan with the surviving stones forming part of a side chamber. This view must have influenced later writers who speak of the monument, without much justification, as a Passage Grave. Prichard was puzzled by the tall stone at the east end. He could recognise that it might have been the portal to a chamber but he could not link it satisfactorily with the other stones. He preferred, rather limply, to consider it a separate *maenhir*. He recorded that a large pit had been dug in front of it but he did not refer to any disturbance in the western chamber. He also mentioned the 'barrow' in the field to the west of Dinas which he considered to be some

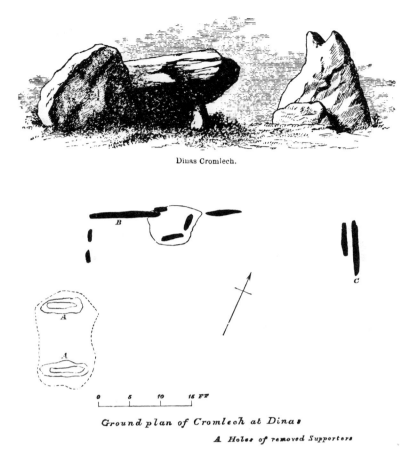

Dinas Cromlech.

Ground plan of Cromlech at Dinas

A Holes of removed Supporters

Fig. 41. Hugh Prichard's plan of the tomb in 1871
(reproduced from *Archaeologia Cambrensis* for 1871 with the permission of the editor).

sort of fortified platform, recognising that it was largely natural. Dry weather in 1970 revealed that it was, in fact, entirely natural.

The next reference to the site—apart from its inclusion in J. E. Griffith's *Portfolio of Photographs of the Cromlechs of Anglesey and Carnarvonshire* of 1900—is in E. Neil Baynes' survey *The Megalithic Remains of Anglesey* (Baynes 1911). Baynes maintained the separation of the chamber and the eastern stone but his discussion of these two was somewhat inconsistent. In discussing the *maenhir* he said that it "may have formed the end of a long chamber" but "the alignment of some stones close by, which are believed to have formed part of a passage dolmen, does little to confirm this theory." (Baynes 1911, 75). However, when he had described these western stones in the first section under 'Dolmens' he had compared the monument to Trefignath (ibid, 44) which he had dscribed as a 'Gallery Grave' (ibid, 42). Such a comparison must imply an interpretation of the remains as a single long structure with an impressive entrance. Apart from this comparison in an aside he made no explicit interpretation, but gave a summary of Hugh Prichard's description. In 1911 the monument had been placed under the guardianship of the Commissioners for the Preservation of Ancient Monuments by the owner, Lord Sheffield, and in expressing the hope that they would remove ivy and tidy the site Neil Baynes

revealed that the hole in front of Stone 1 was then still open.

The Royal Commission *Inventory of Ancient Monuments in Anglesey*, published in 1937 but written some years earlier, still speaks of the tomb as a Passage Grave but definitely interprets the remains as part of a single long structure with Stone 1 as a portal (RCHAM 1937, no. 3). While preparing their plan they investigated the likely site of the other entrance stone and found what they considered to be a stone hole with substantial packing (Stone 9).

In 1936 Professor W. F. Grimes published his important discussion of the megalithic monuments of Wales. In this work he compared Din Dryfol (Ty'n Drifol) to Trefignath and Hendrefor, a trio which was to remain linked in all other subsequent comments on the Anglesey tombs (Grimes 1936, 119-20). He also drew specific analogies between these tombs and the northern Irish, Scottish, and Manx cairns, another conclusion which strongly influenced later writers. In 1950 G. E. Daniel's study repeated the same view of Din Dryfol as a single, long segmented gallery with a tall entrance stone at the east end (Daniel 1950, 86, 186). Professor Piggott's influential survey of the *Neolithic Cultures of the British Isles* included Trefignath, Din Dryfol and Hendrefor as outlying colonies of the Clyde Carlingford Culture, claiming virtual identity between Trefignath and the Irish Court Cairns

(Piggott 1954, 179). In *Megalithic Enquiries* published in 1969 the present writer was rather more circumspect about the identity of cultures on either side of the Irish Sea and preferred the neutral term 'Long Grave', but the essential interpretation of the three tombs, Trefignath, Din Dryfol, and Hendrefor, as long segmented galleries remained unchanged (Lynch 1969, 114-15, 297). In 1970 the discussion was, in essence, the same, with the addition of some details from the 1969 season of excavation (Lynch 1970, 32-33). It was only the excavation of Trefignath in 1977-79 and the revelation that three separate tombs were involved, that forced a reconsideration of the apparent similarities and dissimilarities within this group of Anglesey Long Graves.

History of the Excavation

This monument first aroused the interest of the author when she noticed stones protruding through the grass in front of the large portal stone at the east end. Having excavated with Prof. T. G. E. Powell at Dyffryn Ardudwy where undisturbed blocking had protected important forecourt deposits, she felt confident that, though much of the tomb was obviously damaged, valuable material and information might be retrieved. These hopes were not to be fulfilled in the manner expected.

In the summer of 1969 one month's work was undertaken with two groups of eight students from University College of North Wales. In that year the southern half of the chamber area was excavated, together with the long eastern trench, chasing the elusive blocking which turned out to be a relatively recent road. In the following summer, another month's work was done with a similar work force and Trenches L—Za were opened. These covered the northern half of the chamber and investigated the cairn. However the problem of the shape and size of the cairn was not satisfactorily resolved by these trenches. This uncertainty was one of the factors which delayed the production of the report.

During the 1970 season the capstone and the fallen stone (3) were lifted out of the way, to be replaced in their original positions when the trenches were filled in. The only other element of restoration carried out after the excavation was the straightening of Stone 8 which has been leaning against the portal stone. This work was carried out by the Department of the Environment architect and masons based at Caernarfon.

In 1976 Dr C. A. Smith was appointed Inspector of Ancient Monuments with responsibility for North Wales and one of his first projects was the excavation of Trefignath, a tomb with obvious similarities to Din Dryfol. The success of the excavations at Trefignath and the relevance of the results to the much less clear situation at Din Dryfol led to the resolve to undertake a final season of excavation in the hope of solving some of the outstanding problems. Consequently a short season of two weeks with nine students was

worked in the summer of 1980, when the south side of the cairn, which was known to be well preserved, was investigated with gratifying results. Two trenches (α and Δ) were cut right across the cairn to establish its width and the area of Chamber Two was re-excavated in order to check that no post holes had been missed.

Acknowledgements

The excavation was financed throughout from the Guardianship Fund of the Department of the Environment (now the Welsh Office Conservation and Land Division), and it gives me great pleasure to acknowledge the help and encouragement given by Dr M. R. Apted, who was Principal Inspector during the first excavations, and by Dr C. A. Smith in 1980. I am particularly grateful to Dr Smith for urging me to complete the work on the site, managing to arrange the finance in a much less liberal climate, and finally for forcing me to complete this report promptly. Without his encouragement it is unlikely that the final essential excavation would have taken place. I am also grateful to Mr Whincap, the Department of the Environment architect, and his staff, for arranging for the removal and restoration of the fallen stone in 1970.

The owners of Fferam Rhosydd, Messrs Idris and Kenneth Jones, and the late Mr Glyn Jones took a very helpful interest in the work and showed us great kindness throughout the time we were there. In 1980 they provided space for a camp site and allowed us to use the facilities of the farm with a generosity for which all those involved with the excavation were deeply grateful. In 1969 and 1970 the students stayed with Mr and Mrs G. Owen in Bethel, but in 1980 everyone had to camp.

In the course of the three seasons many volunteers worked on the site and they all worked with the care and cheerfulness which makes the director's task a pleasant one. The shortcomings of the excavation were not those of the workers, but of the director. It gives me great pleasure to record their names below, with special thanks to Martin de Lewandovicz who acted as Site Assistant in 1980. Previously such a luxury was unknown. Those who worked in both 1969 and 1970 are particularly thanked: Keith Bradshaw, Peter Ketley and Helen Morton. In addition, those who worked in 1969 were: Christopher Barrett, Paul Biancardi, Alan Costall, Philip Langley, Michael Lyons, James Walbran, Margaret Barton, Janet Bye, Susan Davies, Jennifer Lewis, Georgina Plowright, Carol Towler and Ann Williams. In 1970 the volunteers were Robert Evans, Carl Harrison, Richard Kelly, Robin Pollard, Jeremy Whitehouse, Elizabeth Davies, Susan Heywood, Judith O'Nions, Gwyneth Owen, Mary Siraut, Heather Williams, Lindsay Williams and Celia Womack. Those who worked in 1980 were: Arfon Hughes, William R. Hughes, Tim Peck, Julie Edwards, Sarah Fried, Veronica Hathway, Coleen Higgins, Susan Kirk and Hilary Morris. I am also grateful to the Gwynedd Archaeological Trust for the loan of manpower for filling in the trenches opened in 1980.

Finally I should like to thank all those who have helped with specialist reporting and advice. Foremost amongst these is Dr David Jenkins who has provided advice on soil problems over many years, also Dr Pat Denne who has identified a great number of charcoal samples with surprising enthusiasm. I am grateful to Mark Webster, Dr John Conway and Terry O'Connor for their analyses of the pottery, soil and bones, and to Mr George Boon of the National Museum of Wales for his identification of the Romano-British sherd. Jean Williamson has helped with the preparation of the final drawings and Mr C. H. Houlder arranged for the slicing and identification of the stone axe. The results of the pottery analysis are incorporated in the discussion of the more extensive assemblage from Trefignath, but the other specialist reports are placed as appendices at the end of this report. Mr J. G. Scott kindly read the manuscript and contributed many stimulating ideas to the interpretation, although it should not be assumed that he is in entire agreement with its final form.

Din Dryfol Chapter 2:
Excavation Record—the setting of the tomb

The tomb stands on a narrow ledge projecting from the north side of a massive boss of rock and the size and shape of this ledge has undoubtedly influenced the design of the monument. It is approximately 79m long, 30m wide, and about 6m high; it drops away steeply on the north and west; on the south side, cliffs rise above it in a series of tall steps to the bare summit of the rock some 25m above. Only on the east is the approach easy with a gradual ascent to the entrance to the tomb. From the ledge it is possible to reach the summit of the rock by a steep ramp which rises from a point a little south-west of the portal stone (1); the presence of this path may be partly to blame for the severe destruction of the eastern end of the monument.

The impressive portal stone stands at the break of slope and the rest of the monument lies on the level edge behind it, bounded to north and south by ridges of projecting rock whose lines seem to have controlled the direction and size of the cairn. The trough between these two exposed ridges is filled with a stony orange clay providing an approximately level surface through which smaller bosses of rock project. The natural soil sequence runs from this undisturbed yellow/orange clay through a stony orange/brown soil to a light brown humic layer. The depth of soil varies; at the centre of the trough beneath the chambers rock was not reached at a depth of 1m; at the western end, the rock was only some 0.1m below the modern grass. The vegetation of the ridge is rough grass with bluebells and bracken, the bracken roots having deeply penetrated all the archaeological deposits.

The rock is a chlorite schist of the Gwna Series with veins of quartz. It is a delicate light turquoise in colour when first exposed, but weathers to a pale grey. The chamber and cairn are composed of this local rock (Greenly in Baynes 1911, 44, 75), and the slabs would not need to be carried more than a few metres, so the massive scale of the monument need not surprise us.

The Cairn

The vastness of the monument is very apparent. A huge portal stone survives at the east end, marking the entrance to what must have been a series of rectangular chambers stretching behind it for a length of 12.5m. Only the westernmost chamber (Four) survives in any recognisable form. The cairn which covered this structure was long and narrow,

certainly over 47m long and probably 62m long; the overall width was about 15m. Although where it was well preserved, the edge of the cairn was straight, its shape does not seem to conform to any standard design, but rather to follow the line of the rock ridges on either side.

The east end of the cairn had been almost totally destroyed on either side of the chambers for a length of 5.5m. West of this point, the southern side was fairly well preserved, although showing signs of disturbance in places. In this area it was possible to recognise a clear distinction within the cairn material—the stones close to the chambers (the Inner Cairn) were very large, many over 1m long, whereas the outer stones were much smaller, normal, manageable boulders of 0.2-0.3m across. This distinction between an inner and outer cairn could be recognised in trenches cut across the cairn further to the west although the definition was far less sharp. Several small trenches were opened at the far end of the ledge but the presence of a modern wall and the absence of a consistent stone layer, due to extensive robbing in the recent past, made it impossible accurately to define the end of the cairn.

Cairn surviving close to chambers (Trenches C, D, E (1969) and B (1980)) Plan: Fig. 47; Sections: Fig. 48 and Fig. 49. Plates XXIII—XXVII.
Virtually no cairn stones remained in the vicinity of the portal and of the putative first chamber while on the north side of the surviving orthostats there was only a ragged remnant. On the south side, however, the cairn was largely intact and the extension of the excavation in that area in 1980 provided crucial information about its structure and the possible sequence of tomb building. Immediately below the topsoil there was a fairly consistent layer of small stones (Fig. 46). This layer was not very informative since it masked crucial differences between ancient and modern features but it did reveal areas of total stone removal and also the presence of some important modern disturbances.

When this layer of small stones was removed the more massive character of the original cairn was revealed. Some of these stones (such as 6) had projected above the modern grass and had been mistaken for parts of the chamber structure by ourselves and by earlier investigators who had broken its top and dug around it and its neighbour.

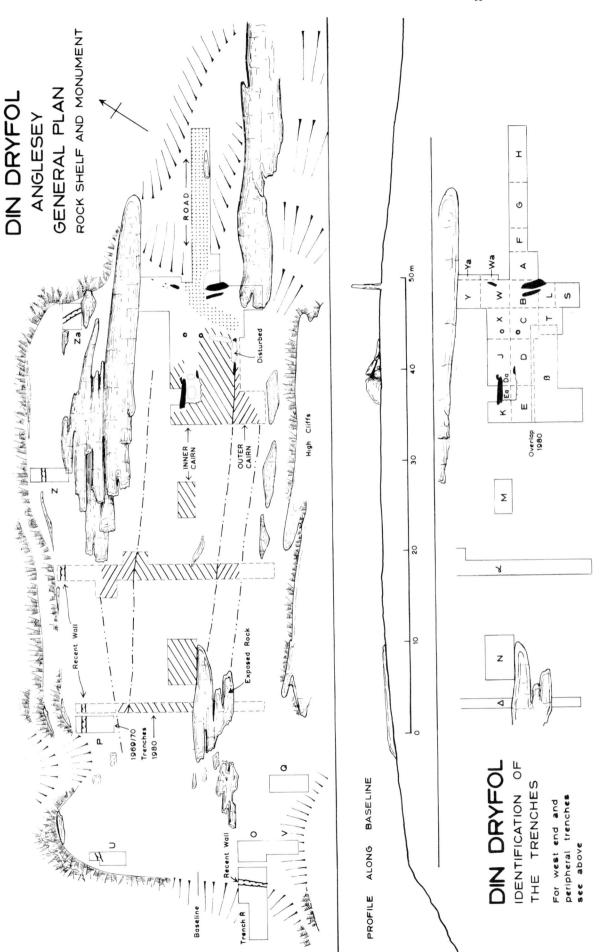

Fig. 42. Site plan showing trenches dug in 1969/70 and 1980.

However exposure of a larger area showed that these huge blocks were simply part of the massive cairn which surrounded the westernmost chamber.

The cairn had been built closely against the back of the orthostats which on the south and west of the chamber had been subsequently removed and only the presence of the cairn stones revealed the position of these uprights. Because of the size of the stones, the cairn was not completely removed in this area but it was possible to observe (in gaps where cairn stones had been previously removed) that no old humus layer survived under it, the stones lying directly on the orange clay subsoil. In places the subsoil had some oak and hazel charcoal on it and two tiny scraps of pottery and some fragments of human bone were found on this surface, but their presence may be due to disturbance of the chamber. Amongst the basal stones of the cairn, but not beneath them, was a soft, very dark brown soil. The origin of this soil is obscure but it covers the subsoil in many areas of extensive disturbance and in Trench S (Fig. 51) contains slag, a fact which suggests that it may belong to an early period of disturbance. How it penetrated amongst the deepest stones of the undisturbed cairn is not clear, but it is a light soil and might perhaps have blown there. It was observed everywhere in both the 1969 and 1980 trenches south of the chambers and was seen to be a layer about 0.1m thick, merging imperceptibly with the paler brown, tough soil in the upper layers of the cairn. In trench β just north of Stone 10 there was a hollow where some of the larger stones had been removed. This hollow was filled with smaller stones set in this soft dark soil with a few scraps of cremated bone, suggesting that it belonged to a period of general disturbance, both in the chambers and amongst the stones of the cairn. The few flint flakes from the upper levels of the cairn in this area may also have been thrown there at that time.

The cairn had been built against the stones of the chamber from the western end towards the east, many of the larger stones being sloped one against the other. In the trench opened in 1980 a clear distinction between an Inner and Outer cairn could be recognised. The Inner Cairn was built of very large slabs, many more than 1m long, while the Outer Cairn was composed of much smaller material which had been laid against the straight edge of the Inner Cairn. This straight edge was easily traced though it did not form a kerb likely to have stood independantly, but consisted of relatively slight stones laid to a line at the lowest level with much larger blocks laid to the same line above them so that the junction was most sharply defined at an intermediate level (Fig. 47).

There was no formal definition of the edge of the Outer Cairn. Formal structure could be observed only at the edge of the Inner Cairn where it could be seen that many of the slabby stones of the Outer Cairn had been set leaning against this edge; beyond this they formed a jumbled mass becoming increasingly thin as the natural surface rose towards the rock ridge. It is probable that this ridge was intended to form the edge of the cairn, but the surviving stones did not reach it everywhere.

In the eastern half of Trench β the nature of the edge of the Inner Cairn changed. Stone 10, a massive orthostatic kerbstone, 1.6m long and 0.75m high, stood on the line and the nature of the disturbance to the east of it suggested that two others had existed there, with a shattered, column-like stone (11) beyond. The quantity of splintered stone showed that the blocks had been broken up with a pick before their removal, a fate which Stone 11 had only partly escaped. It had not been set into a hole but its pointed base had been very firmly wedged by other stones and it still stood securely in spite of the fact that the top had been shattered. The nature of the destruction in this area, dated by a twentieth century cartridge case found at the bottom of one of the holes, suggests that the tips of these kerbstones may have been visible on the surface. The area of disturbance turns northwards forming a deep narrow trench which cut a little way into the subsoil. It is reasonable to suggest that this trench, too, was formed by the removal of upright stones. The presence of a line of stones at this point is very significant for the interpretation of the monument but speculation must be postponed to a later section (Chapter 4).

It could be argued that there is a change in the nature of the Inner Cairn material in this eastern half bounded by upright kerbstones. The stones are smaller and there are very few massive slabs. However there is no formal line of demarcation and the difference may not be a significant one. So little survived of any cairn east of the removed kerb (in Trenches C and T) that no worthwhile comment can be made about it. Moreover the difficulty of distinguishing between the lower levels of the 'road' (see p. 116) and undisturbed cairn makes the identification of the stones shown in Fig. 47 a little suspect.

Central Area of Cairn (Trenches M, N and P (1970) and α and Δ (1980)) Figs. 43 and 44.
In 1970 two rectangular trenches were set out along the approximate centre line of the cairn. These simply revealed the existence of cairn material at these points but did not help to define the extent of the cairn. In 1980 two more intelligently designed trenches were able to establish the approximate width of the cairn and to confirm the distinction between Inner and Outer Cairn seen much more clearly in the area close to the chambers.

Trench M contained very massive cairn material, exactly similar to that found further east. It is obviously part of the Inner Cairn, as would be expected from its position. The large stones were not removed but the soil around them was excavated to subsoil in places. The soft dark brown soil found in the basal layer of the cairn around the chambers was

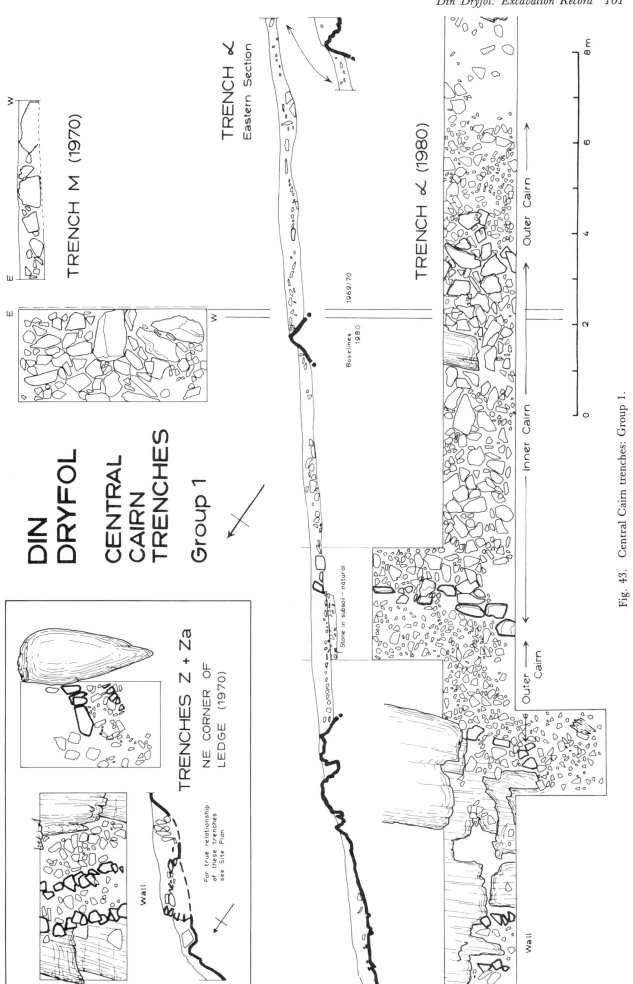

Fig. 43. Central Cairn trenches: Group 1.

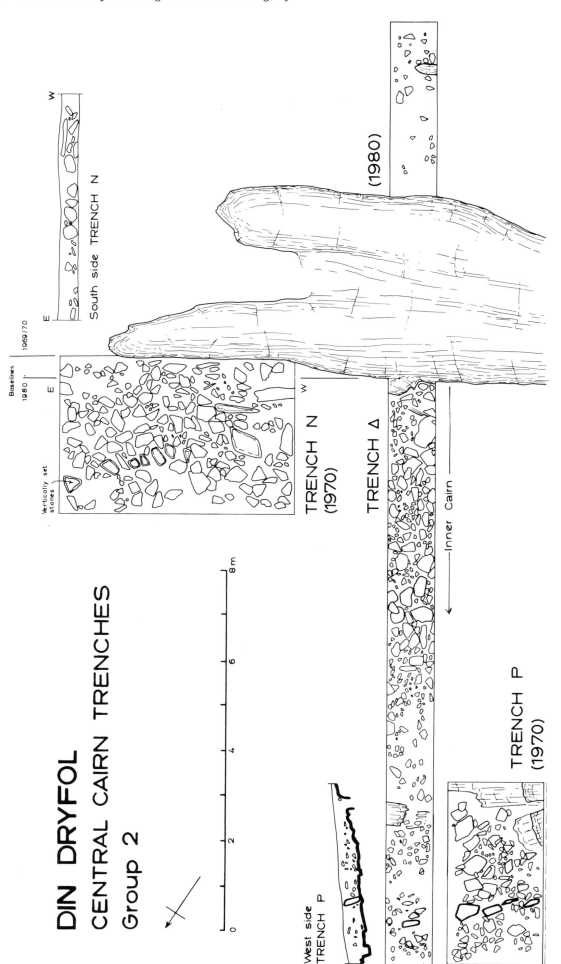

DIN DRYFOL
CENTRAL CAIRN TRENCHES
Group 2

West side
TRENCH P

TRENCH P
(1970)

TRENCH P
(1970)

TRENCH Δ

TRENCH N
(1970)

South side TRENCH N

Vertically set stones

Baselines

1980

1969/70

Inner Cairn

(1980)

Fig. 44. Central Cairn trenches: Group 2.

not found in this trench, nor in the others further west. There was no indication of a pre-cairn humus layer; the stones lay directly on orange subsoil.

The cairn material in Trench α is less obviously massive than in M but larger material could be recognised in the central section and on the north side a line of thin slabs marked the junction of the Inner and Outer Cairns. None of these slabs was set in a stone hole, some had stood upright and had been pushed outwards, others had been leant inwards against the Inner Cairn. This kerb, therefore, was not consistently designed, nor did it look as if it could have been intended to stand as an unmasked edge. In this it resembled the line in Trench β. To the north of it the stones were noticably smaller but formed a compact mass as far as the rock ridge. When the trench was first opened it was thought that the Outer Cairn might have been edged by a line of small upright stones which appeared to continue the line of the ridge. However, further excavation showed that this was illusory and the smaller stones died away without any formal edge.

The southern side of the cairn in Trench α was less satisfactory. There was no clear junction between the Inner and Outer Cairn though a difference in scale could be recognised by the eye of faith. The Outer Cairn material died away on a ragged edge just short of the line of projecting rock.

The cairn material in Trench N formed a fairly consistent layer; it was not exceptionally massive but may be reasonably identified with the Inner Cairn as defined further east. A line of stones running east-west across the trench a little north of centre seemed to be more carefully placed than the others and most of them stood vertically. It is possible that they represent a marking out line down the centre of the cairn. Trench Δ laid out in 1980 revealed an increasingly thin layer of stones running north from the central rock spine. In the light of the evidence from other trenches it was possible to recognise the Inner and Outer Cairn on the north side but there was no formal junction or edge. The modern wall at the north edge of the shelf (see p. 116) is atypical here. Only one face (whether the inner or outer is uncertain) survives, composed of small vertical stones. It is conceivable that much of the material in Trench P belongs to the Outer Cairn, but so little remained that it would be impossible to prove it. An extension to Trench Δ south of the rock spine revealed only a thin and haphazard scatter of stone such as would be expected to occur naturally in the soil in this region. It was assumed, therefore, that the cairn had not extended to the south of the rock and this outcrop had probably been incorporated as the edge here.

The conclusions to be drawn from these trenches are that the cairn continued for at least 34m beyond the end of the chambers; that the distinction between the Inner and Outer Cairn was maintained throughout this length; that the width was largely governed by the presence of the rock ridges on either side, but it may have been gradually reduced towards the west end. This reduction in width would seem to affect the Outer rather than the Inner Cairn which maintains a fairly consistent width of about 9m. The lack of formal edging to the Outer Cairn and the denudation of the western end of the ridge make it less certain that the cairn was tapered and it may have been more strictly rectangular, with a maximum width of about 15m.

Western End of Cairn Trenches Q, V, O, R, U (1970) Fig. 45. Plate XXXVIII
The trenches here were laid out in 1970 in the mistaken belief that walling visible at the top of the slope at the western end of the ledge belonged to the Neolithic cairn. Excavation eventually showed that this wall (also found in Trenches U, P, Δ, α, Z and Za) was modern. The clarification of the size of the cairn which resulted from the 1980 trenches has shown that Trenches Q and V are beyond its southern limits. The stones found in them were all set in light orange/brown soil, the natural soil of the hill; they formed no consistent layer and their arrangement was haphazard. It is therefore reasonable to interpret them as natural. Four pieces of flint were found in Trench V; nothing was found in Q.

In Trenches O and R there had been a good deal of human activity. Charcoal, burnt animal bone, and slag were found in a layer of dirty brown soil filling a hollow just below the western tip of a rock ridge. The line of the crest of this ridge was continued in the northern half of these two trenches by a line of overlapping stones which could be interpreted as a very roughly built wall. It formed a northern boundary to the area of dirty soil and charcoal which was cut at the western end by the modern wall. On the south the soil died away against the rising slope. Although there was a fair amount of stone in Trench O there is no evidence that it belonged to the cairn. The presence of charcoal and slag here would suggest that this was the scene of some later, perhaps Romano-British, activity to which the very roughly built wall was more likely to belong (see p. 115).

The final verdict on these trenches, therefore, is that they failed to establish the position of the end of the cairn. The increasingly thin scatter of cairn material in Trench Δ, the very shallow soil on the NW corner of the ledge and the knowledge that many cartloads of stone had been removed from the west end of the ledge by the previous owner of the farm, all contributed to the decision that it was not worth opening further trenches in this area in order to find the back edge of the cairn which was unlikely to be satisfactorily marked.

The Chambers (Plans: Figs. 46, 47, 50; Sections: Figs. 48 and 49).
The megalithic structure at the east end was, like the cairn, long and narrow (12.5m long by about 1.5m wide) but it had been so thoroughly destroyed that it is difficult to say much more with any confidence.

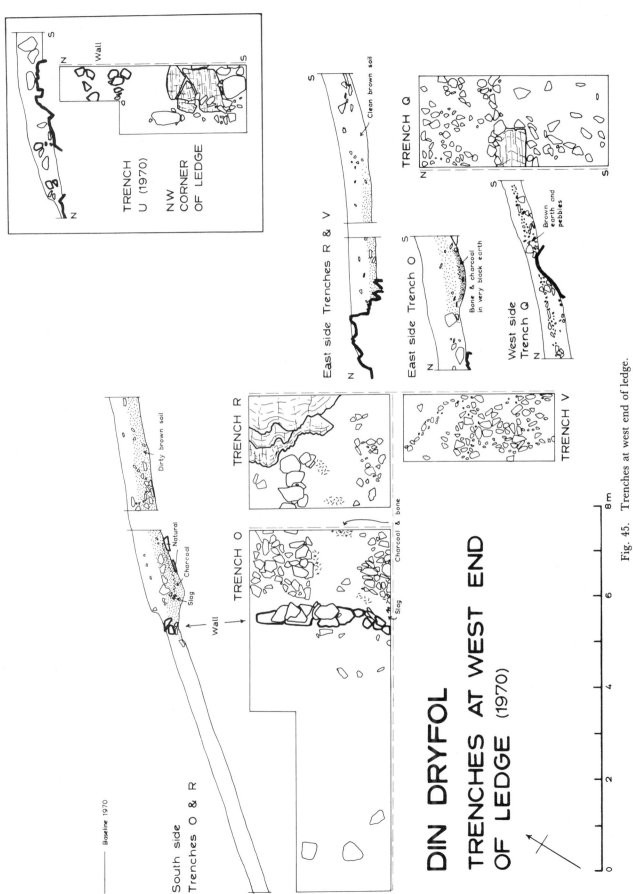

Fig. 45.   Trenches at west end of ledge.

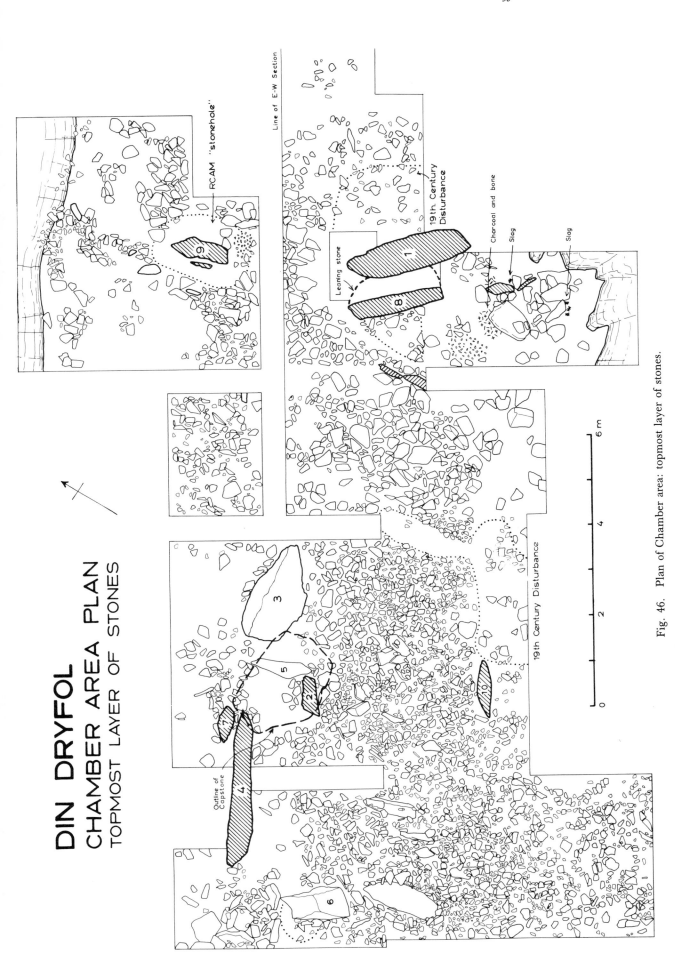

DIN DRYFOL
CHAMBER AREA PLAN
TOPMOST LAYER OF STONES

Fig. 46. Plan of Chamber area: topmost layer of stones.

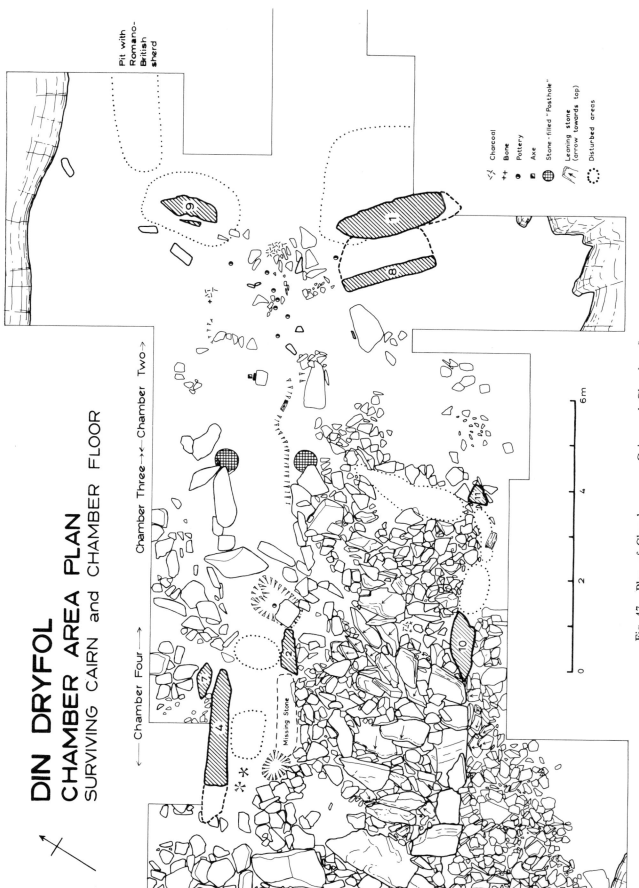

Fig. 47.   Plan of Chamber area: Cairn and Chamber floors.

Moreover, only the huge south-eastern portal was set in a stone hole; all the other surviving orthostats simply stood upon the surface, so that, where the cairn did not survive well, the position of lost stones could not be reconstructed. The present remains—a tall entrance stone at the east end and a rectangular chamber at the west—suggest a series of perhaps four rectangular chambers, but the excavations at Trefignath have shown that such a structure may be susceptible to several different historical interpretations.

The distribution of sherds, concentrated near the portal stone, would tend to confirm that this was indeed the entrance to a chamber, though it must be admitted that there is no other evidence for the nature of the first two chambers. For the third and fourth chambers there is better evidence, though they present difficulties of detailed interpretation. These four putative chambers will be described from the western end since this back chamber (Four) is the best preserved.

Chamber Four

Four stones of this chamber survive. They comprise the north side stone (4); a prop to it (7) whose base was not investigated for reasons of safety; a broken stone on the south side (2), and the capstone which had slipped forward off its supporters sometime before 1871. The line of undisturbed cairn just south of the chamber indicated the position of the southern side stone which must have been about 1.75m long. Its setting could be recognised as a very slight hollow (Fig 49; Section B) but it had not stood in a true stone hole. The position of the back stone was also indicated by the surviving cairn stones. It stood transversely across the chamber where the end of Stone 4 rested on the ground surface, the tip of that stone thus projecting beyond the chamber. The internal dimensions of this back chamber (assuming that Stone 2 is part of it) are 3m by 1m. The height must have been at least 2m judging by the maximum height of the remaining side stone. The tops of both 2 and 7 have been broken, so their present heights are no guide to their former size, though it is very unlikely that they would have been over 2m high. The surviving capstone would have covered about half the chamber and there must have been another over the western end.

Two small hollows in the floor of the chamber at the western end would have been beneath the backstone if they were ancient. They were filled with a softish clay and it was not possible to determine their age or purpose. The status of the larger pit in the south west corner of the chamber is also uncertain. It was quite a sharply cut hole with a filling of orange/brown gravelly clay, similar to the natural subsoil but softer, with a few largish stones in it. This filling, which did not contain any modern material, was divided from the filling of the rest of the chamber by a narrow band of darker clay. It is difficult to interpret this as a stone hole since the other structural stones do not have holes, nor was it obviously a late disturbance like the other pits in the chamber floor.

Disturbances

The whole of the chamber had been deeply disturbed on more than one occasion. However it should be noted that there was no soft dark brown soil in the chamber fill and the disturbances here would all seem to be relatively late. The earliest of the pits dug through the chamber floor was the oval pit at the east end beside Stone 2. This must have been dug before the capstone slipped into its present position. The fill consisted of stones in a sticky brown earth with occasional flecks of burnt bone, some flint implements, and a sherd of glazed crock. Judging from the shape of the rectangular hole in the centre of the floor, the second disturbance took place before the southern side stone was removed. The fill of this hole consisted of brown earth with smallish stones together with a sherd of glazed pottery which joins one from the first disturbance, a few scraps of burnt bone and some waste flint flakes. The longitudinal section (Fig. 48 top) shows that, though the side stone was probably still in position, the back stone had been removed by that stage. At the time of the next disturbance, the side stone had also gone; the disturbance was very probably the occasion of its removal. This disturbance can be recognised in the sections as a spread of brown soil containing a lot of broken stone, together with a few scraps of burnt bone and some waste flint flakes redeposited from earlier diggings. Finally a small square hole had been dug on the south side of the chamber. This was of one spade's width and may perhaps be interpreted as the ill-chosen site for a Ministry sign.

Original Contents of the Chamber

None of the original floor of the chamber survived undamaged. The content of the pits dug through the floor showed that the chamber had probably contained a fair amount of cremated bone, for scraps were found in all parts. Though only a few grammes have survived, two individuals may be recognised. The chamber fill contained eighteen pieces of waste flint and four implements (two scrapers, a strike-a-light, and a fabricator (Fig. 52)), but there was no Neolithic pottery.

Thirty-one pieces of flint, mainly waste, several scraps of burnt bone and two fragments of Neolithic pottery were found amongst the stones of the cairn south of this chamber and Chamber Three. It is conceivable that they had been thrown out of the chambers, Chamber Four being the one most likely to have contained the main deposits.

Junction of Chambers Four and Three

Before the excavation began a narrow stone (5) could be seen beneath the capstone crossing the chamber like a septal slab. However excavation revealed that this stone lay at a high level and did not touch the

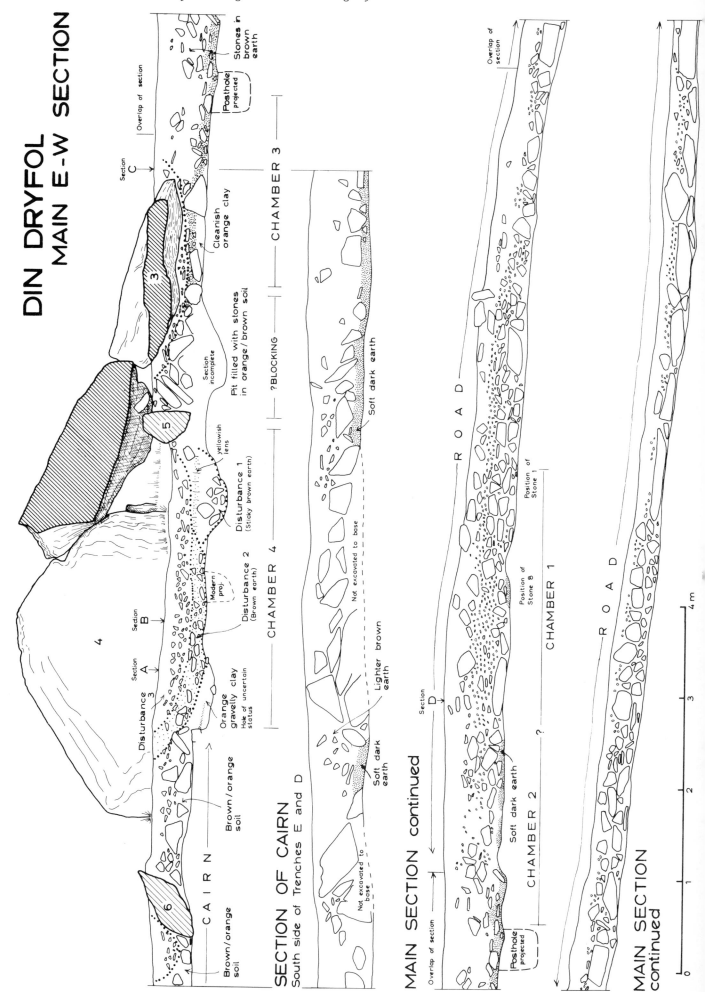

DIN DRYFOL
MAIN E-W SECTION

SECTION OF CAIRN
South side of Trenches E and D

MAIN SECTION continued

MAIN SECTION continued

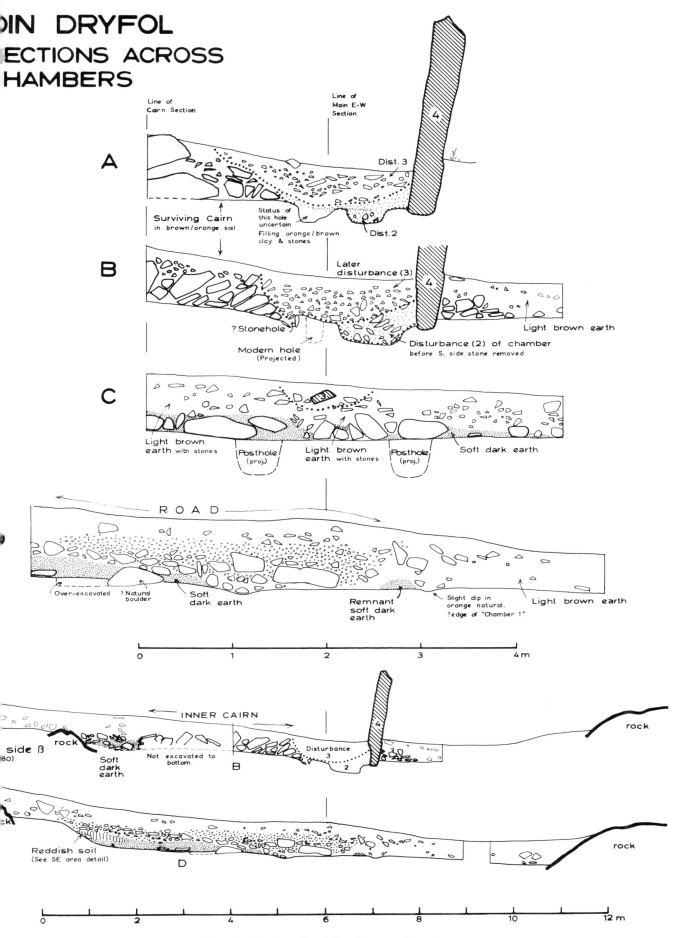

DIN DRYFOL

SECTIONS ACROSS CHAMBERS

Line of
Cairn Section

Line of
Main E-W
Section

A

Dist. 3

4

Surviving Cairn
in brown/orange soil

Status of
this hole
uncertain

Dist. 2

Filling orange/brown
clay & stones

B

Later
disturbance (3)

4

?Stonehole

Light brown earth

Modern hole
(Projected)

Disturbance (2) of chamber
before S. side stone removed

C

Light brown
earth with stones

Posthole
(proj.)

Light brown
earth with stones

Posthole
(proj.)

Soft dark earth

R O A D

Over-excavated

?Natural
boulder

Soft
dark earth

Remnant
soft dark
earth

Slight dip in
orange natural.
?edge of "Chamber 1"

Light brown earth

0   1   2   3   4 m

INNER CAIRN

4

rock

side β
(80)

rock

Soft
dark
earth

Not excavated to
bottom

B

Disturbance
3

2

Reddish soil
(See SE area detail)

D

rock

rock

0   2   4   6   8   10   12 m

Fig. 49.   Sections North-South across Chambers.

floor of the chamber. It would seem, therefore, that there was no formal division between Chambers Four and Three, but it must be admitted that the jumbled stones beneath the capstone and close to the fallen Stone 3 were not well excavated, nor properly understood. In 1969 the southern half of Trench D was excavated before the capstone was moved and this was obviously a mistake which led to cramped working and a poor record.

The situation is complicated by the absence of any stone, or any seating for a stone, which could have matched Stone 2 and by the discovery of a shallow pit filled with large stones just east of Stone 2. This pit (about 1m long by 0.8m wide but only 0.2m deep— really an irregular scoop) ran diagonally into the chamber area and was filled with three layers of large stones, the intermediate ones laid approximately flat and the lowest ones pressed hard into the bottom of the pit. Beneath the flat stones were four fragments of Neolithic pottery and a few scraps of oak charcoal. There was no modern material in this pit and the lack of a complete section makes it difficult to show whether the stone filling was continuous with the upper filling of Chamber Three. The status and purpose of this pit must therefore remain uncertain. It is too shallow and irregular to have held a stone, but its exclusively ancient contents make it difficult to prove that it results from later disturbance.

Chamber Three

Although it certainly existed as a rectangular chamber, the reconstruction in detail of Chamber Three presents many problems. The first is its size; it is undoubtedly 1.2m wide, but it is uncertain whether it directly adjoined Channel Four (making it 3.5m long) or whether it was separate, a squarer chamber only 2m long. Moreover it seems to to have combined elements of wood as well as stone and it is possible that the stone may have included laid stones rather than orthostats. Finally it is difficult to reconcile the surviving features as revealed by excavation with the situation shown on Hugh Prichard's plan of 1871 where he shows Stone 3, now fallen, standing along the northern side (Prichard 1871 and Fig. 41).

The most important but most unexpected features of this chamber were two circular holes (0.4m in diameter and 0.38m deep) set 1.2m apart at the eastern end. These holes were very neatly cut, with vertical sides and a flat base. They did not have the appearance of stone holes which are normally much more irregular, because few stones are circular, but rather looked as though they had been dug for wooden posts about 0.3m in diameter—a medium size tree trunk. When found, these holes were filled with stones, dropped vertically into them, their tips projecting a little way above the old ground level (Plate XXIX). These stones were certainly not packing stones: they filled the entire hole and the only feasible interpretation is that posts had been carefully removed and the holes filled up with these

stones. Such a thing can only have happened before the posts had rotted.

Projecting over the edge of each 'posthole' was the tip of a large flattish stone, the first of a line of such stones running westward for 2m on the south and 1.6m on the north. At this point the lines are broken by large stones lying transversely across the chamber and the situation beyond is jumbled and confused. These jumbled stones are large and they overlie the shallow pit described above. The largest ones lying across the chamber are not firmly placed upon the floor of the chamber but rest on a few smaller stones. Their status as intentionally placed stones is therefore uncertain, but it is conceivable that they may represent, in some way, the back of the chamber. By contrast the northern and southern lines of stones do appear to be carefully chosen and carefully placed and they could have formed the lowest course of a rough stone wall. The fact that they overlap their 'postholes' in identical fashion would suggest that both were put into position when the posts were standing. If this argument is accepted it means that the posts cannot be dismissed as part of a separate, earlier, structure.

The problem of Stone 3 remains acute. If its present position and Prichard's plan are any guide it should have been standing on top of the large diamond-shaped transverse stone and on the long stone which projects over the 'posthole'. This would have left a gap of 1.6m between it and Stone 4 and a more awkward gap of about 0.4m between it and the putative post at the entrance to Chamber Three. Whether such an insecure seating would have been contrived for an orthostat is another question. There is a gap in which it could have stood just to the north of the line of flat stones, but this would place it outside the line of the chamber (Fig. 47). There is no room for it to have stood to the south of the flat stones. On the south side of the chamber, however, there is a gulley in this position between the stones filling the chamber and the line of flat stones which could then be interpreted as the basal layer of cairn material backing the lost orthostat (Fig. 50). A stone in such a position would not be well aligned with the 'posthole' but the gully, so obvious in plan, is difficult to explain in any other way.

Whatever the nature of the sides of this chamber, the stones lying on its floor would seem to confirm its rectangular shape (Fig. 50). Forward of the transverse slabs they tend to be aligned east-west and they look as if they were placed in position when some form of walling was still present. They rest on a fairly clean subsoil surface but some dark brown soil was found amongst those in the centre of the chamber area and it lapped over the lines of flat stones and penetrated the smaller stones in the area of Chamber Two. The presence of this soil suggests that this chamber had, at the least, been unroofed at an early date (p. 115). The upper layer of filling beneath Stone 3 contained light brown earth and broken stone, a superficial disturbance of the top of the chamber fill after the capstone had slipped, but before Stone 3 had fallen.

To sum up the inevitably inconclusive arguments relating to this chamber, one may say that the postholes at the east end should be contemporary with the laid stones which overlap them, and these stones seem to define the north and south sides of a space about 2m long; that the west end of the chamber may be marked by the large transverse stones, although they are less carefully set than the stones at the side; that Prichard's plan cannot be disregarded since it is correct in respect of other surviving stones, and that therefore the north side of the chamber must have been formed by Stone 3, perhaps standing on top of the laid stones and so aligned with the posts, or perhaps standing, misaligned, to the north. The south side may have been similarly formed with a misaligned orthostat, or one standing on the laid stones.

The jumbled stones to the west do not conform to the width or alignment of the chamber in the same way as the eastern filling and they may thus be judged to lie outside it, a more or less formal blocking between Chambers Four and Three. On this interpretation the back of Chamber Three would either be formed by a precarious orthostat, as the sides, or by rough dry-walling. The roof of this chamber in contrast to Chamber Four, would seem to have been lost at an early stage for soft dark earth had percolated among the stones of its filling. Although the north side, rather surprisingly, survived until after 1871, the south side must have gone much earlier, for this area had not received the attention of treasure seekers in the way the more obvious Chamber Four had done.

Original Contents of the Chamber

The floor of the chamber was clean, there was no sign of bone, pottery, or charcoal trodden into it. However some pieces of human bone were found thrown onto the cairn to the south so it is possible that this chamber had held a burial deposit, but, if so, it must have been very much smaller than that in Chamber Four. It is probable that the stone filling was an intentional, Neolithic, deposit and not the result of destruction; however, nothing was found in it. No flints were found and the five fragments of pottery came from the pit close to Stone 2, a feature which is not strictly relevant to this chamber if one believes that it lies beneath material blocking Chamber Four.

Chamber Two

Virtually no structural features of this chamber survive. A large flat stone very like those in Chamber Three, lies on the appropriate line on the south side, with a cluster of small stones at its eastern end. The chamber area was re-opened and these stones re-examined in 1980, lest another 'posthole' might have been overlooked. Nothing was found; the stones lay directly on the orange clay subsoil. The only other indication of the existence of this chamber was a slight hollow in the subsoil running from Chamber Three through this area. On its line was a small firmly set vertical stone, but this and other small upright stones in the vicinity were far too small to have any structural significance and were probably stones occuring naturally in the drift. On the north side there were very few stones except superficial ones in a light brown soil.

The chamber filling survived slightly better than its sides in that a band of smallish stones could be recognised in its western end, continuing the filling of Chamber Three (Fig. 50). These stones in Chamber Two were smaller, less tightly packed, and were intermixed with the dark brown soil which occurred in patches on the chamber floor. In the eastern half of the chamber this filling became confused with the lowest level of the road whose construction had removed most of the dark brown soil (Fig. 48, third line). The fact that this filling can be recognised abutting that of Chamber Three suggests a continuous structure at this point, in contrast to the break postulated between Chambers Four and Three.

No burnt bone was found in the area of this chamber; the only significant find was the shattered blade of a stone axe which had been burnt (Fig. 52). It was found on the floor of the chamber area and must have been broken *in situ* but this could have happened when the chamber was first destroyed or when the road was built.

Chamber One

The division between Chamber Two and Chamber One is an arbitrary one. The distance of 5m between the 'postholes' and Stone 1 would seem to be too long for a single chamber, so it may be divided approximately in half. This would produce a second chamber 2m long from the 'posthole' to the tip of the flat stone on the south side; judging by the breadth of the filling its width should be the same as Chamber Three, about 1.2m. Chamber One would then have been 2.8m long, but might have been a good deal broader if the positions of Stones 1 and 9 are a true indication of the width of the entrance.

The immense portal stone (1) and the scatter of Neolithic pottery and charcoal trodden into the floor are the best evidence for the existence of this first chamber. So minimal is the evidence that it could be equally consistent with the interpretation of this area as a narrow forecourt, but the term 'chamber' will be retained for convenience. Several small stones were found embedded in the subsoil here at the entrance but they were clearly part of the natural drift, the floor of the chamber having been damaged by the construction of the road which had also removed almost all the soft dark earth. It had survived in a few patches to indicate that it might originally have covered this chamber area as it did the disturbed area to the south. The twenty-seven small sherds and scraps of pottery were scattered within an area of

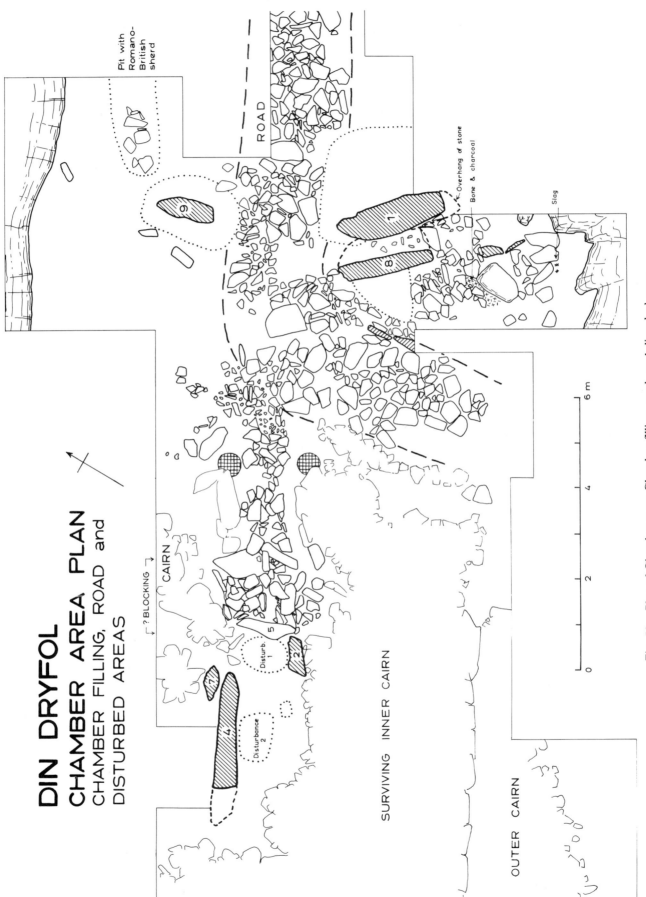

DIN DRYFOL
CHAMBER AREA PLAN
CHAMBER FILLING, ROAD and
DISTURBED AREAS

Fig. 50.   Plan of Chamber area: Chamber filling, road, and disturbed areas.

approximately two square metres and had been deeply trodden into the surface. At one point a small patch of oak charcoal and some bone (both animal and human) had also been trodden in. The area involved corresponds reasonably well to that of the suggested first chamber.

The southern portal stone is both broad and tall, standing at the head of the slope and at slight angle to the line of the chambers. It is tapered, 2.6m broad at the base but only some 0.5m wide at the top. It stands 3.3m high above the old ground level and is set 0.5m into the ground. This is the only stone to be set into a stonehole but the details of the original arrangement have been completely destroyed by a large pit dug around the base of the stone in the nineteenth century. Nothing was found in this hole, but its digging had disturbed part of the road so it post-dates that feature. When Prichard described the site in 1871 it was open, but after 1911 it was refilled.

On the northern side there is no comparable stone. In the 1930s the Royal Commission claimed to have found the hole for the missing stone (RCAHM 1937 xli; 2, no. 3), but excavation of the area in 1970 failed to produce convincing evidence for it. The base of a sizeable stone (9) which the Commission had taken to be a packing stone, was found there but no deep stone hole could be recognised, only the relatively shallow disturbance caused by the Royal Commission investigation itself (Pl.XIV). Stone 9 had been quite a large stone, it was 1.2m long but only 0.35m high. It had a flat top surface as if the upper part of the stone had been sheared off and, if it is really to be considered the northern portal stone, this must have been what happened. A sliver of the back of the stone had been broken off, but it remained in position, a hint of the violence that this stone may have suffered. Even so it is unlikely that it could have matched its companion for size. It stands 2.5m north of Stone 1, a surprisingly wide entrance, if these are the true portal stones.

Immediately behind Stone 1, leaning against it when the excavation began, was another large slab, Stone 8. It was assumed at the outset that this stone was in a derived position, thrown there when the chambers were destroyed. However it was found to be standing on the undisturbed subsoil and therefore its status must be acknowledged to be uncertain. A double portal is not unknown amongst megalithic tombs, but there is no hint of a duplicated portal on the north side and it is possible that Stone 8 belongs, not to the tomb, but to an area of later activity just south of it. Its line is continued by a row of small stones, some of which are later than dark brown soil containing slag, although when first cleared there was a temptation to interpret them as part of a formal front edge to the cairn.

The Front of the Cairn

The northern side of the front of the cairn was virtually bare of stone even when the area was first stripped. When the superficial stones had been removed only one or two small stones were left. Those that stood vertically were noted, but none was more than 0.3m high and it was not possible to produce any convincing edge to the cairn here. Stones observed to the north of the rock ridge (Trench Za, Fig. 43) were investigated in case the cairn had extended beyond the ridge, but they were found to belong to a modern wall. The general configuration of the cairn would suggest that it was bounded on the north by the rock ridge, extending forwards to give the impression of a deep forecourt.

Whether or not this impression of a forecourt was intentional one cannot say. There were no Neolithic features in the area in front of the entrance to the tomb. The pottery was definitely within the area of the putative chamber and, if there had been any blocking in front of the portal it had been entirely removed by a Romano-British pit, by the road, and by the large hole dug in front of Stone 1. The only feature earlier than the road observed in the long eastern trench was a shallow scoop containing dark earth, mixed charcoal, and a scrap of burnt pig bone. It was found in the southern side of the trench, 6m east of Stone 1 and is as likely to be Romano-British as Neolithic.

The front of the cairn on the south side looked more promising. If the line of the Inner Cairn edge is projected it emerges 0.8m south of Stone 1 and it seems inevitable that the gap between the rock and the stone must have been filled in some way by the cairn. Nothing was found in line with Stone 1, but a row of three stones was found, set back a little in line with Stone 8. Two of the stones were vertical, the other leaning against the sloping rock (Fig. 51) and there appeared to be a line, perhaps the southern edge of the cairn, running west from the upper stone. However the first of these upright stones was standing on a layer of reddish soil overlying soft dark brown earth containing slag (Fig. 51 Sections 1 and 2) which must cast doubt upon the Neolithic date of the structure here.

The material between Stones 1 and 8 was difficult to excavate and was not informative. No dark brown soil was found amongst the jumbled stones, but a piece of slag was disovered there. The absence of the soft dark soil might suggest either that it had been dug away or that Stone 8, leaning against Stone 1, had protected this area from the spread of this soil. The second explanation might be the more likely in view of the situation in Fig. 51 Section 2, but it must be admitted that the sequence of events in this area was not satisfactorily resolved.

The Destruction of the Tomb

If the excavation has shown little else it has revealed that the monument had been very severely disturbed on more than one occasion. This destruction began at an early date, judging by a Romano-British sherd from a pit close to Stone 9. It will be argued that the spread of the soft dark brown soil may give an indication of the extent of the disturbance at this time

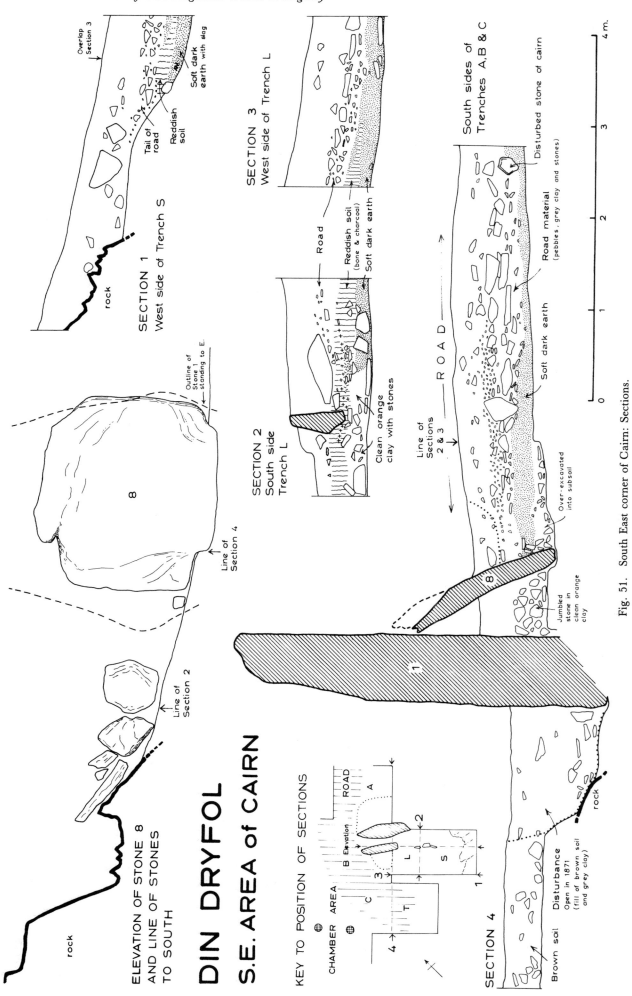

SECTION 1
West side of Trench S

Overlap
Section 3

Soft dark
earth with slag

Tail of
road

Reddish
soil

rock

SECTION 3
West side of Trench L

SECTION 2
South side
Trench L

Road

Reddish soil
(bone & charcoal)

Soft dark earth

Clean orange
clay with stones

ELEVATION OF STONE 8
AND LINE OF STONES
TO SOUTH

8

Line of
Section 4

Line of
Section 2

Outline of
Stone 1
standing to E.

rock

DIN DRYFOL
S.E. AREA of CAIRN

KEY TO POSITION OF SECTIONS

ROAD

CHAMBER AREA

A

B Elevation

C

L

S

T

2

3

1

4

South sides of
Trenches A, B & C

Disturbed stone of cairn

Road material
(pebbles, grey clay and stones)

Soft dark earth

Line of
Sections
2 & 3

ROAD

Over-excavated
into subsoil

8

Jumbled
stone in
clean orange
clay

1

rock

SECTION 4

Disturbance
Open in 1871
(fill of brown soil
and grey clay)

Brown soil

Fig. 51. South East corner of Cairn: Sections.

0 1 2 3 4 m.

when the first two chambers would seem to have been removed. The next serious phase of destruction involved the building of a road up the slope and across the site of Chambers One and Two. Finally more limited, but no less serious, disturbance took place in the surviving chambers and on the southern edge of the Inner Cairn.

Romano-British Disturbance

The dating of this early period of destruction hangs upon the identification of a single abraded sherd of Samian. This sherd has been identified by Mr George Boon of the National Museum of Wales as part of a Dragendorf 37 bowl of South Gaulish manufacturer and Late Flavian date. This is the only closely dateable object found. It comes from the fill of an elongated pit just east of Stone 9. This shallow pit had a filling of stone and dark soil and contained many very large lumps of charcoal, a few scraps of burnt bone, a flint scraper (DD.Wa.1.) and a utilised flake as well as the Samian sherd. Its purpose is unknown; the large lumps of charcoal might suggest some limited industrial acitivity, but there was no evidence for burning in the pit itself. The bone was mainly unidentifiable but included two fragments of human rib; the charcoal was mixed, chiefly oak, hazel, alder, and willow, a combination found with deposits of slag elsewhere on the site.

In the area of denuded cairn in the vicinity of this pit, three rectangular whetstones were found, together with some pieces of slag. The lumps of slag, though not of themselves closely dateable, are similar to those from Din Lligwy (Baynes 1908, 198-98). Several Anglesey hut sites have produced evidence for metal-working, and it is reasonable to suggest that the slag at Din Dryfol belongs to this Romano-British horizon when the ruins of the tomb may have provided shelter for some small-scale industry. Lumps of slag were found in many parts of the excavation, notably in Trenches T and S and between Stones 1 and 8, in the vicinity of the pit near Stone 9, in the upper layer of the cairn in Trench D, and from the material of the later road above Chambers One and Two. It was also found in Trench Z and at the west end of the cairn, associated with charcoal and burnt animal bone in Trench O.

In trenches S and T the slag was found in the layer of soft dark soil which formed an important horizon at the east end of the monument. The origin of this soil is obscure, its colour was a rich dark chocolate brown and its texture was very soft and loamy (see Appendix IV). It had a very high organic content and phosphorous level, suggestive of human interference. It was unlike the buried topsoil beneath the west end of the cairn and would seem to represent an accumulation or introduction of compost-like material over the exposed stones and other disturbed areas during some phase of considerable human activity. In Trenches S, L, and T it formed a fairly consistent layer resting directly on the orange subsoil. In Trenches B, C, X, and J it occurred at the

same level, but only in patches, and the evidence of the sections (Fig. 48 third line) suggests that this was because it had been largely removed by the construction of the road. In Trenches D, E and β it was found amongst the basal layer of cairn stones (Fig. 48 second line). Although some stones appeared also to be set on it, the larger stones could be seen to rest directly on the orange subsoil, so the dark soil cannot be explained as a pre-cairn humus layer, which in any case it did not resemble in texture, being too loose and soft. It is possible that it blew over the cairn from a source somewhere in the area of Chambers One and Two which must have been already destroyed. It was found amongst, but not under, the stones filling Chamber Three, presumably then at least partly ruined; but it did not blow into Chamber Four which must have been protected by its sidestones and capstones at that time, nor did it reach across the cairn as far as Trench M. This soil did not contain dateable objects; only charcoal and scraps of burnt bone were found in it amongst the cairn stones. The bone may have been derived from the chambers, for most of it is human. In Trench S the dark soil contained a lump of slag and was overlain by a spread of reddish soil containing three fragments of burnt human bone and a fair amount of mixed charcoal. The red soil ran under a large flat slab and one of the stones of a sort of false facade to the cairn (see p. 113), suggesting that some rough structure had been built here, although there was no formal hearth (Fig. 51 Section 2). In this corner of the cairn it could also be shown (Fig. 51 Section 4) that the dark soil had been cut into by the foundation of the road, so it may be stratigraphically located between the destruction of Chambers One and Two and the building of the road. If the presence of slag may be used as an indicator of Romano-British date, it would seem that this is the period of maximum destruction at the east end of the tomb.

The presence of slag may also be used to link the disturbance at the east end with the activity at the west end, revealed in Trenches O and R (Fig. 45 and Pl. XVII). Just beneath a rock outcrop there was a hollowed area without stones, filled with dark soil (dirtied by charcoal, not the rich organic soil of the east end), and containing charcoal, burnt animal bone, a lump of slag, and a small piece of daub (R5). Stones in the northern half of the trench were laid in such a way that they might be interpreted as the foundation of a very rough wall which, with the outcrop, might have formed a smaller shelter (p. 103 and Fig. 45). However the hollow contained no formal hearth and there were no incontrovertible signs of structure. The only other finds from the area were a core trimming flake and three pieces of waste flint from the topsoil in Trench V.

The only securely dated Romano-British activity at the site is the digging of the pit near Stone 9, but it is reasonable to link with this a good deal of other damage, notably the destruction of Chambers One and Two, and part of Three. The distribution of slag would suggest that there was some small-scale metalworking here and *ad hoc* shelters would seem to have been contrived in the ruins for this purpose. The valley of the Gwna immediately around Din Dryfol was, in the first few centuries AD, perhaps more densely populated than at any other period. Prichard records (1871, 301) that "there is scarcely an old tenant on either side of this part of the Gwna who has not a history to relate of intricate stone walls cleared away from his meadows, of hut-foundations and floors broken up to make room for the plough, or querns or other wrought stones consigned in fragments to his drains, and of smaller antiquities long ago presented to friends or otherwise disposed of." Good records survive of at least four hut groups within 1km of the tomb (Prichard 1871, RCAHM 1937, 2, nos. 5 and 6) and a copper cake was found in a spring nearby (Prichard 1871, 308), underlining the connection with metalworking. It is not surprising, therefore, that the major phase of destruction should belong to this period.

The Road (Plan Fig. 50, Section Fig. 48).

The excavation had been undertaken because it was believed that stone blocking remained in position in front of the entrance to the tomb. This belief was shown to be unfounded for the stones belonged to a road running up the gradual eastern approach to the ledge and turning across the site of the front chambers towards the steep path up to the top of the rock. This road must be linked to the track from Plas Bach which crosses the Gwna just on the other side of Dinas, but this north-westerly spur is not shown on any map. Both eighteenth century estate maps (UCNW Bodorgan 1579 and Penrhos II. 773) show the road from Plas Bach and the river crossing, but there is no sign of a continuation round the north west side of Dinas rock. At that time the road turned north to Dindryfwl mill at approximately SH 398 725, as the present footpath does now. The excavated road is well made and its building must have represented a considerable effort, but its purpose is not obvious. It simply dies away after turning towards the cliff. It may perhaps have been used for removing stone from the cliffs although there is no positive evidence that they have been quarried. A cart could certainly not be taken to the top of the hill and a road would not be necessary for those on foot, nor for animals.

Half the width of the road was excavated for a length of 17m east of Stone 1. It had an average width of 2.5m and had been carefully built with a kerb of larger stones for most of its length; its foundation was a layer of flat slabs with two further layers of stone above them on the crest of the hill. The top surface was finished with a spread of small pebbles. This construction was neatest at the bottom of the slope (Fig. 48, bottom line), but the pebble layer was thickest where it had reached the crest and turned across the line of the chambers. The road had no formal end, it simply died away in Trench T

without any sign that it had been deliberately destroyed (Fig. 50).

The date of the road is uncertain but it is most likely to belong to the late eighteenth or early nineteenth centuries. Stratigraphically it post-dates the dark soil and predates the pit in front of Stone 1 which was open in 1871. This pit can be seen (Fig. 46) to bite into the side of the road and several larger stones above the pebble layer (Fig. 48) have been thrown from this disturbance onto the surface of the road. Presumably the road was not a visible feature in 1871, for Prichard does not mention it. Slag was found in some quantity in the make-up of the road in Trenches C and A, also a flint flake, a hammerstone (Fig. 52), and a plough pebble.

Eighteenth to Early Twentieth Century Disturbances

Chamber Four was first dug into before the capstone had slipped or the south side stone had been removed (Figs. 48 and 49). It is possible that the backstone and the western capstone had already gone by then and entry was made from the west end, for Chamber Three has not been so extensively dug. Two pits (Disturbances 1 and 2) were dug through the floor of Chamber Four, pits which contained glass and sherds probably of eighteenth century date. Joining sherds showed them to be essentially contemporary, though the section suggests a sequence. Subsequently a more comprehensive disturbance (3) took place, involving the breaking of a lot of stone and probably the removal of the south stone. All this must have taken place before 1871, by which time the southern stone had certainly gone and the surviving capstone had slipped. The pit in front of Stone 1 had also been dug shortly before this date and remained open until 1911. There may have been some other, unidentified, excavations into the cairn south of Chamber Four—the origin of Prichard's story of a stupendous cromlech in this area. Stone 3 did not collapse until after 1871, its fall perhaps due to some digging beside it.

The deep but narrow disturbance along the line of the Inner Cairn edge in Trench β may be dated to the period 1890-1918 by the Kynoch Gastight cartridge case found at the bottom of the hole close to Stone 10. Since the monument was placed under official guardianship and protection in 1911 one must assume that the digging belongs to the early part of the period! It is thought that this 'investigator' must have been chasing a line of stones whose tips were just visible on the surface, though the ferocity of the destruction would seem to suggest more than just idle curiosity.

The date of the modern wall around the ledge is unknown. A piece of glass and some slag were found in its core but they do not provide close dating. Only the basal level survived; the rest had probably fallen to the bottom of the slope where its modern equivalent now stands. It had been quite a well-made wall, 0.8-1.2m wide at the base with an inner and outer face and a rubble core (Pl. XVIII). At the west end where it was cut into the slope it only had an outer face (Fig. 45). It is unlikely that the construction of this wall did much damage to the monument, but it caused some trouble to the excavation since it was thought at first to be the edge of the cairn—hence, the number of small trenches which trace its line (Figs. 43-45).

The final period of destruction was not evidenced in the excavation, but it was reported by Messrs Jones that their predecessors at Fferam Rhosydd in the earlier part of this century had removed many cartloads of stone from the western end of the ledge.

Din Dryfol Chapter 3: The Finds

The finds from the excavations at Din Dryfol were not plentiful, but they were sufficient to reinforce and confirm the conclusions that could be drawn from the structural evidence given in Chapter 2. They fall into three groups: the prehistoric material, pottery and flints coming from the chambers and from probably derived positions in the cairn and disturbed areas; a loosely related group of Romano-British material from areas of disturbance, and a few modern objects which help to date the latest phase of destruction.

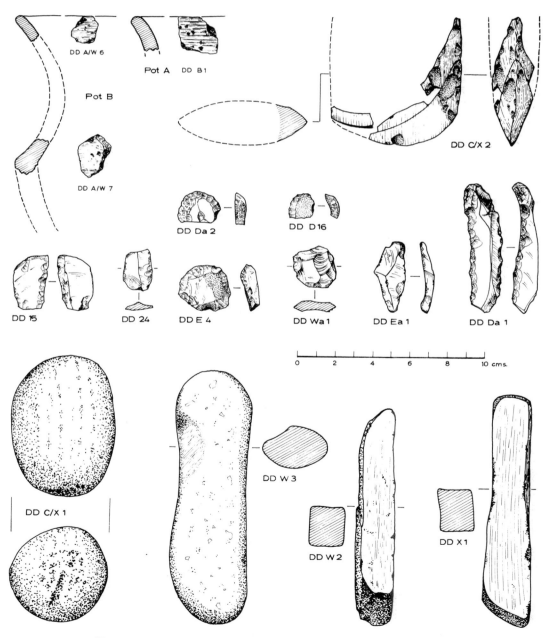

Fig. 52.   Prehistoric and Romano-British(?) Finds from Din Dryfol.

Neolithic Finds

Pottery

The twenty-seven pieces of Neolithic pottery found on the floor of Chamber One constituted the most important group of material from the site, however they amount to only 40gm in weight and no pot can be fully reconstructed from them, even on paper. The largest sherd is less than 600mm^2 in area. The fabric, however, is distinctive and the shape is that of an open shouldered bowl. Three different pots may be distinguished by slight variations in colour and surface treatment but in terms of distribution they are intermingled.

All three are without grit with a slightly vesicular texture and well-burnished surface, the burnishing done with a narrow instrument with a rounded point. The average thickness is 9mm; some sherds are 10mm and others 7mm thick but the significance of this cannot be judged since their position on the pot is unknown. All are grey/brown throughout and have been well fired. Pot A, represented by eleven sherds, may be distinguished by having both inner and outer surfaces well burnished; Pot B has only the outer surface burnished, a surface which is a little paler than Pot A. The presence of two everted rims and some concave sherds show that both these pots were open shouldered bowls (Fig. 52). The shape of Pot C is less certain since only six tiny sherds survive. It is thinner than the others and has a matt surface.

Analysis (Part I, Chapter 7) has shown that they indeed contain no stone grit but the voids in the matrix are distinctively rhomboid in shape and it is possible that the clay was originally tempered with calcite. Although almost half of the pottery from Trefignath is macroscopically vesicular in texture and includes no visible grits, rhomboid voids are found only in two of the earlier pots from that site—Vessels D and M. The samples from Din Dryfol were unfortunately too small for heavy mineral analysis so no firm statement can be made about the origin of the silt used. However the comparable Vessel D from Trefignath was analysed and its components suggested that it might have been made on Ynys Gybi, but could not have come from the Din Dryfol area. On the assumption that the technical trick of calcite gritting is a significant link, it may be tentatively suggested that the Class 3 pots (which include all the Din Dryfol sherds) were not made in the Gwna valley. Pot B (sherd Y) contains a little grog, not present in A (sherd X), and is thus linked more closely, by both Principal Component and Link Cluster Analysis, to the Trefignath material (Table 12 and Figs 32-34).

The five sherds from the pit near Stone 2 have the same gritless, vesicular fabric as those from Chamber One, but they probably do not belong to the same pots. Two pots may be represented: Pot D (three sherds) with a thickness of only 5mm and a well-burnished outer surface, and Pot E, two paler, rather thicker sherds with a looser texture. Pot D was

analysed (sherd Z) and the results confirm a close similarity, but not identity, to Pot A (Sherd X).

The three scraps of pottery from amongst the cairn material in Trench B are less vesicular than the others but they are so abraded that no useful comment can be made about them, except that they belong to the same broad Neolithic family as the rest of the pottery.

That family is, in Welsh terms, the Irish Sea Group (Lynch 1976, 65), pots which use a virtually gritless clay with a loose vesicular texture and good surface treatment, usually a horizontal burnishing. The predominant shape is the open shouldered bowl with a sharp but simple carination and a light everted rim. Characteristic assemblages are those from Clegyr Boia in Pembrokeshire (Williams 1952) and Dyffryn Ardudwy in Merioneth (Powell 1973). The pottery from Din Dryfol has all the most important features of this group and, if it is believed that the typological development of this style is from a lighter to a heavier rim and towards a slacker profile, then the Din Dryfol material with its very thin rims, should be among the earlier examples. The closest comparison in rim form, shape, and standard of finish lies with the material from Dyffryn Ardudwy, a group which unfortunately is undated, though it has been judged to be early.

It is obvious that these undecorated shouldered bowls from Wales belong to a more widespread ceramic family: pots made in imitation of leather containers and known in eastern and north-eastern England by the term 'Grimston Ware' (Piggott 1954, 114) and Ireland by various sub-style names—Dunmurray, Ballymarlagh, Lyles Hill, Lough Gur Class I (Case 1961). The elegant, but essentially simple and skeuomorphic design of these pots and their long period of popularity make it difficult to construct a universally acceptable historical explanation of their similarity and distribution. There are those who stress the broadest family relationships and speak of 'Grimston-Lyles Hill Ware' without attempting fine regional or chronoligical divisions (Smith 1974, 106-08); there are those who emphasise the minor stylistic differences and build on them quite elaborate theories of population movement to and fro between the regions (Scott 1978). The present writer would lean towards the former view while recognising that regional groups are present within this material and may, when conjoined with other strands of evidence, illuminate the history of ideas and folk movements within these islands. Thus the Welsh facies of this family may be termed the 'Irish Sea Group' because it is but one of many connections between Wales and Ireland at this time, while specific links with eastern England are less easy to discern. The term, however, should not be taken as implying no contact eastwards, or a priority in Wales or in Ireland, because as yet the chronology on both sides is too broad.

The pottery from Din Dryfol cannot hope to resolve these problems and so wider issues have been left aside. Comparisons within Wales have been quoted and some firmer conclusions may be ventured within the context of Anglesey alone.

Within Anglesey the obvious comparison is with the material from beneath the cairn at Trefignath, pottery which has a date of approximately 3100 bc (HAR 3932). This assemblage has been described in detail elsewhere in this volume and here it is only necessary to point up the similarities and contrasts with the sherds from Din Dryfol. At both sites the predominant shape is the open shouldered bowl but at Trefignath the reconstructed pots (eg E and L) suggest a rather straighter neck with less precisely worked rims. The impression of rather clumsier workmanship is reinforced by a study of the surface treatment; there are no burnished sherds at Trefignath of the quality of those from Din Dryfol and the vesicular wares have only a smooth matt surface, which in many instances has become badly eroded. This difference in quality within what is obviously a similar potting tradition is undoubtedly due to the different nature of the assemblages; that from Trefignath is a domestic group while the pots from Din Dryfol had been chosen for deposition within a tomb. The domestic nature of the Trefignath pottery is emphasised by the greater variety of shapes and fabrics present. Vessels H and J seem to be small hemispherical cups made from heavily gritted clays. Not surprisingly analysis has shown that all this domestic assemblage could have been made locally on Ynys Gybi, whereas the pottery used ritually at Din Dryfol had been brought perhaps for some distance, though probably not from outside the island.

The most specific connection between the two sites is the possible use of calcite grit, inferred from the distinctive rhomboid shapes of the voids left by its dissolution. These voids were seen in all the sherds analysed from Din Dryfol (representing Pots A, B, and D) but only in Vessels D and M from Trefignath (pp. 69-70). Both these pots came from the southern end of the latter site and are firmly stratified in the old ground surface underlying the cairn, thus they are associated with the earliest activity on the site and the radiocarbon date of 3100 bc. No typological comparison can be made with Vessel M whose shape is unknown, but Vessel D was very probably an open bowl with a slight shoulder and an everted, or possibly small rolled rim. As such it is comparable to the pots from Din Dryfol and, it is interesting that Vessel D has a rather more carefully finished surface than most of the other pots at Trefignath, although it does not have a true burnish. Whether or not the technical trick of calcite gritting would indicate a common origin for the Din Dryfol pots and these two from Trefignath, it does add a more tangible strand to the links between the two assemblages which otherwise must rely on rather subjective judgements.

Stone Implements

The most interesting stone implement from the excavation is the broken blade section of a polished stone axe (DD.C/X.2). It was found on the old ground surface in the area of Chamber Two, a part of the monument which had been very thoroughly disturbed, a disturbance during which the axe had been shattered since four fragments of it were picked up close together. However the butt is not present and it is likely that it was already a broken implement when placed in the tomb. The axe had been burnt at some stage.

The surviving pieces suggest an axe 67mm across and perhaps 25mm thick with a pointed oval section (Fig. 52). The blade had been chipped by use but remains sharp. The blade area had been beautifully polished, but flaking scars are still visible on the side. The rock has been identified by thin section (AN 58) as a siliceous crystal tuff (W. J. Phillips per C. H. Houlder *pers.comm.*). This is not a common rock type but may be found, for example, in Lower Paleozoics in Wales, the Lake District, and other parts of western Britain. The axe is not a recognised factory product and its origin cannot be pinpointed.

This is the only stone axe to have been found in a megalithic tomb in North Wales (Lynch 1969, 150, 161, 166). This is perhaps surprising in view of the quantity of axes made in the area and the relatively frequent discovery of axes inside tombs in Scotland and Ireland where they have sometimes been placed in obviously significant positions (eg. Doey's Cairn, Dunloy (Evans 1938, 63)).

The excavations produced seventy pieces of waste flint of which six showed some signs of use. All except three were rather poor quality pebble flint such as may be picked up on Anglesey beaches. The material was widely scattered and pieces were found in most of the trenches opened. The bulk of it came from the cairn south of the chambers (twenty-seven pieces) and the disturbed fill of Chamber Four (eighteen pieces). The badly denuded area of cairn to the north of the chambers produced only two pieces; eleven were found in the make-up of the road to the east of the tomb and eleven came from the trenches on the ledge west of the chambers, most of these (eight) being found in Trenches O, R, and V, where there was evidence for disturbance, probably Romano-British in date.

Only eight implements were found. They have a distribution similar to that of the waste flints. Three came from the cairn south of the chambers, four from Chamber Four and one from an area of Romano-British disturbance. However, most of these are of much better quality flint, only one of them is obviously a beach pebble. The implements consist of two worked blades (both broken), four scrapers, a large fabricator and a smaller pointed piece which has been used as a strike-a-light at both ends. None of these tools is especially diagnostic either of date or cultural context and all are quite appropriate to a Neolithic tomb. The fabricator and strike-a-light are types which are thought to have a generally later Neolithic context, but thick rods of fabricator type have been found at Hembury so they are unlikely to be confined to the later horizon (Piggott 1954, 78 and 359).

The nature of the implements may be best appreciated from the drawing (Fig. 52) and they need little individual description. DD.15, a parallel sided blade with steep working and a little gloss on the dorsal ridge and shallower working on the underside, was found amongst the cairn material in Trench β. The smaller blade, DD.24, comes from the same context. The well-made scraper, DD.E.4, comes from a hollow in the cairn material close to the back of Chamber Four from which it might have been thrown out. It is made from a dark glossy flint with a white chalky cortex and is very typical of Neolithic scrapers. DD.Da.2 is made from a pale grey flint, has been slightly burnt and the resultant pitting has obscured the working. It comes from the pit under the capstone in Chamber Four. The tiny scraper (DD.D.16) also comes from the disturbed fill of Chamber Four. It might be a Mesolithic survival since it is the only implement to be made from a beach pebble. The strike-a-light (DD.Ea.1) comes from the same context; all the edges have been chipped by use and both ends have been rubbed smooth. The fabricator (DD.Da.1), made on a thick curved flake of maroon/brown flint, has been heavily worked from both faces on each side but does not show much sign of wear on the ends. DD.Wa.1, a very battered piece of speckled grey flint, seems to have been part of a scraper. It was found with another piece of utilised flint in the pit which produced the sherd of Romano-British pottery.

Burnt Bone

The eighteen small samples of bone were kindly examined by Dr T. P. O'Connor, whose report is given in full in Appendix I.

Of forty-two fragments from the disturbed fill of Chamber Four, twelve could, with certainty, be identified as human. The remains of two individuals were present; an adult represented by six fragments of long bone cortex, and an immature individual (apparently sub-adult rather than juvenile) represented by six fragments of parietal bone.

Bone from disturbed areas near the entrance to the tomb included both human and animal bones (sheep, sheep/goat, pig, and cattle or horse), but most of the identifiable scraps from amongst the cairn stones immediately south of Chambers Three and Four were human. On the other hand all the identifiable bone from the far end of the cairn was animal, and may be confidently assigned to a later period.

Romano-British Material
Pottery

The only incontrovertible Romano-British piece is a single sherd of very abraded pink pottery from the elongated pit close to Stone 9. It is a small piece, 30 × 35mm and only 4mm thick; both surfaces have been lost, and there is only a hint of a small beaded rim. However it has been recognised by Mr George Boon of the National Museum of Wales as part of a bowl of Dragendorf Form 37 of South Gaulish manufacture and Late Flavian date—that is, late first century AD.

Stone Implements

A piece of a possible quern came from Trench S in an area with dark soil, slag, and burnt bone, a corner of the cairn which seems to have been the scene of Romano-British activity (see p. 115). It has no obvious features of a quern except that it is a suitable stone, perhaps foreign to the district (a coarse granite with much mica) with one very flat, smooth surface. It is too small for useful comment on its shape, except to say that it cannot be the top half of a beehive quern.

An oval hammerstone was found in the make-up of the road above Chamber Two (DD.C/X.1 Fig. 52). It is a well-cemented sandstone with signs of abrasion at either end. It is not an artefact in the true sense but it is similar to hammerstones found in the nearby hut circles and now in the Plas Bach collection in Bangor Museum (Griffith 1892, nos. 1 and 3).

Three whetstones were found in the area of the denuded cairn just north of Chambers One and Two (Fig. 52). All three are elongated pebbles; only one has been much used and since that comes from the topsoil it is possibly a relatively modern scythe sharpener. The date of the others is also uncertain since they have no firm stratigraphic position. DD.W.2, a rectangular piece of fine sandstone, was found close to the old ground surface, but in light brown soil. Only one side shows any sign of use. DD.W.3 is a beach pebble of fine grained igneous rock. It has a natural hollow which shows some sign of artificial wear. DD.X.1 has been sliced to a rectangular shape, and has been much whetted on all four sides. It is made from a smooth, fine grained siltstone and is possibly modern.

Slag

Slag was found in many parts of the excavation and it has been argued elsewhere (pp. 115-16) that it probably belongs to the Romano-British period. Analysis (Appendix III) has shown that it cannot be positively identified as the residue of iron-working, but that this is its most likely origin. 1.7 kg was found. Most of it came from the eastern end of the cairn where, significantly, it was found in the soft dark soil which had covered the destroyed chamber there. The largest quantities were, however, found in Trenches S and T, an area of heavy disturbance, and in the make-up of the later road. It was also found occasionally in the upper levels of the surviving cairn but none was found in the fill of Chambers Three and Four. A single piece was found in Trench O at the western end of the cairn.

Charcoal (see Appendix II)

The slag was often associated with charcoal. It was seldom possible to distinguish between Neolithic and Romano-British charcoal, but the results seem to suggest that the earlier material was predominantly oak and hazel, whereas the later charcoal included a mixture of many species. Alder, hazel, willow, and oak were a common combination in disturbed areas, with blackthorn, cherry, birch, and heather or bilberry (the latter more likely in view of the modern vegetation) occurring occasionally.

Burnt Bone

Much of the bone from disturbed areas probably came originally from the chambers since it included scraps of human bone, but the burnt bone from Trench L and Trench O (at the west end) is unlikely to have come from that source. The seventeen fragments from Trench L were mainly unidentifiable but included six pieces of rib which might be human. All the identifiable pieces from Trench O were sheep or sheep/goat. They had been burnt to a high temperature, perhaps food bones accidentally reburnt in an 'industrial' hearth.

Modern Material

Modern finds were not plentiful, but some of them are significant because they enable certain disturbances to be dated. The most important find in this connection is the Kynoch Gastight cartridge case from the edge of the Inner Cairn. Enquiry with the makers elicited the information that this type was made between 1890 and 1918. The two sherds of brown glazed crock from Chamber Four are joining sherds from the same pot. It cannot be closely dated, but is considered by Mr Peter Davey (*pers. comm.*) to be Buckley Ware, probably of eighteenth century date since the fabric is thinner and finer than the nineteenth century material. The joining sherds come from the oval pit beneath the capstone and the large rectangular pit in Chamber Four, and show that these two disturbances were contemporary.

The quartz 'plough pebble' from the surface of the road could have been brought in as road metalling and is therefore not directly relevant to the date of the road. The practice of pressing pebbles into the sole of a plough to protect the wood from wear is known from several parts of Europe during the twelfth to sixteenth centuries (Fenton 1962-63; Lerche 1970). In Wales it is thought that the use of pebbles was superseded by the use of iron nails towards the end of the Middle Ages so that these characteristically worn stones should be of broadly mediaval date (*pers. comm.* Dr Ilid Anthony and staff of St. Fagans Museum). It is not impossible for the road to be mediaeval, disused and overgrown before the eighteenth century estate maps were drawn up, but it is more likely to be later. In any case the position of the plough pebble amongst the surface metalling does not provide good dating evidence.

Din Dryfol, Chapter 4: Discussion

In very broad terms the interpretation of the monument is not difficult. It is an example of the monumental stone tombs built during the earlier Neolithic in many parts of western Europe and Britain. The long cairn, the architectural emphasis on the entrance with its tall portal(s), and the series of simple rectangular chambers are all features which can be found in various combinations in the northern part of the Irish Sea province. The neutral term 'Long Grave' may usefully be retained to describe this rather basic local member of the family which includes Clyde Tombs, Court Cairns, and Portal Dolmens. The pottery, fragments of five different bowls, also belongs to a widely distributed Irish Sea tradition.

The interpretation of the structure in detail, however, and its history of building present several difficulties and its damaged state prevents their conclusive solution. The problem centres upon whether the line of chambers was built as a single unit or whether it may be broken down into two or even three separate phases of activity. The significant points in this argument concern the posts removed from the entrance to Chamber Three, the stones removed during the destruction of the Inner Cairn edge at the end of the last Century, and the status of the jumbled stones to the east of Chamber Four.

The Tomb as a Single Unit

The strongest argument for this view is the position of the tomb in relation to the ledge on which it stands. Stone 1 stands just at the head of the sloping approach; with the entrance centrally placed between two rock ridges, the builders would thus have exploited to the full the natural advantages of the site. By comparison the position of the entrance to Chamber Three lacks definition. Such arguments, however, are subjective and it is difficult to know how much weight should be given to them.

As a single unit the tomb would be a very large one, not so much in the number of chambers (probably four) but in the scale of these chambers, stretching for a distance of 12.5m. However, apparently unitary monuments of this length are to be found in Scotland (Clettraval, Uist 12 (Henshall 1972, 616)), the north of Ireland (Moytirra East, Co. Sligo (De Valera 1960, Pl. V)), and the Isle of Man Cashtal yn Ard (Piggott 1954, 156)), so that size alone is no argument against a single period of building. Such long chambers normally have some formal division between the compartments. At Din Dryfol there is no surviving evidence on this point. It is normal for the septal or jambs to be firmly set because of their structural role, but here one cannot be certain that they would have been embedded. The stones apparently blocking Chamber Four would mean that the end chamber could scarcely have been used in the same way as the others, even if it had been constructed at the same time.

The Tombs as Two Units

There are several arguments which can be brought forward to suggest that the monument may be broken down into two units; Chambers Three and Four built first, with Chambers One and Two added at a slightly later date.

The fact that the posts which must have stood at the entrance to Chamber Three had not rotted *in situ*, but had been removed and their holes carefully filled in, shows that they must have been fully accessible. Furthermore, this change of plan must have occurred during the lifetime of an exposed timber, not more than a hundred years or so after they were set up.

The restricted and specific nature of the modern disturbance of the cairn edge just south of these postholes is also relevant. It has been argued above (p. 100) that these holes were dug by someone who was chasing a line of stones whose tips must have shown on the surface. It may be suggested, therefore, that two kerbstones stood between Stones 10 and 11 and that others had stood between Stone 11 and the postholes, forming a front edge or facade to the Inner Cairn.

This interpretation would envisage a primary monument with a chamber divided into two compartments set in a long straight-sided cairn which had an edge defined by large stones, either laid or upright, which ran up to Stone 11, then turned north to provide a front to the cairn abutting tall posts which formed the entrance to the tomb. Such a combination of stone and wood would have been unusual but the general design could be matched in many areas, though the double compartment would have been rare in Wales itself.

Before the entrance posts had rotted they were removed and one may imagine that this was done when Chamber Two was built. Since we know nothing of the structure of Chamber Two, except

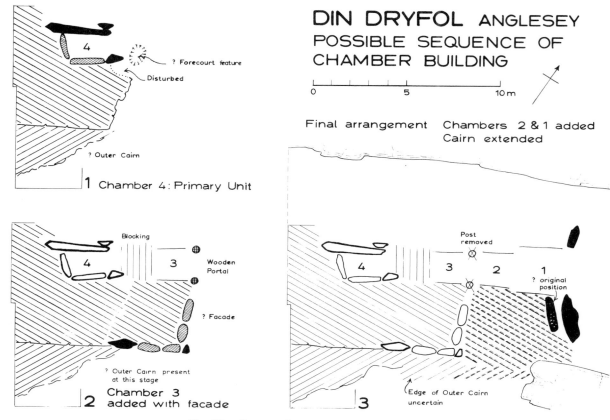

Fig. 53. Suggested sequence of construction.

that it abutted directly onto Chamber Three, we cannot know why this should have been thought necessary, but it does indicate that the interval between the primary tomb and its extension was not a long one. The cairn would also have been extended, engulfing the earlier front (or façade if it warranted that name) but unfortunately very little of that added cairn survives. Its wholesale destruction might suggest that it was more attractive to later pillagers, and this might be another argument for a difference in date. The same might be said of the differential destruction of the two groups of chambers, but both these points are speculative since so little of either remains.

It is questionable whether the Outer Cairn material should assigned to the later phase. When the cairn was extended eastwards was it also widened? Structurally it is obvious that the Outer Cairn material was laid against the edge of the Inner Cairn but it is not quite so certain that this edge was ever designed to be exposed. Moreover the relationship of the Outer Cairn material to the rock ridges on either side would suggest that it had been part of the original design. The absence of cairn material south of Stone 11 precludes a satisfactory answer to this question.

The Tomb as Three Units
It is possible to argue that the primary unit described above could itself be divided into two chambers of different date. There are certainly differences in the

construction of Chambers Three and Four, not only the use of wooden entrance posts in Three, but also the probable use of laid stones. Moreover the height (2m) of Chamber Four could not have been matched by Chamber Three. Even if Stone 3 was propped on the laid stones it would only have been 1.40m high.

The difficulties of understanding the junction of Chambers Three and Four have already been described (p. 107). These difficulties were partly the result of poor excavation and partly the inadequacy of the evidence. Since Stone 5, originally interpreted as a septal, was found to lie at a high level, one view of this junction might be that there was no formal division between the two parts of the chamber. Another view might be more radical, claiming that any communication between the two was completely blocked and that they are essentially separate structures. In this view, the pit near Stone 2 would be a forecourt feature in front of Chamber Four and the jumbled stones, including 5, would be a blocking. Chamber Three would then have been built in front of this blocking, the transverse slabs being the base of its back wall. This would give a chamber size of 2m × 1.20m.

Support for this view might be sought in a study of the Inner Cairn. There is a change in the nature of its edge approximately opposite Stone 2 and the stones of the eastern part of the Inner Cairn are smaller than those of the west. However there is no formal demarcation to the change in stone size, which does not correspond exactly with either the change from laid to upright kerbstones, or the assumed front of Chamber Four.

Mr J. G. Scott, who has most kindly read this report, has suggested an alternative interpretation which would divorce the wooden posts from the stone chambers altogether. In his view the two posts might have seen as part of a porch to a mortuary structure whose eastern and western ends were defined by posts set in the shallow pit just east of Stone 2 and in the deeper pit of uncertain date at the west end of Chamber Four. This wholly wooden structure would then have been replaced by the stone Chamber Four with 'Chamber Three' as a narrow, dry-built forecourt partially blocked at its inner end and extending forward to the position of the demolished porch. Thus he would see the cairn belonging to a two-unit structure, as described above but those units being a chamber (with the burial deposit) and a forecourt (without burials), not a double chamber. He would agree that Chambers Two and One must be an addition and that at that time the eastern half of his forecourt might have been incorporated as part of the new sequence of chambers.

The present writer is loth the accept this interpretation because she feels that the precisely positioned stones overlapping the postholes demonstrate the contemporaneity of the two structural forms and that, if the jumbled stones are accepted as blocking, they cut across any link between Chambers Four and Three. Nor does she feel that the shallow pits are likely to be postholes since they contrast markedly with the others. However the evidence on none of these points is conclusive and therefore as many alternative interpretations as are feasible should be rehearsed.

Nevertheless, in spite of the uncertainties which attach to many points, the preferences of the writer may be seen in the sequence outlined in Fig. 53, in which the first two structures are single chambers, the one quite orthodox, the second very unusual in construction and associated with a quite monumental straight facade. The interval between the first two phases is unknown, but that between phases 2 and 3 must have been short, though the evidence for the existence of this later interval is much the more convincing.

The dating of megalithic tombs is a notoriously difficult problem. Comparison of building styles provides only a very broad chronology and the surviving contents may come from an unhelpfully long period of use. Two conclusions may be drawn from the pottery at Din Dryfol. Firstly there is no essential difference between the sherds from the primary and tertiary units, suggesting only a relatively short interval between phases 1 and 2, as well as 2 and 3, where, in any case, the structural evidence demands a rapid sequence. Secondly, because the distribution of the pottery near the entrance is restricted to the putative area of Chamber One, there is no reason to suggest that it belongs to a period of pre-tomb activity, and it may therefore be used to provide a *terminus ante quem* for the building of this chamber and, more firmly still, for the earlier units. Finely-made, undecorated shouldered bowls are normally considered to belong to the earlier Neolithic (Powell 1973, 44-46), though it must be admitted that their currency was a long one (Savory 1980, 221). However the simple, everted rim, very well burnished surfaces and, in particular, the technical similarity to the dated pottery from Trefignath, all combine to suggest that a date of approximately 3,000 bc would be appropriate for the construction and use of this tomb, placing it probably amongst the earlier monuments on the island. The absence of any indisputably late Neolithic material would suggest that this tomb, unlike many others, was not in use for a very long period.

Because of its badly damaged state, Din Dryfol has added little to our knowledge and understanding of the rituals of burial practised by its builders. The presence of cremated human bone within the disturbed Chamber Four demonstrates that cremation was practised by the users of the primary unit, as is the case in the majority of tombs in the Irish Sea area. The few flint tools and fragmentary sherds are also typical of the material found in other tombs in Wales and Ireland and do not warrant the term 'grave goods'. The presence of a broken stone axe is more unusual for Wales, but axes have been found in tombs elsewhere.

In tombs of this 'Long Grave' family the entrance area is normally emphasised both architecturally and by evidence of ritual activity. Although the chamber was high, the entrance to Chamber Four was not especially impressive, but there may have been a forecourt pit just outside it. Apart from this poorly understood pit, there is no evidence for activity—hearths or pits—in front of either Chamber Three or Chamber One. Since so little is known of the structure of Chamber One, except that it may have been wider than the others, it could be suggested that this area was not so much a chamber as a narrow forecourt in the manner of Annaghmare (Waterman 1965) or Shanballyedmond (O'Kelly 1958). In that case the scatter of sherds near Stone 1 would be derived, as in several other tombs, from some exterior ritual activity rather than burial ceremonies. However this point cannot be pressed in the absence of any firm evidence. Forecourt activity has been recorded at Pant y Saer, Bryn yr Hen Bobl, and Bryn Celli Ddu in Anglesey (Lynch 1970, Chap. 2). all probably later monuments, and at the final phase at Trefignath, but not at the earlier chambers there. Possibly, therefore, this aspect of religious activity was not a feature of the earlier Neolithic in the island. The absence of carefully laid blocking material is perhaps unusual in the context of 'Long Graves' but, again, this was not found against the earlier chambers at Trefignath. It is just possible that Chamber Three was filled with stone as were some Irish Court Cairn chambers (e.g. Tully (Waterman 1978, 9)), but, in view of its history of destruction, no firm statement can be made about the date of these stones.

The discovery that the entrance to Chamber Three had originally been built of wood is one of the more unexpected results of the excavation. The occasional use of wood in what are essentially stone monuments may have been more common that we now think, for it cannot be recognised except under excavation conditions. Recent excavations in Brittany have shown that gaps in a stone alignment were filled with wooden posts (Le Roux, 1979), and the use of wooden props in the construction of megalithic tombs must have been commonplace. Nevertheless the discovery of structural postholes in stone chambers is very rare; the few examples are dispersed, and it is as yet too early to attempt a coherent discussion.

Pairs of posts like those at Din Dryfol have been found at the complex megalithic site on Guernsey, Les Fouillages (Kinnes 1982, 26). Amongst several independent structures beneath a trapezoid mound was a two-compartment rectangular chamber with tall stones at one end and a pair of posts at the other. Inside the chamber were three complete Danubian pots and this stage of the monument is associated with a radiocarbon date of 3,600 bc. A similar pair of postholes was found during the excavation of Browndod, a Court Cairn in Co. Antrim (Evans and Davies 1934-35). This is a four-chambered monument with a deep 'lobster claw' forecourt. Uncharacteristically the portal stones of the chamber are set at right angles to the facade and project across its line. Immediately in front of these stones and in line with them are two circular holes 0.3m across and 0.30m deep. The excavators said that they had 'the appearance of post holes', but no packing remained in them (Evans and Davies 1934-35, 79-80). They were filled with a flecked black and red 'sealing' which extended into the first chamber. This material was interpreted as a disturbance layer of uncertain date, but the postholes are unlikely to be the result of disturbance since they are very neatly made and partly rock-cut. Unfortunately it is not possible to suggest a structural function for them since they duplicate the stone portal. The isolated and aberrant Court Cairn at Shanballyedmond, Co. Tipperary, had a final kerb of wooden posts (O'Kelly 1958), and the forecourts at Cohaw, Co. Cavan, had been closed at some date by wooden fences (Kilbride-Jones 1951). Postholes in the chambers at the same site might be the result of disturbance.

Les Fouillages, Browndod, Shanballyedmond, Cohaw, and Din Dryfol cannot be considered a coherent group; they are architecturally distinct, geographically dispersed and probably separated in time. In contrast, Lochill, Slewcairn, and Doey's Cairn, Dunloy, which all combine wooden and stone structures, do seem to be a genuinely related group (Masters 1981, 167-68). However the way in which the two materials are combined in these monuments differs from that at Din Dryfol, for the wooden element forms a complete and distinct structure, recognisably similar to the post and dry-walled burial chamber at Dalladies Long Barrow (Piggott, 1974). The wooden structures in this interesting—and early—North Irish Sea group (of which Ballafayle on the Isle of Man may also be a member (Masters 1981, 168)) consist of two or three large multi-postholes set in line down the length of a narrow chamber which has been deliberately fired. This chamber is variously combined with a stone porch or entrance, and, in the case of Dunloy, with a fully Irish antechamber and facade (Evans 1938, Collins 1976). Din Dryfol has none of the features of this group, and they are only relevant to the discussion to the extent of showing that the combination of wood and stone was architecturally acceptable within the Irish Sea area at a date round about 3,000 bc.

Turning to broader historical issues, it is difficult to categorise either phase of Din Dryfol, or to relate it at all precisely to contemporary tombs in Wales, Ireland, or Scotland. The virtual absence of the eastern elements and the uncertainty about whether the primary unit was a single or double chamber, as well as the structural problems of Chamber Three make worthwhile discussion very difficult. The rectangular chambers, long cairn, and tall entrance stones make it clear that it belongs to the 'Long Grave' family which is dominant in many parts of the Irish Sea province. It may be significant that tombs of this family are those most frequently changed and adapted (Corcoran 1972), as Din Dryfol was at least once. These tombs are widespread on both sides of the Irish Sea and may be divided into regionally distinct groups: the Clyde Tombs of south-west Scotland with their significant sub-groups of proto-megaliths (Scott 1969), the Irish Court Cairns (de Valera 1960), and the Portal Dolmens which may be found both in Ireland and in Wales (Lynch 1976), with a modified version in Cornwall.

The best known Welsh representative of the 'Long Grave' family is the Portal Dolmen, exemplified by the West Chamber at Dyffryn Ardudwy, Tan y Muriau on Lleyn, or the fine but damaged monument in Carnedd Hengwm South (Lynch 1969). However this style of tomb, dominant in North Pembrokeshire and on the mainland of North Wales, is not reliably recorded in Anglesey. Drawings of the destroyed tomb at Llanfechell (Daniel 1950, Pl. III) suggest that it could have been a Portal Dolmen, but no other tomb could be confidently classified as one, although some closed square chambers do exist. Because of its high entrance stones the eastern chamber at Trefignath comes close to the type, but the classic H-shaped portal is not present. The same is true of Din Dryfol and neither should be classified as a Portal Dolmen.

The sequence of building at Din Dryfol is uncertain and one cannot be sure whether the units were single or double chambered tombs. It may be relevant to note, however, that there are no two-chambered Portal Dolmens in Wales (Lynch 1969, 125), although the form is present in Ireland and the duplication of chambers is certainly common within the broader 'Long Grave' family. Since it is probable that at least one of the phases at Din Dryfol was two-chambered, this removes the monument a little further from the classic Welsh Portal Dolmens.

The Irish Court Cairns are regularly two- or four-chambered (de Valera 1960, 23-25), but are never found without a monumental facade and forecourt, indeed it is their most characteristic feature. Although its scale and plan may vary, a concave facade is almost universal, and the absence of such a feature from Din Dryfol—and from Trefignath as well—is the strongest argument for rejecting the Court Cairn link which has often been mentioned in the past (Lynch 1969, 114).

There is, however, one recently excavated Irish monument which does exhibit some telling parallels with Din Dryfol. This is Barnes Lower, Co. Tyrone, an unusual Court Cairn with a virtually flat facade and a multiplicity of subsidiary chambers (Collins 1966). It could be clearly demonstrated that the main chamber had been built in two stages, for a flat facade of substantial, but not very high, orthostats in line with the entrance to Chamber 3 had been engulfed by additional cairn material in exactly the manner suggested for Din Dryfol. This added front element of the tomb is interpreted by the excavator as two segmental chambers built in dry-walling (in contrast to the orthostatic build of the back ones). The chambers are badly ruined and it is just conceivable that the added element may have been a very narrow forecourt like that at Annaghmare, Co. Armagh (Waterman 1965), for the final facade is also unusually flat, more like the front of a 'lobster claw' cairn than a true forecourt. Such an interpretation is also possible in relation to Chamber One at Din Dryfol. There is a further link with Din Dryfol in that at Barnes Lower the back unit (Chambers 3 and 4) might itself be sub-divided. There is a change in the lie of the cairn stones, but no buried facade, in line with the junction of these two chambers between which access is blocked by a high closing slab. This presents a dilemma similar to that of the possible separation of Chambers Three and Four at Din Dryfol.

The structural history of Barnes Lower is thus very similar to that suggested for Din Dryfol, but the design of the chambers and the cairn does not provide a strikingly close parallel. However, the possible existence of a primary single chamber with a closed H-shaped portal may be a significant pointer in the search for the origins of the Irish Court Cairn, the one member of the 'Long Grave' family whose development has as yet resisted illuminating dissection (Scott 1969, Henshall 1972, Corcoran 1973). Din Dryfol and Barnes Lower might, therefore, be equated on a general rather than a specific level as monuments atypical of their regional group but revealing within their development the basic elements from which their individual traditions were to be built.

The elements present at Din Dryfol, the rectangular chambers, the tall portal and flat front but minimal forecourt activity, are found most frequently in combination in south-west Scotland where comparable histories of addition and adaptation have often been demonstrated (Scott 1969, Henshall 1972). Precise parallels, however, are difficult to quote because so little structure remains at Din Dryfol, and because the putatively earlier chambers in Scotland (Henshall 1972, Fig. 4) are themselves quite varied, greater standardisation of construction and size being a feature of later monuments. If Chamber Four at Din Dryfol had formed a single unit on its own it might be compared to Ardmarnock (ARG 17) in plan, if not scale. In scale it would be closer to the back chamber at Cairnholy II (Henshall 1972, Fig. 3). In both these Scottish examples the chamber is formally closed by a high septal, but at Din Dryfol there is no evidence that such a septal existed, and the junction of Chambers Four and Three is an area of particular uncertainty. One can say little about the structure of Chamber Three; but if the northern side stone (3) had been propped on the long flat stone which lies there at present, such an arrangement could be paralleled at Brackley in Kintyre (Scott 1955), just as the combination of wood and stone may be paralleled in the region, albeit in a rather different way. Very little can be said about Chambers One and Two but, if the inner portal (Stone 8) is in its true position, this duplicated entrance, too, can be found amongst the Clyde tombs (e.g. Brackley and Crarae (Scott 1955, 1961)). Although several Scottish tombs have deep semi-circular facades in the Irish manner, the flat facade is rather more common, and many of the putatively early sites have no extra stones flanking the entrance (Henshall 1972, catalogue of plans). On the other hand, the facade is conspicuously rare in Wales itself, so its absence from Din Dryfol should not be seen as a peculiarly Scottish trait.

Of the three main branches of the 'Long Grave' family, therefore, Din Dryfol would seem to lie closest to the Clyde tombs but because of its damaged state the parallels can only be of the most general kind. A similar relationship is argued in the case of Trefignath which shares several features with Din Dryfol and, of the Anglesey tombs, is obviously the closest to it. Here again the problem of whether one may consider Din Dryfol Chamber Four in isolation is relevant. If one may, it is clear that the central chamber at Trefignath is a good parallel for it—a simple box with entrance stones. However the dry-walled cuspate forecourt, present at both later stages at Trefignath is not found at Din Dryfol and the addition of chambers is differently organised. At Trefignath the three single chambers remain separate and distinct units, whereas the surviving evidence at Din Dryfol suggests rather the formation of a continuous gallery of at least three chambers. The arrangement is not reliably recorded elsewhere in Wales except at the enigmatic monument, Cerrig

Llwydion, near Cynwyl Elfed in Carmarthenshire. The other 'Long Grave' in Anglesey, Hendrefor, near Llansadwrn, has two groups of collapsed stones about two metres apart and, in view of the evidence from Trefignath, may represent two distinct chambers, as might the less obviously related tomb at Presaddfed (Lynch 1969, 115-16 and 123). Din Dryfol, therefore, must now be recognised as a rather more unusual monument than was originally thought. Before they were excavated, Din Dryfol, Trefignath, and Hendrefor might be linked together with some confidence; now Din Dryfol with its long gallery stands apart from the other two, though remaining recognisably part of the same broad family.

The similarity of the pottery from Trefignath and Din Dryfol underlines this relationship, although that from Trefignath is less obviously associated with the use of the tomb. The undecorated bowls at Trefignath come from the 'quarry' at the end of the monument and from beneath the cairn so that they certainly predate the central chamber, and probably the western one as well. The technical link (p. 119) between some of this pre-cairn pottery and the sherds from the chambers at Din Dryfol would, therefore, suggest that Din Dryfol is the earlier monument, contemporary, at the very latest, with the western chamber at Trefignath. This chamber may be identified as a small Passage Grave with short passage opening to the north, a stylistic group to which the date of 3,000 bc would seem appropriate (Lynch 1975). The chronological relationship between these two tombs belonging to different megalithic traditions, demonstrates that the variety of tomb-building styles which is such a feature of Neolithic Anglesey, was present in the island from a very early date.

Appendices

I. REPORT ON THE CREMATED BONE FROM DIN DRYFOL, ANGLESEY

by T. P. O'Connor, Environmental Archaeology Unit, York

Eighteen samples of cremated bone were submitted for examination and identification. The bone was all highly calcined, indicating burning at a high temperature. Most fragments were in the same range 3mm to 10mm maximum dimension. Inevitably, the majority could not be identified.

Of forty-two fragments from the chamber area, twelve could with certainty be identified as human. The remains of two individuals were present, an adult represented by six fragments of long-bone cortex, and an immature individual (apparently sub-adult rather than juvenile) represented by six fragments of parietal bone. Only one fragment from the chamber area could be definitely identified as not human, comprising the proximal 20% of a sheep left metacarpal.

Bone from elsewhere in and below the cairn included a few fragments identifiable as human, probably disturbed from the chamber content, and fragments identifiable as sheep, sheep/goat, pig, and a large ungulate (probably cattle or horse). The non-human bone had apparently been subjected to the same high temperature as the human bone.

A full list of identifications is given below.

Bone from Chamber Four

DD.E7
Total: 5 fragments   3 fragments parietal bone, human, immature.
1 fragment ?femur cortex, human, adult.
1 fragment indet.

DD.Ea8
Total: 4 fragments   2 fragments limb bone cortex, human, adult.
2 fragments indet.

DD.Ea9
Total: 3 fragments   1 fragment rib, human.
1 fragment limb bone cortex, human, adult.
1 fragment indet.

DD.Da/Ea 1-8
Total: 9 fragments   1 fragment tibia cortex, human, adult.
8 fragments indet.

DD.Da8
Total: 18 fragments   3 fragments parietal bone, human, immature.
1 fragment ?tibia shaft, human, adult.
14 fragments indet.

DD.D31-32
Total: 2 fragments   2 fragments indet.

DD.D25a
Total: 1 fragment   1 fragment proximal left metacarpal, sheep.

(This last find was from a heavily disturbed area and is probably intrusive F.M.L.)

Bone from under Cairn outside Chamber Four

DD.E3
Total: 16 fragments   4 fragments rib, human.
4 fragments limb bone cortex, species indet.
8 fragments indet.

Bone from amongst Cairn Stones to South of Chambers Three and Four

DD.D13
Total: 2 fragments   2 fragments limb bone cortex, human.

DD.D23
Total: 2 fragments   2 fragments indet.

DD.D24
Total: 1 fragment   1 fragment indet.

DD.ß28
Total: 35 fragments   3 fragments limb bone cortex, large ungulate.
1 fragment rib, species indet.
31 fragments indet.

Bone from Denuded areas, Chamber One and Entrance

DD.W1
Total: 21 fragments   4 fragments rib, ?human.
1 fragment limb bone cortex, small ungulate.
16 fragments indet.

DD.Wa5
(from pit with RB sherd)
Total: 60 fragments   2 fragments tooth enamel, ?small ungulate.
1 fragment scapula, ?small ungulate.
2 fragments rib, human.
55 fragments indet.

Bone from Trenches L and S

DD.L1
Total: 17 fragments   6 fragments rib, ?human.
11 fragments indet.

DD.S4
Total: 3 fragments   3 fragments rib, human

Bone from beneath road to east of Tomb

DD.F3

Total: 2 fragments   1 fragment frontal bone, pig.
                                    1 fragment indet.

Bone from west end of Cairn

DD.O3

Total: 45 fragments   5 fragments rib, sheep/goat.
                                    1 fragment proximal end left ulna, sheep.
                                    39 fragments indet.

II. CHARCOAL IDENTIFICATIONS

by Dr M. P. Denne, Department of Forestry and Wood Science, University College of North Wales, Bangor

Each bag was sampled at random, from the larger pieces. The numbers given are the actual number recorded. The quantity of charcoal in each sample was normally very small.

The following points should be borne in mind: wood structure is quite variable, between trees, between stems, roots and branches, and with environment, etc. Some species (e.g. oak, ash, elm, yew etc.) are so distinctive that this causes no problems, but others can be quite tricky. Alder and hazel, for example, are sometimes clearly distinguishable, sometimes look rather similar, sometimes look like something different until one looks at them microscopically. Some species (e.g. willow and poplar) are so similar that one needs good microscopic sections to distinguish between them, and that would be very difficult with charcoal. Hence in the present samples:

Oak, ash, birch: I am very confident about these records.

Willow: in this situation willow seems more likely, but aspen or black poplar is also a possibility.

Alder, hazel: I am reasonably confident that I have distinguished these two species correctly from each other, but could be mistaken in some samples.

Cherry: probably *Prunus avium,* though could be *P.padus, P.cerasifera,* or *P.spinosa.*

Unknown: likely to be another species, but too small or too distorted for identification.

From possibly undisturbed Neolithic Contexts

From under the cairn south of Chamber Four

E8   Hazel 8
       Oak 4   Weight: approx. 13grm
D37 Oak 4   Weight: 0.40grm

From shallow pit in Chamber Three

D34 Oak   Weight: 0.69grm

From surface of 'Chamber 2'

X2   Oak 10
       Hazel 1   Weight: 1.44grm

From surface of 'Chamber One' entrance

A6   Oak 4   Weight: 0.75grm

From disturbed areas within the chambers

Chamber Four, with cremated bone

Ea8 Oak 2   Weight: 0.39grm

Within area of Chamber Three

C2   Willow 1   Weight: 0.39grm

Amongst surviving Cairn to south of Chambers Three and Four

B31 Oak
       Alder
       Blackthorn,
       hawthorn, or rose   Weight: 3.02grm
B28 Hazel
       Heather or bilberry Weight: 1.57grm
D35 Oak
       Willow   Weight: 0.95grm
D36 Oak 2   Weight: 0.23grm
D23 Alder (probable)   Weight: 0.18grm

Ea 10 west of Chamber Four

       Oak   Weight: 0.79grm

Area south of Chambers One and Two, with slag and bone

?Romano-British disturbance

B11 west of Stone 8

       Alder or hazel 4
       Gorse or broom 2
       Willow 1
       Oak 1   Weight: 1.10grm
S5   Oak 4
       Alder 3
       Hazel 7
       Willow 1   Weight: 21.50grm
S6   Hazel 7
       Willow 6
       Alder 3
       Oak 1   Weight: 17.95grm
L1   Willow (probable) 5
       Oak 2
       Hazel 2
       Unknown, poss.
       willow root   Weight: 2.27grm
L2   Alder 8   Weight: 3.10grm
C3 above road
       Oak   Weight: 1.71grm

From pit with Romano-British sherd

Wa8 Oak 19
    Hazel 16
    Alder 14
    Willow 10
    Ash 1   Weight: 80.50grm

From west end of cairn with slag and animal bone

O5 Oak 7
    Hazel 7
    Willow 6
    Alder 7
    Ash 1
    Birch 1
    Cherry 1   Weight: 26.48grm
O6 Oak 7
    Hazel 3
    Willow 2   Weight: 8.90grm

R6 Alder 5
    Oak 3
    Hazel 3   Weight: 7.50grm

Beneath road east of tomb

F3 with pig bone
    Oak 2
    Hazel 2
    Alder 1
    Heather (probable) 1 Weight: 3.15grm
G4 with slag
    Ash 3
    Hazel 3
    Oak 1
    Willow 1
    Birch (probable) 1   Weight: 0.86grm

III. ANALYSIS OF SLAG SAMPLES FROM DIN DRYFOL, ANGLESEY

by Dr D. A. Jenkins, Department of Bio-chemistry and Soil Science, University College of North Wales, Bangor.

Four samples have been analysed by arc spectrography and by X-Ray diffraction with the following results:

Source/ trench:	S	T	W/A	Y/W
Macrofeatures:	Earthy brown; grey vesicular micro-crystalline patches.	Dense, dark green/ grey; micro-crystalline; brown weathered surface.	Dark brown, vesicular earthy.	Light, vitreous; vesicular grey material.
Crystalline phases detected by XRDA and unidenti-fied peaks:	Fayalite (FE_2SiO_4)	2.51 and 2.155A	Quartz (Magnetite?) 2.84 and 2.47A	Quartz Cristobalite

Trace Elements (contents in ppm. on the log scale $10^{n/8}$):

Be	<5.6	7.5	10	<5.6
Co	24	<4.2	<4.2	24
Cr	56	75	130	42
Cu	42	<10	<10	<10
Ga	10	7.5	5.6	3.2
Mo	42	32	24	7.5
Mn	>1%	>1%	>1%	1%
Ni	24	1.0	1.0	24
Sn	<10	<10	10	<10
Ti	3200	4200	1%	3200
V	420	750	750	130
Y	<3.2	<3.2	<3.2	5.6
Yb	<1.0	18	24	<1.0
Zn	560	420	320	<240
Zr	1300	1800	1800	180

Not detected in any sample:

Ag (<1.0ppm); Au (<56ppm); As (<750ppm); Bi (<56ppm); Cd (<420ppm); Ge (<10ppm); Pb (<10ppm); Sb (<130ppm); Tl (<10ppm).

Comments

These samples carry relatively high levels of such lithophilic elements as Mn, V, and Zr which would be expected in slags; the levels of Zn and Mo seem unusually high, although the latter has been found in several local Fe-rich slags. The dark brown colour of S, T, and W/A and the presence of fayalite (S) and magnetite (W/A?) indicate that these slags are iron-rich. There is no positive evidence, however, in these analyses that the slags were associated with smelting for such specific metals as silver, gold, copper, lead, or tin.

IV. REPORT ON SOIL ANALYSIS OF SAMPLES FROM DIN DRYFOL

by Dr J. S. Conway, Department of Biochemistry and Soil Science, University College of North Wales, Bangor.

Eight soil samples from various parts of the cairn were analysed in order to elucidate their probable origin. Munsell colours were determined on air dried samples and on ignited (500°C) samples; percentage loss on ignition (500°C for four hours) was measured; and soil phosphorus concentration was also determined.

The samples fall into three clear groups: the dark chocolate brown material which occurs amongst the lowest stones in the cairn and in areas where the cairn has been robbed out; the other dark soils from beneath the cairn; and the natural subsoils of the area.

The first group, samples 1, 2, and 7, are dark reddish-brown (5YR3/3) with high organic content and a fairly high iron content, evidenced by their ignited colours (5YR3/4). Phosphorus values are also very high, with the exception of sample 2 from near Stone 8. These properties indicate direct human interference.

The second group, samples 5 and 6, are dark yellowish-brown (10YR4/3-4/4), again with a fairly high organic content and high phosphorous values, although more in keeping with an original topsoil. Possibly these are contaminated either with the dark reddish soil or possibly with charcoal, bone, or slag, or perhaps both. Any of these materials would cause the elevated values recorded.

The final group, samples 3, 4, and 8, are typical of the leached B-horizon of the local soils (Trisant-Gaerwen series), brownish-yellow (10YR6/4) with very low organic content and phosphorous levels as expected.

Discussion

The dark reddish-brown soil would seem to represent a buried A horizon, perhaps not in the sense of a true old ground surface, but of an accumulation of organic-rich fine material percolating down between the stones of the cairn. In appearance this material is closely comparable with the equivalent material from the cairn at Capel Eithin, though the phosphorous levels at Din Dryfol are considerably higher (Capel Eithin 1500-2000 ppm).

Little can be said concerning samples 5 and 6 as they both contained charcoal and bone, either contaminates being sufficient to distort the analysis of the soil itself. The natural subsoil samples are again similar to equivalent levels from Capel Eithin, Gaerwen, Anglesey.

Sample no.	Colour		% L.O.I."	Total P @ p.p.m	Location
	Air dry	Ignited			
1.	5YR3/3	5YR3/4	39	3000	SE corner Trench C
2.	5YR3/3	5YR4/6	25	1500	W. of Stone 8 Trench B
7.	5YR3/2	5YR3/4	25	3250	Trench B
5.	10YR4/3	5YR4/6	19	2500	Beneath cairn Trench E
6.	10YR4/4	5YR5/4	18	2250	S. of base line Trench O
3.	10YR6/4	5YR6/6	6	550	Entrance area Trench W
4.	10YR8/4	5YR6/8	7	400	Between Stones 1 and 8
8.	10YR6/4	5YR6/6	5	875	Natural subsoil

' Munsell colour
" at 500°C
@ Perchloric acid digestion, mean of three replicates.

Bibliography

Alexander, J. and Ozanne, P.C. and A., 1960. 'Report on the Investigation of a Round Barrow on Arreton Down, I.o.W.', *PPS*, 26, 263-302.

Antiquity, 1972. 'Editorial', *Antiquity*, 46, 265.

Antiquity, 1981. 'Editorial', *Antiquity*, 55, 81-9.

Aubrey, John, 1980. *Monumenta Britannica Parts 1 and 2* ed. by John Fowles, Dorset Publishing Co.

Ball, D. F., 1963. *The Soils and Landuse of the District around Bangor and Beaumaris,* Memoirs of the Soil Survey of England and Wales, H.M.S.O.

Barber, A. J. and Max, M. D., 1979. 'A New Look at the Mona Complex (Anglesey, North Wales)', *Journ. Geological Society London,* 136, 407-32.

Baynes, E. N., 1908. 'The Excavations at Din Lligwy', *Archaeologia Cambrensis,* (6th series), 8, 183-210.

Baynes, E. N., 1909. 'The Excavation of the Lligwy Cromlech, in the County of Anglesey', *Archaeologia Cambrensis,* (6th series), 9, 217-31.

Baynes, E. N., 1911. 'The Megalithic Remains of Anglesey', *Transactions of the Honourable Society of Cymmrodorion,* 3-91.

Baynes, E. N., 1914. 'Some Dolmens of North Wales', *Proceedings Llandudno and District Field Club,* VIII, 48-60.

Bell, M., 1977. 'Excavations at Bishopstone, Sussex. The Flint Industries', *Sussex Archaeological Collections,* 115, 19-39.

Beswick, P., 1977. 'Report on the Shale Industry at Swine Sty', *Transactions of the Hunter Archaeological Society,* 10, 207-11.

Brewster, T. C. M., 1963. *The Excavation of Staple Howe,* Scarborough.

Britnell, W., 1979. 'The Gwernvale Long Cairn, Powys', *Antiquity,* 53, 132-4.

Britnell, W., 1980. 'Radio Carbon Dates for the Gwernvale Chambered Tomb, Crickhowell, Powys', *Antiquity,* 54, 147.

Britnell, W., 1981. 'Trelystan', *Current Archaeology,* 78, 201-5.

Britnell, W., 1982. 'The excavation of Two Round Barrows at Trelystan, Powys', *PPS,* 48, 133-201.

Britnell, W., 1984, in W. J. Britnell and H. N. Savory, *Gwernvale and Penywyrlod,* Cambrian Archaeological Association.

Burenhult, G., 1980. *The Archaeological Excavation at Carrowmore Co. Sligo, Ireland 1977-9,* No. 9 Theses and Papers in North European Archaeology, Institute of Archaeology, University of Stockholm.

Burton, J. E., 1914. 'Trearddur Bay, Site of Ancient Camp', *Archaeologia Cambrensis* (6th series), XIV, 307-08.

Calkin, J. B., 1953. 'Kimmeridge Coal-Money', *Proceedings Dorset Natural History and Archaeological Society.*

Carr, A. D., 1982. *Medieval Anglesey,* Llangefni, 1982.

Cambrian Archaeological Association, 1870. 'Twenty-fourth Annual Meeting held at Holyhead on Tuesday 23rd August and Terminated on the Following Saturday', *Archaeologia Cambrensis* (4th series), I, 353-72.

Clark, J. G. D., Higgs, E. S. and Longworth, I. H., 1960. 'Excavations at the Neolithic Site at Hurst Fen, Mildenhall, Suffolk; 1954, 1957, and 1958', *PPS,* 26, 202-45.

Collins, A. E. P., 1966. 'Barnes Lower Court Cairn, Co. Tyrone', *Ulster Journal Archaeology,* 29, 43-75.

Collins, A. E. P., 1976. 'Dooey's Cairn, Ballymacaldrack, Co. Antrim', *Ulster Journal Archaeology,* 39, 1-7.

Corcoran, J. X. W. P., 1969. 'The Cotswold-Severn Group' in Powell, T. G. E. *et al. Megalithic Enquiries in the West of Britain,* 13-104, Liverpool.

Corcoran, J. X. W. P., 1972. 'Multi-Period Construction and the Origins of the Chambered Long Cairn in Western Britain and Ireland' in Lynch, F. and Burgess, C. (eds), *Prehistoric Man in Wales and the West,* 31-64, Bath.

Corcoran, J. X. W. P., 1973. 'The Chambered Cairns of the Carlingford Culture, an Enquiry into Origins' in Daniel, G. E. and Kjaerum, P. (eds), *Megalithic Graves and Ritual,* 105-16, Jutland Archaeological Society.

Cunliffe, B. and Phillipson, D. W., 1968. 'Excavations at Eldon's Seat, Encombe, Dorset', *PPS,* 34, 191-237.

Daniel, G. E., 1950. *The Prehistoric Chamber Tombs of England and Wales,* Cambridge.

Daniel, G. E., 1963. 'The Personality of Wales' in Foster, I. Ll. and Alcock, L. (eds), *Culture and Environment,* 7-23, Routledge.

De Valera, R., 1960. 'The Court Cairns of Ireland', *Proceedings Royal Irish Academy,* 60, C 9-140.

Evans, E. E., 1938. 'Doey's Cairn, Dunloy, Co. Antrim', *Ulster Journal Archaeology,* 1, 59-78.

Evans, E. E. and Davies, O., 1934. 'Excavation of a Chambered Horned Cairn, Browndod, Co. Antrim', *Belfast Natural History and Philosophical Society,* 70-87.

Fenton, A., 1962. 'Early and Traditional Cultivating Implements in Scotland', *PSAS,* XCVI, 264-317.

Gibson, E. (ed), 1695. *William Camden's Britannia.*

Giot, P. R., 1960. *Brittany,* Thames and Hudson.

Glenn, T. A., 1914. 'Exploration of Neolithic Station near Gwaenysgor, Flintshire', *Archaeologia Cambrensis,* (6th series), XIV, 247-70.

Gough, R., 1789. *William Camden's Britannia.*

Green, H. S., 1980. *The Flint Arrowheads of the British Isles,* BAR, 75.

Greenly, E., 1919. *The Geology of Anglesey, Vols 1 and 2,* Memoirs of the Geological Survey U.K. London H.M.S.O.

Gregory, S., 1963. *Statistical Methods and the Geographer,* Longman.

Griffith, J. E., 1892. 'British Antiquities found at Plas Bach near Cerrig Ceinwen, Anglesey, *Archaeologia Cambrensis,* (5th series), IX, 242-3.

Griffith, J. E., 1900. *Portfolio of Photographs of the Cromlechs of Anglesey and Caernarvonshire.*

Grimes, W. F., 1936. 'The Megalithic Monuments of Wales', *PPS,* 2, 106-39.

Grimes, W. F., 1939. 'The Excavation of the Ty-Isaf Long Cairn, Brecknockshire', *PPS,* 5, 119-42.

Grimes, W. F., 1945. 'Early man and the soils of Anglesey', *Antiquity,* 19, 169-74.

Grimes, W. F., 1960. *Excavations on Defence Sites 1939-45, I: Mainly Neolithic—Bronze Age,* M.o.W. Archaeological Reports 3, London.

Henshall, A. S., 1972. *The Chambered Tombs of Scotland Vol 2,* Edinburgh.

Herity, M., 1974. *Irish Passage Graves,* Irish University Press.

Herity, M. and Eogan, G., 1977. *Ireland in Prehistory,* Routledge.

Holgate, R., 1980. *The Location of Megalithic Chambered Monuments in Anglesey: An Indicator of Life in the Neolithic* unpublished dissertation in the Institute of Archaeology, London.

Houlder, C. H., 1968. 'The Henge Monuments at Llandegai', *Antiquity,* 42, 216-21.

Hunter, M., 1975. *John Aubrey and the Realm of Learning,* Duckworth.

Iversen, J., 1973. *The Development of Denmark's Nature Since the Last Glacial,* Danmarks geologiske Undersögelse V Raekke No. 7c Reitzel, Copenhagen.

Jacobi, R. M., 1979. 'Early Flandrian Hunters in the South-West', *Devon Archaeological Society Jubilee Proceedings,* 48-93.

Jacobi, R. M., 1980. 'The Early Holocene Settlements of Wales' in Taylor, J. A. (ed), *Culture and Environment in Prehistoric Wales,* 131-206, BAR, 76.

Jermy, A. C. and Tutin, T. G., 1968. *British Sedges: a Handbook to the Species of Carex found Growing in the British Isles,* Botanical Society of the British Isles.

Jones, H. L., 1855. 'List of Early British Remains in Wales, No. III', *Archaeologia Cambrensis,* (3rd series), I, 18-27.

Keeley, H. C. M., 1977. *Interim Report on the Soils of Trefignath, Anglesey,* A.M.Lab.Report 2300.

Keeley, H. C. M., 1979. *Interim Report (II) on the Soils of Trefignath, Anglesey,* A.M.Lab.Report 2716.

Kinnes, I., 1982. 'Les Fouaillages and Megalithic origins', *Antiquity,* 56, 24-30.

Leisner, G. and V., 1965. *Die Megalithgräber Der Iberischen Halbinsel,* Madrider Forschungen Band I, Berlin.

Lerche, G., 1970. 'The Ploughs of Mediaeval Denmark', *Tools and Tillage,* 1:3, 131-49.

Le Roux, C.-T., 1979. 'Circonscription de Bretagne: St. Just', *Gallia Préhistoire,* 22, 526-30.

L'Helgouach, J., 1965. *Les Sépultures Mégalithiques en Amorique,* Rennes.'

Llwyd, A., 1833. *A History of the Island of Mona,* Ruthin.

Lynch, F. M., 1969. 'Megalithic Tombs of North Wales' and 'The Contents of Excavated Tombs in North Wales' in Powell, T. G. E., *et al. Megalithic Enquiries in the West of Britain,* 107-74, Liverpool.

Lynch, F. M., 1970. *Prehistoric Anglesey,* Anglesey Antiquarian Society, Llangefni.

Lynch, F. M., 1975. 'Excavations at Carreg Samson Megalithic Tomb, Mathry, Pembrokeshire', *Archaeologia Cambrensis,* CXXIV, 15-35.

Lynch, F. M., 1976. 'Towards a Chronology of Megalithic Tombs in Wales' in Boon, G. C. and Lewis, J. M. (eds), *Welsh Antiquity,* 63-79, National Museum of Wales, Cardiff.

Maltman, A. J., 1978. 'Serpentinites and Related Rocks of Anglesey', *Geological Journ.,* 12, 113-38.

Manley, J. and Healey, E., 1982. 'Excavations at Hendre, Rhuddlan: The mesolithic finds'. *Archaeologia Cambrensis* CXXXI, 18-48.

Marshall, D. N. and Taylor, I. D., 1977. 'The Excavation of the Chambered Cairn at Glenvoidean, Isle of Bute', *PSAS,* 108, 7, 1-39.

Masters, L., 1981. 'Chambered Tombs and Non-Megalithic Barrows in Britain' in Evans, J. D., Cunliffe, B. W. and Renfrew, C. (eds), *Antiquity and Man,* 161-76, London.

Megaw, J. V. S. and Simpson, D. D. A., 1979. *Introduction to British Prehistory,* Leicester U.P.

Moore, P. D., 1973. 'The Influence of Prehistoric Cultures upon the Initiation and Spread of Blanket Bog in Upland Wales', *Nature,* 241, 350-53.

Morris, L., 1818. 'A Short Account of Holyhead Church . . . in a Letter to Brown Willis Esq.', *Cambrian Register,* III, 212-18.

Newcomer, M. H., 1971. 'Some Quantitative Experiments in Handaxe Manufacture', *World Archaeology,* 3, No. 1, 85-93.

Norman, C., 1977. 'A Flint Assemblage from Constantine Island, North Cornwall', *Cornish Archaeology,* 16, 3-9.

O'Neil, B. H., St.J., 1936. 'Excavations at Caerau Ancient Village, Clynnog, Caernarvonshire', *Antiquaries Journ.,* 16, 295-320.

O'Nualláin, S., 1972. 'A Neolithic House at Ballyglass near Ballycastle, Co. Mayo', *Journ. of the Royal Society Antiquaries of Ireland,* 102, 49-57.

O'Riordáin, S. P., 1954. 'Lough Gur Excavations...', *Proceedings Royal Irish Academy,* 56, C, 297-459.

Owen, N., 1775. *A History of the Island of Anglesey.*

Peacock, D. P. S., 1977. 'Ceramics in Roman and Medieval Archaeology' in Peacock, D. P. S. (ed), *Pottery and Early Commerce,* 21-33, Academic Press.

Petersen, M., 1965. *History Under the Sea,* Washington.

Piggott, S., 1954. *The Neolithic Cultures of the British Isles,* Cambridge.

Piggott, S., 1974. 'Excavation of the Dalladies Long Barrow, Fettercairn, Kincardineshire', *PSAS,* 104, 23-47.

Pollard, A. M., Bussell, G. D. and Baird, D. C., 1981. 'The Analytical Investigation of Early Bronze Age Jet and Jet-like Material from the Devizes Museum', *Archaeometry,* 23, 139-67.

Powell, T. G. E., Corcoran, J. X. W. P., Lynch, Frances and Scott, J. G., 1969. *Megalithic Enquiries in the West of Britain,* Liverpool.

Powell, T. G. E., 1973. 'Excavation of the Megalithic Chambered Cairn at Dyffryn Ardudwy, Merioneth, Wales', *Archaeologia,* CIV, 1-49.

Pritchard, H., 1871. 'Mona Antiqua: Tyn-Trefoel or Dindryfal, Cadmarth and Dinas Cromlech', *Archaeologia Cambrensis,* (4th series), II, 300-12.

Pugh, E., 1816. *Cambria Depicta: a Tour through North Wales.*

RCAHM, 1937. *Inventory of the Ancient Monuments of Anglesey,* H.M.S.O.

Renfrew, C., 1976. *Before Civilization,* Penguin.

Ritchie, J. N. G., 1970. 'Excavation of the Chambered Cairn at Achnacreebeag', *PSAS,* 102, 31-55.

Roberts, E., 1958. *The County of Anglesey: Soils and Agriculture,* Memoirs of the Soil Survey of Great Britain, H.M.S.O.

Rowlands, H., 1723. *Mona Antiqua Restaurata.*

Saville, A., 1979. 'Further Excavations at the Nympsfield Chambered Tomb, Gloucesterchire, 1974', *PPS,* 45, 53-91.

Saville, A., 1980. 'Five Flint Assemblages from Excavated Sites in Wiltshire', *Wiltshire Archaeological Magazine,* 72/73, 1-27.

Savory, H. N., 1976. *Guide Catalogue to the Early Iron Age Collections,* National Museum of Wales.

Savory, H. N., 1980. 'The Neolithic in Wales' in Taylor, J. A. (ed), *Culture and Environment in Prehistoric Wales,* 207-32, BAR, 76.

Scott, J. G., 1955. 'The Excavation of the Chambered Tomb at Brackley, Kintyre, Argyll', *PSAS,* 89 (1955/6), 22-54.

Scott, J. G., 1961. 'The Excavation of the Chambered Cairn at Crarae, Loch Fyneside, Mid Argyll', *PSAS,* 94 (1960/1), 1-27.

Scott, J. G., 1964. 'The Chambered Cairn at Beacharra, Kintyre, Argyll', *PPS*, 30, 134-58.

Scott, J. G., 1969. 'Clyde Cairns of Scotland' in Powell, T. G. E., *et al. Megalithic Enquiries in the West of Britain*, 175-222, Liverpool U.P.

Shepherd, W., 1972. *Flint: its Origin, Properties and Uses*, London.

Smith, C., 1978. 'Trefignath Burial Chambers', *PPS*, 44, 445.

Smith, C., 1979. 'Trefignath Burial Chambers', *PPS*, 45, 340.

Smith, C., 1981. 'Trefignath Burial Chambers, Anglesey', *Antiquity*, 55, 134-6.

Smith, I. F., 1965. *Windmill Hill and Avebury*, Clarendon.

Smith, I. F., 1974. 'The Neolithic' in Renfrew, C. (ed), *British Prehistory: a New Outline*, 100-36, Duckworth.

Stanley, W. O., 1867. 'Mona Antiqua. The Cromlech at Trefignath', *Archaeologia Cambrensis* (1867), 234.

Stanley, W. O., 1870. 'On the tumulus in Plas Newydd Park, Anglesey', *Archaeologia Cambrensis* (4th series), I, 51-8.

Stanley, W. O., 1871. 'The Chambered Tumulus in Plas Newydd Park, Anglesey', *Archaeological Journ.*, 28, 85-96.

Stanley, W. O., 1874. 'Cromlech at Trefignath', *Archaeological Journ.*, 31, 1-2.

Stanley, W. O., 1874. 'Proceedings at Meetings of the Royal Archaeological Institute, 5th June 1874', *Archaeological Journ.*, 31, 296-7 and 301-2.

Wainwright, G. J., 1959. 'The Excavation of a Mesolithic Site at Freshwater West, Pembrokeshire', *Bulletin of the Board of Celtic Studies*, XVIII, part II, 196-205.

Wainwright, G. J., 1962. 'The Excavation of an Earthwork at Castell Bryn-Gwyn, Llanidan Parish, Anglesey', *Archaeologia Cambrensis*, CXI, 25-58.

Wainwright, G. J., 1972. 'The Excavation of a Neolithic Settlement on Broome Heath, Ditchingham, Norfolk, England, *PPS*, 38, 1-97.

Wainwright, G. J. and Longworth, I. H., 1971. *Durrington Walls, 1966-68*, Society of Antiquaries.

Waterman, D. M., 1965. 'The Court Cairn at Annaghmare, Co. Armagh', *Ulster Journ. Archaeology*, 28, 3-46.

Waterman, D. M., 1978. 'The Excavation of a Court Cairn at Tully, Co. Fermanagh', *Ulster Journ. Archaeology*, 41, 3-14.

Way, A., 1871. 'The Cromlechs of Anglesey', *Archaeological Journ.*, 28, 97,108.

White, S. I., 1981. 'Excavations at Capel Eithin, Gaerwen, Anglesey 1980', *Transactions of the Anglesey Antiquarian Society*, 1981, 15-27.

Williams, A., 1952. 'Clegyr Boia, St. David's, Pembrokeshire: Excavation in 1943', *Archaeologia Cambrensis*, CII, 20-47.

Williams, H., 1923. 'The Romano-British Site at Rhostryfan, Caernarvonshire', *Archaeologia Cambrensis*, LXXVIII, 87-113 and 291-302.

Williams, J. Ll. and Jenkins, D. A., 1976. 'The Use of Petrographic Techniques in Assessing the Provenance of Sediments used in Ceramics' in Davidson, D. A. and Shackley, M. L. (eds), *Geoarchaeology*, 115-36, Duckworth.

Williams, L., 1950. 'The Development of Holyhead', *Transactions of the Anglesey Antiquarian Society*, 1950, 51-70.

abbreviations used: *PPS* —Proceedings of the Prehistoric Society.
PSAS—Proceedings of the Society of Antiquaries of Scotland.

XXI.   Din Dryfol. Dinas rock with tomb on lower shelf. View from north

XXII.   Din Dryfol. Air view from east by courtesy of RAF Valley. 1969 trenches open

XXIII. Din Dryfol. Trench β, 1980 from the east showing distinction of Inner and Outer Cairn. Metric scale in 50cm divisions

XXIV. Din Dryfol. Trench α, 1980. NE extension from west showing distinction of Inner and Outer Cairn. Metric scale

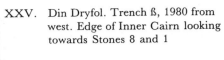

XXV. Din Dryfol. Trench ß, 1980 from west. Edge of Inner Cairn looking towards Stones 8 and 1

XXVI. Din Dryfol. Trench ß, 1980. Junction of Inner and Outer Cairn from east. Metric scale

XXVII. Din Dryfol. Trench ß, 1980. Stone 10 and Inner Cairn with areas of nineteenth century disturbance. View from top of Stone 1

XXVIII. Din Dryfol. Trench ß, 1980. Stones 11 and 10 with view of disturbed section beyond. Cartridge case was found at base of this disturbance. View from north

XXIX.   Din Dryfol. Baulk X/C 1970.
Postholes at front of Chamber
Three from north. Northern hole,
with scale, still filled with stone,
southern one fully excavated

XXX.   Din Dryfol. Baulk X/C 1970. Posthole at front of Chamber Three fully excavated with original packing
remaining

XXXI.   Din Dryfol. 1969. View of Chamber Four from back (west). Disturbed fill of chamber below finds tray; cairn backing missing stone on right

XXXII.   Din Dryfol. 1969. Area of Chambers Three and Four from east; cairn and chamber filling

XXXIII.   Din Dryfol. 1970. Area of Chambers One and Two from east. Small ranging poles standing in Chamber Three postholes. Foot scale

XXXIV.   Din Dryfol. Trench W 1970 from south. Remains of road in foreground, Stone 9 beyond. Note dislodged sliver to left of main block. Foot scale

XXXV. Din Dryfol. Trenches A, F, G, H 1969. View up road from east. Lowest level of road exposed

XXXVI. Din Dryfol. Trench A 1969. Detail of pebble surface of road. Scale in centimetres and inches

XXXVII.   Din Dryfol. Trench O 1970.
          Foot scale lying at back of
          recent wall. View from south

XXXVIII. Din Dryfol. Trench Z 1970.
          Recent wall at edge of rock
          shelf, view from west.
          Foot scale